# Milton
## in Early America

# Milton
# in Early America

GEORGE F. SENSABAUGH

PRINCETON, NEW JERSEY

PRINCETON UNIVERSITY PRESS

1964

✧

Publication of this book has been aided by the Ford Foundation program
to support publication, through university presses,
of works in the humanities and social sciences

✧

Printed in the United States of America
by the Vail-Ballou Press, Inc., Binghamton, New York

for George and David

## PREFACE

On the tercentenary of Milton's birth, Charles Francis
Adams announced to members of the Massachusetts Historical Society that *Paradise Lost* had left but a single discernible mark on the life of the Bay Colony. Such a challenging
statement, which in view of the occasion paid strange homage
to Milton, called out an immediate response. Within two
months Adams himself reported to the Society that evidence
belying his earlier assertion had come to his hands; and since
that time scholars have shown that Milton inspired the literary
community of early America not simply in New England but
in the middle and southern colonies as well. Scholarship has
now turned up enough information to suggest that, relatively
speaking, Milton influenced poetry in early America as much
as he affected poetry in eighteenth-century England, and, as
Raymond Dexter Havens revealed long ago, that impress was
deep and significant. Yet the query Howard Mumford Jones
posed in the early thirties—what is really known about American interest in Milton?—remains largely unanswered. The
effect Milton had on the moral, spiritual, and intellectual life
of early America has never been systematically explored.

To measure American interest in Milton from Colonial days
through the first twenty-five years of the Republic is the task
of the present inquiry. Even early in this formative period of
American life signs pointed to Milton idolatry and to a phenomenal response to his art. Cotton Mather of Massachusetts
and William Byrd of Virginia early succumbed to the spell of
his poetry. John Adams, Benjamin Franklin, and Thomas
Jefferson showed in various ways that they marveled at the

breadth of his mind. If New Englanders spoke of him first, and disclosed in their writings the impress of his language and thought, they did so not because of any special Puritan affinities but because among early settlers they sooner honored libraries and schools. Wherever books clustered, Milton was present; whenever he was present, he made himself felt. As centers of culture increased on the seaboard interest in his name and works eventually so grew that by the end of the eighteenth century he had become a nationally recognized figure, admired by citizens of the entire American community. His singular powers to instruct and inspire so appealed to Americans searching for ideals and values that for a few decades they deferred to what he had said.

To exaggerate the importance of any one man in cultural history is a common failing among scholars. Perhaps the present inquiry has fallen into the very trap it has tried to avoid. But this much is clear: for a while in American history Milton moved through the whole cultural community, impressing not only poets but also editors and free-lancers, statesmen and lawyers, schoolmasters and doctors and clerics. This hardly means that other voices out of the past failed to make themselves heard. Nothing could be further from the truth. From the classical world Homer, Virgil, and Horace still spoke with a commanding authority, along with Plato, Aristotle, and Cicero. Lactantius and Clement of Alexandria, Luther, Grotius, and Beza still shaped sermons and theological tracts. Ramus dichotomized early American minds as perhaps no other one man. Among modern authors Shakespeare and Pope seemed so timely that Americans praised them regularly in essays and poems, often quoting their sayings and sentiments. But none impressed on Americans distinct modes of feeling and speaking; none etched on their minds visions of a transcendent world through which mundane activity could be read and assessed. Milton had precisely this effect on early Americans, and this is why his influence assumes such significance.

Scholars have already shown Milton's impress in other countries of the Atlantic community, particularly in England, where his influence might be expected to be greatest. John Walter Good pointed out in 1915 how powerfully Milton moved through the multiple forms and phases of English life in the eighteenth century. Seven years later, Raymond Dexter Havens focused on his effect upon English poetry. Early in the present century J. G. Robertson disclosed how Milton had reached over into Germany and France to affect literary expression, especially in the latter country, where he left a distinct mark on early Romanticism. Scholars have even searched for Milton's tracks in such far away lands as Poland, Persia, and Japan. Such studies have verified Milton's appeal to people all over the world, as well as the power of his language and thought. But during the time he most affected these countries none stood precisely in America's position. None had attempted to carve a new nation out of a new land, none groped for an idiom to celebrate New World experience. That Americans looked to Milton during the time of their national youth, that he in turn affected their sensibilities and gave them a voice to articulate what was uppermost in their own minds and hearts is therefore of singular interest. At this particular moment in American history Milton played a role he could play nowhere else: he could and did become an inextricable part of a country seeking national identity.

From the very beginning this inquiry presented problems of method and scope. To record every mark Milton made during the period under discussion, to find every reference to his name and works or to ferret out every piece that by chance might show a trace of his hand proved to be infeasible. Newspapers and magazines, as well as sermons, almanacs, and fugitive tracts are available in such overwhelming numbers that no one could ever hope to examine them all. Such an abundance of source material dictated a wide and representative sampling rather than an attempt at complete coverage—wide enough to discover recurrent patterns of imitation and reference, representative enough to suggest that further research would only confirm their design, not alter their contours. Even representative sampling turned up enough evidence to make organization difficult.

American dependence on England for standards of judgment and taste dictated an even further limitation in scope. Americans obviously plagiarized English authors, obviously reprinted English essays and books, obviously found their vogue for Miltonic verse in the vogue that flourished in England. Yet to pursue such relationships beyond occasional comment would encompass peripheral questions, answers to which, however interesting to cultural history, would blur the main aim of the inquiry. The only practical solution to such a basic procedural problem lay in focusing directly on American interest in Milton as revealed in American imprints, with only cursory glances, if that interest appeared to spring from abroad, toward lands of ultimate origin. For of central importance to the task at hand was not to uncover lines of inter-Atlantic communion, but to assess how Americans responded to Milton as a growing national self-consciousness turned their eyes to the past. During such a derivative period an American imprint was enough to declare American interest.

Titles have often been shortened and normalized, unless for some reason it seemed wise to retain the originals. Biographical facts have been taken from accepted authorities. Quotations from Milton have been transcribed as they appeared in American imprints, uncorrected by reference to standard editions. Doubtful ascriptions still remain doubtful, since attempts at positive identifications have proved to be, for the most part, vexingly futile. Dates have been interpreted flexibly. Books first printed long after the time of their known composition, for example, have been discussed in a context either early or late in accordance with the particular problem under examination. Several bibliographical problems have defied solution. Neither Sabin's *Bibliotheca Americana*, nor Evans' *American Bibliography*, nor Wegelin's *Early American Poetry*, nor Jantz's *The First Century of New England Verse* could clear up a number of questionable dates, authors, and titles. Unsigned articles in magazines and silent borrowing from English and even from other American journals have received little comment simply because a brief investigation of such practices produced little or no fresh information. It is sufficient to say that editors and columnists pilfered from one another without shame. Only a glance at Frank Luther Mott's *A History of American Magazines* shows how annoyingly anonymous most magazine writing was in the early years of American journalism.

Standard works on American literature and civilization have contributed to the story here told. Moses Coit Tyler's *A History of American Literature*, Perry Miller's *The New England Mind*, and Thomas Jefferson Wertenbaker's series of volumes I found particularly useful. More recent works such as Louis B. Wright's *The Atlantic Frontier*, Norman Foerster's *Image of America*, and the encyclopedic *Literary History of the United States* furnished many facts and ideas. Unpublished theses and dissertations which opened up insights and codified information are too numerous to mention by name. I am grateful to the editors of *American Literature* and of *The Huntington Library Quarterly* for permission to incorporate, in changed form, material previously published. To the staffs of the Library of Congress, the Huntington Library, the Houghton Library at Harvard, the Sterling Library at Yale, and the John Carter Brown Library and the Harris Collection of American Poetry at Brown University I am appreciative for many courtesies and much help. To Miss Patricia

Brehaut I owe special thanks for secretarial assistance. I am indebted to James Holly Hanford and Leon Howard, who kindly sent me a number of leads, and to David Levin, Virgil K. Whitaker, and Louis B. Wright, who read the manuscript and made useful suggestions. I am also indebted to the American Philosophical Society and to Stanford University for grants-in-aid which allowed me to complete this project earlier than otherwise would have been possible.

GEORGE F. SENSABAUGH

*March 1, 1963*
*Palo Alto, California*

# CONTENTS

# Milton
## in Early America

ONE

# An Image of Greatness

John Milton appeared to early Americans as a man of titanic stature. Few dared speak ill of his name; most praised him as one of England's most illustrious sons and extolled his lofty thought and sublime style. William Livingston, the Colonial poet-lawyer of New York, placed the "Great *Milton* first" on his list of "far-fam'd bards" that had "grac'd *Britannia's* isle." [1] John Adams recorded in his prepresidential diary that Milton's "Powr over the human mind was absolute and unlimited," that "His Genius was great beyond Conception, and his Learning without Bounds." [2] John Blair Linn, an arbiter of letters in the early days of the Republic, implied that Milton was "not only the first poet, but one of the most eloquent rhetoricians, and gigantic reasoners, that the English nation ha[d] ever produced." [3] Such praise placed Milton alongside John Locke and Sir Isaac Newton in a triune of great Englishmen, whose equal but distinctive genius Americans often acclaimed in one reverent breath. So great was Milton's stature

[1] *Philosophic Solitude: Or The Choice of a Rural Life. A Poem* (New York, 1747), p. 32. Livingston became the first governor of New Jersey in 1776.

[2] *Diary and Autobiography of John Adams,* ed. L. H. Butterfield (Cambridge, Mass., 1961) I, 23. Adams recorded this judgment on April 30, 1756.

[3] *The Powers of Genius, A Poem, in Three Parts* (2nd edn., Philadelphia, 1802), pp. 147–148. For an account of Linn as poet and critic, see Lewis Leary, "John Blair Linn, 1777–1805," *William and Mary Quarterly,* IV, Third Series (1947), 148–176.

from Colonial years through the first quarter century of the Republic that his shadow eclipsed even Homer and Virgil.[4] Few authors except the inspired prophets and singers of Scripture could stand up against him, and sometimes Americans invested Milton himself with the sacred mantle of Isaiah and David.[5]

Such veneration and praise only tokened how far he had penetrated into the life of the land. Schoolmasters quoted his words to illustrate points of grammar and rhetoric, and recommended his language and style. Moralists presented his Eve as an ideal of womanly virtue and found in his picture of prelapsarian bliss a design for nuptial love. Ministers transposed his lines into rubrics of worship, cited him to support their positions, and so absorbed his vast images that their congregations envisioned the Christian story not as depicted in Scripture but as described in *Paradise Lost*. Politicians applauded his stand on civil and ecclesiastical freedom, and, after his epic had become a common possession, turned his portraits of evil and of good into propagandist devices to fight party disputes of the day. But none called on him more often than aspiring young authors. Fired with nationalistic ambition, poetasters invoked the muse for the appearance of a second Milton on American shores and attempted to reach greatness themselves by imitating his language, syntax, and verse forms. From New England to the Carolinas Americans asked Milton to witness their thought or speak their deepest convictions. For a moment in history he commanded an authority rarely granted any person, in any country, at any time.

So phenomenal a response to the man and his works sprang

---

[4] See, for example, John Blair Linn, in *The Literary Magazine and American Register*, I, no. 1 (October 1803), 15–16. Linn wrote a series of "Critical Notices" under the pseudonym "I. O."

[5] See Ezra Sampson, *Beauties of the Bible. Being a Selection from the Old and New Testaments. With Various Remarks and Brief Dissertations* (Hudson, 1815), p. 153.

less from values commonly held than from contradiction and paradox. As Americans shaped their discourse according to neoclassic principles of taste,[6] they answered warmly to the high rhetoric of *Areopagitica* and to the grand style of *Paradise Lost*. As they embraced current ideals of the Enlightenment, they instinctively read their experience in terms of Reformation theology and Renaissance views. The commonsensical stance of the era failed to weaken the hold of the old rhetoric or to replace long-established, analogical habits of mind. Augustan modes of expression might inform, but sublime passages still moved heart and soul. Ideas of perfection and progress might inspire hopes for the future, but concepts of original sin and of a hierarchical universe still satisfied needs of the spirit. Such paradoxes, far from alienating Milton in the American community, in fact drove him deeper into the general consciousness. If Americans wrote for the age in Popean couplets, they aspired to write for the ages in Miltonic language and style. If they saw man and the world in a new philosophical light, they measured his journey through life against the old Christian values Milton had pictured in *Paradise Lost*.

Americans spoke of him so often and made him such an intimate part of their lives that before the eighteenth century closed he had become a household and a community word. He had in truth by that time achieved national prominence; and if his rise to such recognition left a chaotic story, a tale scattered and sometimes obscure, it nevertheless held the stage steadily, reaching a climax within the first fifteen years of the new century. After this time he gradually faded from the national

---

[6] For an account of the influence of Addison and his followers on American prose, see Howard Mumford Jones, "American Prose style: 1700–1770," *The Huntington Library Bulletin*, no. 6 (November 1934), pp. 115–151. For an analysis of the influence of Pope in America, see particularly Agnes Marie Sibley, *Alexander Pope's Prestige in America, 1725–1835* (New York, 1949).

scene, but that should in no way lessen interest in his cultural achievement. For popular praise of the man and his works told only a small part of the story: at the peak of his fame he gave Americans eyes to see visions and a tongue to speak from the soul. His vast imagery, particularly as seen in *Paradise Lost*, opened vistas not so much on actual and mutable nature as on transcendent and unchanging reality. His voice—commanding and vibrant—not only guided the course of early serious verse but also informed the moral, spiritual, and intellectual life of the nation. Sharpening values, enlivening faiths, even shaping dreams of a "Western Millennium," he ministered singularly to the needs of the country in the time of its national youth. No wonder Americans saw him as a man of towering stature; no wonder they called him the "Great Milton." So phenomenal a figure in letters and life at so crucial a moment in American history merited no lesser acclaim.

## II

Why Milton could play such a significant role in early American life can be readily seen. He had spoken so often to so many topics of perennial human concern that most men, whatever their callings, could respond to something he said. Politics? He had constructed arguments for individual freedom, as well as for an ordered society. Love? He had held for divorce, yet had presented the highest ideals of nuptial companionship. Religion? He had fought bitterly against ecclesiastical tyranny but had supported the central Christian position. To these and to other matters of permanent interest he brought an abundance of learning, a clear hierarchy of values, and a power of expression that stamped his pronouncements with the indelible marks of a master. What he said appeared to express archetypes of experience representing the variety and richness of human thought and activity. Because he could speak to most men, his fame grew; because his fame grew, he spoke with greater authority. A further glance at his titanic image, therefore, coupled with an account of how and why it developed, should properly preface any attempt to recount his role in American life. His phenomenal fame reflected and at the same time prefigured the nature of his imprint over the land.

The first published testaments about Milton presented him simply as a great inspired poet. Cotton Mather had early implied Milton's greatness by borrowing some "colours" from his eloquent language to elevate several events in his own *Magnalia Christi Americana,* but few references to Milton the man appeared before 1714. In this year a poem entitled *Written in the Inimitable Paradise Lost* described him as the "Great *Milton*" whose "*Daring Muse*" had come "down from *Blest Abodes*" and caught "on fire with an Immortal Flight" [7] —a sketch hinting that he had been divinely inspired. Yet at this early date Americans drew back from investing Milton with the mantle of Scriptural authors. A letter in *The New England Courant* could add only that Milton was "lofty" and that he sang "in his own inimitable Strain"; [8] and the famous Mather Byles could admit only that Milton's poetry was far superior to his own, a judgment no one has ever cared to deny. [9] Such random comments, however, gave Milton little distinction: many poets, living and dead, had merited similar praise.

But in 1728 James Ralph sketched a portrait that singled

[7] *Select Essays, With Some Few Miscellaneous Copies of Verses Drawn By Ingenious Hands* ([Boston], 1714), pp. 10–11. Reproduced by Charles Francis Adams in "Milton's Impress on the Provincial Literature of New England," *Proceedings of the Massachusetts Historical Society,* XLII (1908–1909), 163.

[8] *The New England Courant,* no. 48 (June 25–July 2, 1722), p. [1].

[9] *Poems on Several Occasions* (New York, 1940), pp. 25–34. Reproduced from the edition of 1744, with an introduction by C. Lennart Carlson. Byles's judgment is found in the poem, "Written in Milton's *Paradise Lost,*"

Milton out in the fraternity of laureate poets. Born in America, Ralph left for England in 1724, where he soon published under a London imprint three volumes of poems whose prefaces and contents, among many things, assessed the literary scene of the day. He satirized Pope,[10] argued that blank verse was the true form of poetry,[11] and assailed the "servile imitators" of Milton, saying that they and their works would be "buried in oblivion together." Such remarks on the state of poetry allowed him to praise Milton for his sublimity. Only Milton, he declared, could be "happy in the sublimest subject"; only Milton possessed the "fancy and judgment to manage it." [12]

So warm was Ralph's praise and so moving was his response to sublimity that Milton appeared as a living figure before him. "There *Milton* stands," he exclaimed in *The Muses' Address to the King*, "with elevated front/ And eye sublime." So clear and majestic a picture asked that Ralph comment upon the nature of Milton the man and upon the effects of his verse. He declared that Milton's genius was "Unbounded, vast, and bold," that indeed it was "matchless in its flame,/ Its strength, its energy." That such genius would create poetry of the highest order and that such poetry in turn would possess powers to pierce man's very soul should be only expected. Winged with rapture, Milton bore man up to the skies, opening every source of "admiration, transport, love, esteem and joy." [13] If Ralph failed to say that Milton's lips had been touched with hallowed fire from the altar, he came perilously close to so doing. He perceived that Milton had special powers to inspire and transport, that Milton could speak so intimately to mind and heart

which appeared first in *The New England Weekly Journal*, no. XXII (August 21, 1727).

[10] See *Sawney. An Heroic Poem. Occasion'd by the Dunciad* (London, 1728).

[11] *Night: A Poem* (London, 1728), Preface.

[12] *ibid.*, p. viii.

[13] *The Muses' Address to the King: An Ode* (London, 1728), pp. 13–14.

that Ralph could see him enfleshed and could envision the greatness of the man through the sublimity of his poems. To Ralph, Milton could never be a poet nearly anonymous. More than Dryden or Pope, more even than Shakespeare, he was a personality to be felt and a power to move.

For the next decade or so Americans presented the same vibrant picture. Before becoming the President of William and Mary College, William Dawson saw Milton as a "Great Chieftain" whose "steepy Heights" he himself had attempted to climb.[14] John Adams, the poet-preacher of Newport and Cambridge, extolled Milton for having inspired Mather Byles in his verse in imitation of *Paradise Lost*, implying that no better evidence of Milton's immortality could be found than in Byles's poem and that no better recommendation could be made for the piece itself than that it mounted with "ardour" to Milton's "godlike heights." As a great and profound poet and as a model of sublimity Milton merited fame that should "resound from shore to shore." [15] In such an atmosphere of praise Nathanael Ames announced in his *Astronomical Diary* for 1744 that *Paradise Lost* was a "divine Poem" and that Milton was the "best of English poets," [16] and a Harvard student spoke of "tow'ring *Milton's* lofty flights" [17] and the *American Magazine* of his "true Sublime." [18] As mid-century approached, the image of Milton as the most sublime English poet had become so widespread that the *American Magazine*, desiring to furnish details about the man and his work, reprinted the text of Elijah Fenton's short critical biography. But as yet Milton remained simply a great man and a sublime

[14] *Poems on Several Occasions* (New York, 1930), p. 8. Reproduced from the edition of 1736, ed. Ralph L. Rusk.

[15] *A Collection of Poems* (Boston, 1744), pp. 6–8.

[16] Boston, 1744, in a prefatory comment to the "Courteous Reader."

[17] *The American Magazine* (February 1744), p. 258, *"An Epistle from* Cambridge."

[18] *ibid.* (April 1744), pp. 341–348, "The Art of Preaching, in Imitation of Horace's Art of Poetry."

poet. A new dimension in the portrait had to await an appraisal of Western poets in William Livingston's *Philosophic Solitude*, a youthful poem assessing literature and life.

William Livingston received his education at Yale College and apparently there began his serious study of literature. The classics he certainly knew, as well as the most significant authors in English. A commendatory verse prefacing his *Philosophic Solitude* spoke of the wide range of his reading and of how he had conversed with angels and with *"the mighty dead,"* naming, among others, Virgil and Milton as representing his heritage in poetry, and Newton and Locke as his illuminators in prose. Livingston himself claimed that among those who had most improved the human mind Virgil came first, but immediately following him, and first in Britannia, came the "Great *Milton.*" To Livingston, Milton was all that he had been to earlier Americans: a man of "tow'ring thought," the "Parent of song," the mighty poet "fam'd the world around." But he was more, too. Taking the step that James Ralph had hesitatingly put forward and then reluctantly withdrawn, Livingston placed Milton in the hallowed circle of singers and prophets divinely inspired.

Livingston to be sure was not quite prepared to secure Milton in the Scriptural canon, but he saw God Himself as the source of Milton's inspiration and power, saw a divine Spirit guiding his genius to envision the glories of the heavenly world:

> His glowing breast divine *Urania* fir'd
> Or G O D himself th' immortal Bard inspir'd.[19]

With this couplet Livingston presented Milton as indeed "peerless" among the authors he named. Neither Dryden nor

---

[19] *Philosophic Solitude: Or The Choice of a Rural Life. A Poem,* pp. V, 32.

Pope nor Watts, who followed on his roster of poets, could be placed in his class. For the American image of Milton now encompassed a bit of divinity, now reflected a Spirit that elevated man's soul and cleared his mind in ways only Scripture could do more efficaciously.

Before long Americans would place Milton in the hierarchy of angels, but in the meantime they simply rebrushed the pictures Ralph and Livingston had already drawn. In *The Choice,* Benjamin Church added a few exclamations and hyperboles without changing any essential feature, simply saying that the immortal Milton was a genius so famous that to exalt either the man or his works would be to commit an impertinence. Judged by his own statement, Church could be easily deemed one of the most impertinent critics in eighteenth-century America:

> H A I L Briton's Genius, *Milton!* deathless Name!
> Blest with a full Satiety of Fame:
> Who durst attempt Impertinence of Praise?
> Or sap insidious thy eternal Bays?
> For greater Song, or more exalted Fame,
> Exceeds Humanity to make, or claim.
> These to peruse, I'd oft forget to dine,
> And suck Refection from each mighty Line.[20]

If Church failed to mention Milton's divine inspiration, Mrs. Anne MacVicar Grant supplied the missing stroke in the portrait now becoming widely accepted. In her reminiscences of manners before the Revolution, she recalled the high position Milton had held in the household of Colonel Schuyler, where, as the daughter of a British officer stationed near Albany, she matured in an atmosphere of unusual literary cultivation and charm. Mrs. Grant often spoke of her own and of Madame Schuyler's admiration for Milton; but, what is sig-

[20] *The Choice* (Boston, 1757), p. 8.

nificant here, she took Milton's invocation to *Paradise Lost* "quite literally," declaring that she "had not the smallest doubt of his being as much inspired as ever Isaiah was." [21] No one else in early America made quite so bold a claim, but ministers had already implied such an equality by citing Milton and Scriptural authors as peers.

The approach of the Revolution turned Americans to Milton's prose and added another dimension to his developing portrait. Long known in America as a controversialist, Milton now began to appear as a powerful reasoner on civil and ecclesiastical freedom, particularly in the sermons of Jonathan Mayhew, who claimed him as one of his mentors. The powers of reasoning which Mayhew silently admired, John Adams openly praised in his *Diary* for 1765, saying that Milton's control over the human mind was absolute and unlimited and that his genius was without bounds. Thirty years later, subsequent to sharp national debates on the nature of government, Adams became disenchanted with some of Milton's proposals,[22] but as events moved toward hostilities with England he and other Americans praised Milton's polemical tracts. Andrew Eliot even implied that Milton should be famed more for his prose than for his poetry. Writing to Thomas Hollis in appreciation of a gift of Milton's pamphlets, Eliot declared that they "who consider that very great man only as a poet of the first rank know less than half his character. He was every thing." [23] Such admiration for Milton's powers of thought led in 1770 to an edition of *Considerations Touching the Likeliest Means to*

[21] *Memoirs of An American Lady: With Sketches of Manners and Scenery in America, as They Existed Previous to the Revolution* (London, 1808), II, 151–153. For comment on this book, with a reference to Milton, see *The Monthly Anthology and Boston Review*, VI (April 1809), pp. 274–280.

[22] *A Defence of the Constitutions of Government of the United States of America* (London printed, Boston reprinted, 1788), pp. 295–300.

[23] *Collections of the Massachusetts Historical Society*, IV, Series 4 (Boston, 1858), 412.

*Remove Hirelings out of the Church,* to which was attached selections from *Of Reformation in England, An Apology for Smectymnuus,* and *Animadversions upon the Remonstrant's Defence against Smectymnuus.* The explicit purpose of this publication, an editorial comment explained, was to give the "vulgar" as well as the "rich and great" an "opportunity of seeing the opinion of the celebrated J O H N   M I L T O N , on a subject of such universal concernment as the G O S P E L method of rewarding its P R E A C H E R S . ' ' But however much the editor of these reprints admired Milton's prose, he could not refrain from adding a word about Milton's poetic genius, and about *Paradise Lost.* He declared that the "sublime genius" of the learned Milton "expanded beyond the limits of this lower World, and animated him to compose P A R A D I S E   L O S T , a Work which continueth to *amaze,* to *astonish,* and to *delight* mankind." [24]

Such praise for both his poetry and prose presented pretty faithfully the image of Milton that prevailed on the eve of open hostilities with England. As a poet, Milton ranged in divine realms, revealing to the imagination scenes unperceived by uninspired mortals. As a polemicist, he turned to affairs of Church and State, solving through his acute powers of reason issues vexing the day. If he could elevate, he could also persuade, and Americans recognized this combination of powers to be unusual enough to warrant special comment. Whether writing with his left hand or his right, Milton was superlatively great.

Perhaps this is the reason that during the Revolutionary period Americans saw Milton as a cultural hero, capable of inspiring the country and of guiding its people to higher intellectual and spiritual planes. Nathaniel Ames the Younger

[24] *An Old Looking-Glass for the Laity and Clergy of all Denominations Who Either Give or Receive Money Under Pretence of the Gospel* (Philadelphia, 1770). This also appeared under a New Haven imprint in 1774.

envisioned in his *Astronomical Diary* for 1769 some "future
L O C K S '' and a "second N E W T O N '' on American shores,
another ''S H A K E S P E A R E '' or ''S O M E  M I L T O N , ''
who would

plan his bold impassion'd Theme
Stretch'd in the Banks of Oxellana's Stream.[25]

Benjamin West conjured up much the same dream in his *New
England Almanack*. Hailing America as the *"glorious Seat"*
of all that was good and great, West pictured her "free-born
*Sons*" extending her glories through the *"Earth's wide
Realms"* and visualized America herself becoming the *"blest
Abode"* of "Newtons, Miltons, Youngs *and* Addisons!" [26]

The vision of future glory to be won by Americans imitating
*"the mighty dead"* appeared in sharper detail after the British
surrender. Reciting some extravagant verse in a Fourth of
July oration, the Reverend William Rogers viewed the new
age then happily rolling to a utopian climax and saw a future
"Bright with the splendors of her mid-day beams," a time that
would bring forth "a Homer and a Milton," whose "pomp
and majesty of song" would give "immortal vigor" to deeds
achieved "by heroes in the fields of fame." [27] A similar prospect
quite overwhelmed a commencement orator at the University
of Philadelphia. America would have, he predicted, poets that
would "eternize, in song, their native groves and rivers"—
poets that would "equal the daring sublimity of Homer, the
correct majesty of Virgil, or the nice delicacy of Horace—and,
to come down to more modern times, the *evangelical strains* of
Milton." [28] By now Milton had become to Americans not only
one of history's great figures, worthy of emulation and praise,

[25] *An Astronomical Diary* (Boston, [1769]).
[26] *The New England Almanack* (Providence) for 1774.
[27] *An Oration, Delivered July 4, 1789* (Philadelphia 1789), p. 21.
[28] *The Columbian Magazine Or Monthly Miscellany* (October 1786),
p. 85.

but also a hero leading America toward a cultural utopia. Toward the end of the Revolutionary period a few voices challenged such extravagant views. In reporting a Shakespearean Jubilee in England, *The Boston Magazine* repeated some words Mr. Garrick had spoken on that occasion: if "you want still a greater authority than Milton's, for the unequalled merits of Shakespeare, consult your own hearts." [29] And in one of his sermons Nathanael Emmons asserted that the "works" of Homer, Shakespeare, and Milton constantly verged "toward oblivion," whereas St. Paul's pronouncements had survived the ravages of time and would "grow in beauty as they grow in age." [30] But such judgments were rare.

More often Americans saw Milton as the supreme author of all time. Samuel Dexter, in a poem *The Progress of Science*, told a Committee of Overseers at Harvard College that Pope was "tuneful" and that all could feel Shakespeare's "divine" force; but he added that Milton was "Our modern Homer, and sublimest bard." [31] Some verses by a callow youth addressed to Timothy Dwight in praise of *The Conquest of Canäan* raised Milton to an even more exalted position. Homer, Virgil, Tasso—all could claim greatness, this youth maintained; yet Milton alone he thought "god-like" and most sublime, though he now had a rival in Dwight! [32]

Such uncritical praise of early American achievements in poetry makes literary judgment of the time suspect, but Milton himself seldom lost his preeminence. A note to Dwight's poem *The Triumph of Infidelity* explained that Milton possessed "clear and intuitive moral optics," that he rose "in his

[29] *The Boston Magazine*, II (1785), 130.

[30] *A Sermon Preached at the Installation of the Reverend David Avery* (Providence, [1786]), pp. 23–24.

[31] *The Progress of Science* ([Boston], 1780), p. 8. The poem was issued in 1790 under a New York imprint with the notation "Never Before Published."

[32] *The American Magazine* (March 1788), pp. 265–266, "To the Author of the Conquest of Canaan."

moral conceptions, with no unhappy imitation of the scriptural sublimity"; [33] and an anonymous author in *The Royal American Magazine* declared that Milton stood in advance of the ancients, as well as of Shakespeare. If Shakespeare had equalled if not exceeded the sublimity and beauty of earlier writers, even more could be claimed for Milton, he said. For in Milton "every excellence of all the ancients" was "heightened"; these excellences and "innumerable others" moved "beyond all comparison above them." Milton's genius disdained "to be confined within the limits of this world, launched into the infinite abyss, and created others for itself." [34] The scope of his vision secured him a unique place among the most celebrated authors of the Western world.

## III

Such an image of greatness in Colonial and Revolutionary times emerged from a widely scattered body of work by a diverse group of writers. Perhaps no one American in that early age grasped the whole picture at once, though even the most casual observer stressed Milton's sublimity. As the new nation began to grope for cultural identity, as Americans sought to strengthen their schools, clarify their beliefs, stabilize their government, and create a fresh and vigorous literature they turned to great men of the past, hoping to discover guide lines in their exciting adventure. The result was a flood of periodicals and books, of orations and sermons and fugitive poems, many of which mentioned Milton or cited his works. Even almanacs began to tell stories about him,[35] and as evidence of

[33] *The Triumph of Infidelity: A Poem* (1788), pp. 20–21, in a note signed "Scriblerus."

[34] *The Royal American Magazine* (Boston, April 1774), pp. 127–128, in an essay taken "from a late publication."

[35] See, for example, *Farmer's Almanack, For the Year of Our Lord 1798* (Portland); *Beers's Almanac For the Year of Our Lord, 1799* (Hartford); *The New-England Diary and Almanac, 1809* (Leominster); and *Johnson's Almanac, for the Year 1810* [Philadelphia]. The most widely told anecdote

their esteem Americans published between 1787 and 1815 twenty-eight editions of his poetry. Out of this heightened activity a more complex and a more authoritative Milton emerged, tailored to fit specific needs of the day. Americans now saw him as a combined scholar and genius, as a witness for Christianity and as a spokesman for God, as a consummate artist who served as a pattern and touchstone of excellence for poets and critics. The period of Milton idolatry was at hand. Debate over the merits of classical learning shaped the figure of Milton the scholar.[36] Milton's love of ancient languages and literatures could not be gainsaid; evidence of their effect on his manner and matter appeared in nearly all he had written, particularly in his early poems and in *Paradise Lost*. Defenders of ancient culture therefore pointed to Milton as an example of greatness springing from a knowledge of Latin and Greek, an argument that seemed almost self-evident after the appearance in England of James Beattie's *On the Utility of Classical Learning*, interest in which reached American shores during the early Republic. As might be expected, the image of Milton the scholar appeared most often in centers of knowledge. Leonard Woods informed the graduating class of Harvard University in 1796 that, among others, Milton had brought honor to England, that he had fostered the seeds of freedom and had contributed to the progress of reason, taste, philosophy, and true religion.[37] Thomas Thacher presented an almost identical view, saying that the illustrious names of

was this: Milton, asked whether he would instruct his daughters in different tongues, replied, "No, sir, *one tongue* is sufficient for a woman."

[36] See, for example, *The Literary Miscellany*, I (1805), 15; and David Graham, *The Pioneer, Consisting of Essays, Literary, Moral and Theological* (Pittsburgh, 1812), pp. 97–107. For a discussion of the educational problem, see Richard D. Mosier, *The American Temper: Patterns of Our Intellectual Heritage* (Berkeley, 1952), under "The Republican Education," "The Critique of Classical Education," "The Utilitarian Learning," and "The Curriculum and the Culture," pp. 134–140.

[37] *Envy Wishes, then Believes. An Oration, Delivered at Commencement, Harvard University, Cambridge, July 20th, 1796* (Leominster, 1796), p. 8.

"Milton, Locke, and Newton" would be forever inscribed "in the annals of learning and philosophy." [38] As scholars speaking to scholars, Thacher and Woods saw the advantage of placing Milton high on the roll of men known for their command of the past.

Yet Milton's obvious learning embarrassed poets and critics in a literary community now struggling to emerge from the domination of neoclassical principles. Romantic doctrine demanded that a poet be an original genius, not a classical scholar: *poeta nascitur, non fit.* But the plain fact was that Milton had trained himself from his youth to write the sublimely original *Paradise Lost.* Americans resolved the dilemma of conflicting doctrines by presenting Milton as a union of creativity and learning, as a combined scholar and genius who had produced art superior to what either could achieve individually.

No American argued this position more assiduously than John Blair Linn, pastor of the First Presbyterian Church in Philadelphia and poet and critic for *The Literary Magazine and American Register.* Basically romantic, Linn nevertheless adhered to the eighteenth-century school of taste as mirrored by Scotch rhetoricians like Hugh Blair and Lord Kames, particularly in his poem *The Powers of Genius,* in which he assessed a number of English authors. Here he asserted that Milton was a true original not only in his poetry, which was sublime, but also in his "political and miscellaneous productions," which were "mines of intellectual gold." Yet if Linn considered Milton an example of original genius, he also saw him a learned scholar. If he could state that to impose laws upon genius was like "hoppling an Arabian courser," he could nonetheless conclude that Milton's knowledge, far from impeding him, actually prepared his wings for a flight:

[38] *A Discourse on the Errors of Popery, Delivered in the Chapel of the University in Cambridge, May 8, 1805* (Cambridge, 1805), p. 24.

The Muse of Milton in his infant days
Lisp'd in sweet numbers, pour'd prolific lays,
With dauntless soul his little arms he spread
To grasp the wreaths which hung from Homer's head.
Rous'd by the wonders of the classic page,
He gave to study all his early age;
In thirst of knowledge and his favourite lore,
He sought instruction on a foreign shore,
Courted the Muses in Italian plains
Where his lov'd Tasso pour'd his melting strains.
. . . Crown'd with th' applauses of imperial Rome,
He turns his footsteps toward his native home;
There gives to Wisdom all his studious hours,
And gives expansion to his mighty powers;
At length prepar'd, he spreads his wings for flight
And seeks the realms of uncreated light . . .[39]

A note to these couplets confirmed Linn's position. "The voice of criticism," he said, had pronounced Milton "the most learned among the poets"; but he added that Milton's "vast information, while it did not restrain," nevertheless "regulated his flight."

Such an exercise in semantic legerdemain allowed Linn to enhance the image of Milton as America moved belatedly from the neoclassical to the Romantic period. No one ever denied Milton's great genius; now it was combined with, indeed was regulated if not restrained by, a surpassing command of scholarly knowledge.

The image was so important to the literary scene of the early Republic that Americans presented it in widely various contexts. An article "On Independent Genius" in *The New York Magazine* implied that "genius alone, unaided by learning," could not have produced *Paradise Lost*, though it was admitted "that Milton soared rapidly to perfection, unconscious of the existence of any superiority in those compositions,

---

[39] *The Powers of Genius, A Poem, in Three Parts*, pp. 37, 56–57, 147.

the principles of which he is supposed to have imitated." [40] An essay "On Poetical Expression" in *The Literary Magazine and American Register* asserted that Milton knew how "*to build the lofty rhyme*," yet had introduced into his creations "all the happiest idioms of every language with which his extensive learning was acquainted." "Hebraisms and Grecisms, Latinisms and Italianisms, poured themselves into his copious mind," and what came out was not a pedantry of style, but a language that attempted "to seize on those felicitous expressions which more nicely reveal our sensations." [41] If a knowledge of foreign idioms could produce a precision of style, comprehension of music could enhance rhythm and meter. Americans therefore stressed not simply Milton's command of words but also his knowledge of musical terms.

*The Port Folio* particularly wished to develop this part of the Miltonic image. An essay "On Music" in this journal pointed to Milton's allusions to Grecian numbers in *Paradise Lost,* as well as to the beneficial effects of harmony as seen in the Lady's song in *Comus,* all of which confirmed the opinion that Milton's "learning was as extensive as his invention was grand." [42] A subsequent issue of the same journal directed further attention to Milton's knowledge of music by citing several lines from his poems.[43] But *The Mirror of Taste* gave the fullest account of Milton's understanding of this sister art. In a series of articles, some of which apparently stemmed from a larger essay or book perhaps originally published in England, this journal deplored the great ignorance most poets had displayed in their comments on melody and rhythm. Joseph Addi-

---

[40] *The New York Magazine Or Literary Repository,* New Series (January 1797), pp. 25–26. This essay may have been copied from an English journal.

[41] *The Literary Magazine and American Register,* V, no. 30 (March 1806), 172–176.

[42] *The Port Folio,* III, no. 31 (July 30, 1803), 242–243.

[43] *ibid.,* III, no. 32 (August 6, 1803), 251–253.

son had disclosed woeful gaps when he discussed Italian opera; and Sir William Temple, in speaking of modern music, had revealed gross limitations of mind. Pope had shown "no pleasure in the combinations of sounds," nor had Robert Southey or Mrs. Barbauld. But the "very reverse" was "the case with Milton": he spoke and wrote "of music not only with all the grace and fancy of a poet, but with the correctness and precision of a musician." His understanding of this art had indeed been "complete." [44]

By 1808 Americans had so fixed in their minds the picture of Milton as a combined scholar and genius that *The Port Folio* saw fit to transcribe from an "elegant authour" some sentiments to confirm it. Milton, the argument reiterated, "was one of the most learned men" England had ever produced; but deference to Romantic doctrine demanded an immediate qualification: "his great learning neither impaired his judgment nor checked his imagination." [45] Late in the period John E. Hall brought the whole picture together. "Milton's mind," he declared in *The Port Folio,* "was fraught with every finer feeling, which led him to indulge in the various and delightful paths of music, poetry, and philosophy: in these he particularly excelled, and he delighted in celebrating their influence over the mind and the heart." [46]

Such a symbol of genius and learning led Americans of the religious community to secure Milton as a witness for Christianity. Among the many great names they asked to testify in behalf of Christian belief, Milton proved to be one of the most satisfying and eloquent. As President of Yale College, Timothy Dwight informed the graduating class of 1797 that Christians far outweighed infidels in achievement and learn-

[44] *The Mirror of Taste and Dramatic Censor,* II, no. 1 (July 1810), 57–60.
[45] *The Port Folio,* V, no. 1, New Series (January 2, 1808), 14–15.
[46] *ibid.,* I, no. 2, Third Series (February 1813), pp. 174–176, under "The Adversaria; Or, Evening Recreations," signed by "J.E.H."

ing: neither Bolingbroke nor Hume nor Voltaire, nor any "list of Infidels" he could readily assemble, could, "without extreme disadvantage," be compared with men like Erasmus or Locke or Newton or Berkeley or Milton. "In no walk of genius," Dwight further maintained, "in no path of knowledge" could "Infidels support a claim to superiority, or equality with Christians." [47] Such an array of witnesses had perhaps been suggested by the argument of the prosecution at the trial of Thomas Williams, who had been convicted in London by Thomas Erskine for selling Thomas Paine's *Age of Reason*. An account of this trial, as well as parts of Erskine's impassioned pleas, had been printed in a London newspaper the summer before Dwight made his address; and in 1798 excerpts from the London story appeared in America. Erskine had summoned a number of witnesses before the bar of public opinion to testify against Paine, but he gave a stellar position to Milton, whom he quoted at length. What Paine had called "but the tale of the more ancient Superstitions of the world" had been, Erskine maintained, the subject of Milton's "immortal song"; and the "mysterious incarnation of our blessed Saviour," which Paine had "blasphemed," Milton had "made the grand conclusion of Paradise Lost, the rest from his unfinished labours, and the ultimate hope, expectation, and glory of the world." [48]

The heralded blasphemies of Paine forced Americans to repeat Erskine's position. In his biography of George Washington, Mason Locke Weems presented as witnesses for the

---

[47] *The Nature, and Danger, of Infidel Philosophy, Exhibited in Two Discourses, Addressed to the Candidates for the Baccalaureate, in Yale College, September 9th, 1797* (New Haven, 1798), Second Discourse, p. 58.

[48] See, for example, *Poor Richard Revived: Or Barber and Southwick's Almanack, For the Year of Our Lord, 1798* (Albany). See also George F. Sensabaugh, "Milton at the Trial of Thomas Paine," *Notes and Queries*, II, no. 5, New Series (May 1955), 212–213.

old piety men like Milton and Boyle, who had "brought the finest education and abilities to the examination of christianity" and had found "the closer their examination of it, the clearer their conviction of its divine truth." How could the virtuous youth of America, in view of such testimony, renounce Christianity and "follow the baseless reveries" of a drunkard like Paine? The Reverend Weems left his query unanswered, but what he said left no doubt where he stood.[49]

In *A Sermon on the Character and Conduct of Zaccheus* Henry Colman summoned Milton to testify that Christianity had "successfully passed the most severe and critical examination." Milton in truth was a witness who, together with Bacon and Newton and Locke, so far outweighed others, that, as Gilbert Wakefield had argued, Colman reported, "if the dispute must be decided by the preponderancy of *genius* and *accomplishments,* such men as Hume and Gibbon" would be but as "the *small dust of the balance* against the *mountains;* as the malignant glimmerings of a taper to the effulgence of a midday sun."[50]

The superiority of Christians over skeptics of the Enlightenment seemed so evident to Jonathan Allen that in a poem on the existence of God he advised "atheists" to follow in the tracks of men like Newton and Milton and Locke, putting special emphasis on the testimony of Milton's great hymn to the Creator in *Paradise Lost,* which he quoted in part.[51] Americans could scarcely muster the principal champions of Christendom without calling on Milton, even as far west as Ken-

[49] *A History of the Life and Death, Virtues, and Exploits, of General George Washington* (Georgetown, [1800]), pp. 69–70.

[50] *A Sermon on the Character and Conduct of Zaccheus: Intended to Promote the Belief and Influence of Christianity* (1810), pp. 9–10 and note.

[51] *A Poem, On the Existence of God. An Ode on Creation. To Which are Added Several Hymns, and an Eulogy on General George Washington* (Haverhill, 1803), p. 24.

tucky, where he appeared in a letter to *The Evangelical Record and Western Review* as a friend of the old piety.[52] No other poet testified more often; no other deposition carried more weight.

Americans considered Milton a prime witness not simply because of his genius and learning but because he had portrayed the verities of Christian belief. Hannah Adams placed him on her list of great Christian authors.[53] The Reverend William Duke praised him because he had written about Christian subjects, saying that Providence had annexed to Christianity the very flower of mankind. Duke admitted that Homer and Virgil possessed genius, and no one, he declared, should belittle the significance of what they had said. But neither, of course, had presented the truths of Christian doctrine as finally revealed in the New Testament. That Milton had done so was precisely one secret of his power and greatness: he had pictured the "terrors of hell, the glories of the divine Majesty, the wonders of redemption, and the awfulness of a general and final judgment." "How poor, how trivial, in comparison," Duke explained, was "the grandest representation of merely human fancy!" Yet Milton should not be praised too highly for writing the truth about man and his destiny: "to suppose that his ingenuity could work up a matter of fiction to such a degree of sublimity and importance" would be to "compliment" him beyond his desert. In short, Milton himself had not imagined the truth, had not himself conjured up the great visions of *Paradise Lost;* he had only described what had been revealed to him and to other Christians in the pages of Scripture. But if Duke drew back from accrediting Milton with too much creative power, he felt no twinge in praising the manner

---

[52] *The Evangelical Record and Western Review for the Year 1812,* I, no. 1 (January 1812), 8–9, in some verses included in the letter.
[53] See Hannah Adams, *The Truth and Excellence of the Christian Religion Exhibited* (Boston, 1804), under *Milton.*

in which he had presented his scenes. Milton's depiction of Christian revelation struck him with admiration and reverence. The "propriety and liveliness" of his "representation" was "scarcely inferior to inspiration" itself.[54]

In a poem delivered at a public exhibition at Cambridge Charles Prentiss saw Milton in much the same light;[55] and *The Literary Miscellany* declared that the subject of *Paradise Lost,* being of universal interest to man, was by its very nature "infinitely higher" than "the conquest of a country, or the founding of an empire": Milton had written truths about which every individual of the human race was "personally, and immediately, and deeply concerned."[56] No wonder *The Boston Spectator* translated Abbé Delille's essay on epic poetry, which presented Milton not as a national poet but as *the* poet of the Christian world. Singing of the Fall of Man and of his future redemption, Delille had said, singing of the present life, the life hereafter, and of the uninterrupted relation between heaven and earth—"what author can be compared to him!"[57]

So incomparable a poet of the Christian story appeared to a number of Americans as something of a prophet himself, inspired like Hebrew writers of old. *The Huntingdon Literary Museum* declared that the best poets often borrowed from Scripture and "adopted the language of the prophets," naming Milton among those who had done so.[58] Ezra Sampson carried the argument further by saying in his *Beauties of the Bible* that a close imitation of Scripture could place an author

---

[54] *A Clew to Religious Truth, Obviating the More Common Suggestions of Infidelity, and Leading the Serious Inquirer into Such an Acquaintance with Christianity as May Avail to the Saving of his Soul* (Wilmington, 1795), pp. 51–52.

[55] *A Collection of Fugitive Essays, in Prose and Verse* (Leominster, 1797), pp. 129–130.

[56] *The Literary Miscellany,* II (Cambridge, Mass., 1806), 377–379.

[57] *The Boston Spectator,* I, no. 15 (April 9, 1814), p. 59.

[58] *The Huntingdon Literary Museum and Monthly Miscellany,* I (Huntingdon, 1810), 566–568, in an essay "The Scriptures."

next to the prophets themselves. To clarify his position he presented a number of examples of Scriptural sublimity, citing passages from Moses and David and Isaiah, as well as from Habakkuk and Daniel. Such passages soared "above the writings of the immortal Homer himself, even as the flight of the eagle is above the orbit of the most daring among ordinary birds." The superiority of Scripture having been demonstrated, Sampson glanced briefly at Milton: "the boast of English poets," "a Christian believer," a "close studier of the beauties of the Bible." From Scripture Milton drew much of "his beautiful imagery," Sampson declared, as well as many of his "noble conceptions" and much of his "astonishing grandeur." So taken was Sampson with Milton's manner and matter that he saw him seizing "the mantle of the Scripture bards," catching "their sacred enthusiasm" and "their etherial fire." To him, *Paradise Lost* was a poem that had no equal in sublimity except the Scriptures themselves.[59]

In a poem delivered before the Philermenian Society of Brown University, Isaac Bailey took the next logical step. Milton's inspiration, he said, came not from "P O E S Y alone" but from a "holier flame," came indeed from the regions of the seraphim themselves, where Milton still sang with that "blessed throng" new hymns now inaudible to mortal man.[60] Apotheosis could hardly go beyond this. Bailey had placed Milton among the highest orders of angels and had implied that he spoke directly for God.

The combined image of learning, genius, and quasi-divinity allowed Americans to assert that Milton was a consummate artist. Who knew as much? Who was more gifted? Who else

[59] *Beauties of the Bible. Being a Selection from the Old and New Testaments. With Various Remarks and Brief Dissertations*, p. 153.

[60] *A Poem, Delivered Before the Philermenian Society of Brown University* (Providence, 1812), pp. 7–8.

was a spokesman for God? Americans of the literary community needed a model to follow, as well as a touchstone of judgment; and in his superlative qualities and deathless achievements Milton supplied both. This completed image of Milton appeared in textbooks and fugitive poems, but chiefly in essays and sketches of significant figures, some of which focused on Milton alone. Occasionally, to be sure, Americans denied Milton a supreme place in the hierarchy of poets, or questioned his art. John Hayes of Dickinson College declared that Virgil, Shakespeare, and Milton alike should yield before the "harmonious song" of Homer; [61] and *The Boston Spectator* presented a similar view.[62] *The Monthly Anthology* maintained that no lines in Milton could "in any one of the essentials of poetry" be "superiour" to Chaucer's description of Creseyde.[63] In much the same vein *The Port Folio* stated in an indifferent sonnet that Shakespeare was Milton's "only fit compeer," [64] and later argued that Shakespeare was Milton's superior in the delineation of manners and character.[65] But Thomas Dermody expressed the majority view in *The Lady's Weekly Miscellany*, where he presented Shakespeare and Milton in a series of contrasts. The "former," he said, "was a man of many faults and many virtues; the latter nearly a pattern of perfection." [66]

Nearly a pattern of perfection. Neither Virgil nor Homer could match him in technical achievement, and in sheer virtu-

[61] *Rural Poems, Moral and Descriptive; To Which are Added, Poems on Several Subjects* (Carlisle, 1807), in the poem "Winter," p. 126.

[62] *The Boston Spectator*, I (November 12, 1814), 188, in an essay "Homer, Virgil, Milton, and Klopstock."

[63] *The Monthly Anthology and Boston Review*, V (April 1808), 209, in an essay on Chaucer.

[64] *The Port Folio*, IV, no. 11 (March 17, 1804), 88.

[65] *ibid.*, II, no. 3, Third Series (September 1809), 257–258.

[66] *The Lady's Weekly Miscellany*, V, no. 6 (December 6, 1806), 44, in an essay "The Genius of Shakespeare and of Milton Contrasted" by the "late Thomas Dermody," the Irish poet.

osity he towered above Ariosto and Tasso, above Camoëns and Klopstock.[67] As *The Rhode Island Literary Repository* said, Milton was the very "prince of epick poets," [68] or, as John Blair Linn averred, the very "first among the poets who were not the prophets of the Lord." [69]

To secure this image in the American mind periodicals often compared Milton with Homer, pointing to specific beauties or excellences that showed him superior. *The Literary Magazine and American Register* argued that *Paradise Lost* excelled the *Iliad* or *Odyssey* because its supernatural machinery was not only more effective but true.[70] A critic in *The Massachusetts Magazine* demonstrated in two consecutive essays that Milton surpassed Homer in the presentation of scenes. "The greatest poets in every age have vied with each other in the description of a moonlight evening," he began; but he could find "among all the treasures of ancient and modern poetry" not "one superiour" for "pleasing imagery" and "variety of numbers" to Milton's picture of evening in Book IV of *Paradise Lost*. Even the famous night scene in Book VIII of the *Iliad* could not stand up against it, nor could Homer excel Milton in describing the dew.[71] But Milton's artistry was not limited to the delineation of scenes. In one of the most popular textbooks of the day Lindley Murray presented him as a

---

[67] See Samuel Low, *Poems* (New York, 1800), I, 84–87; *The Literary Magazine and American Register*, I, no. 2 (November 1803), 91–97; *The Boston Spectator*, I (October 8, 1814), 175; and *idem.*, I (November 12, 1814), 182–183.

[68] *The Rhode Island Literary Repository*, I, no. 5 (August 1814), 268.

[69] *The Literary Magazine and American Register*, I, no. 1 (October 1803), 15–16.

[70] *The Literary Magazine and American Register*, VII, no. 41 (February 1807), 92.

[71] *The Massachusetts Magazine Or Monthly Museum of Knowledge and Rational Entertainment*, II, no. 3 (March 1790), 143–147; and II, no. 5 (May 1790), 288–292. For a contemporary assessment of Milton's powers of description, see Phyllis Mackenzie, "Milton's Visual Imagination: An Answer to T. S. Eliot," *University of Toronto Quarterly*, XVI (1946), 17–29.

master of conjoining rhythm and sense. Milton had made "every line sensible to the ear"; he had mastered the art of marrying accent and thought.[72]

Yet when Americans spoke of Milton as a consummate artist they had in mind chiefly his imagery. Perhaps a majority would have agreed with *The New York Magazine* that "to delineate a subject by its most striking and lively attributes, or the faculty, as Voltaire expresses it, *de bien peindre sans vouloir tout peindre,*" was "certainly one of the great secrets of the art of Poetry." [73] At any rate, Americans seldom tired of commenting on how well Milton had learned this particular secret. *The Monthly Anthology and Boston Review* saw him raised above "solicitude" and "collected and undazzled" despite the marks left by religious and political fanaticism because he knew that he was *"painting for eternity"*; [74] and Joseph Dennie presented him in *The Port Folio* as a bard "of the happiest descriptive powers," who "noted objects not only with the eye of a poet, but with the accuracy of a philosopher." [75]

Pedagogues plumbed the secret of Milton's artistry more deeply. William Smith, onetime Provost of the College and Academy of Philadelphia, declared that Milton's distinction was to leave "something to be conceived beyond the power of words to express," that is, to suggest more than to describe, a method of delineation through which Milton had been able to achieve some of his finest effects.[76] John Quincy Adams presented a similar argument in his *Lectures on Rhetoric and*

[72] *English Grammar, Adapted to the Different Classes of Learners* (New York, 1810), p. 250–255.
[73] *The New York Magazine Or Literary Repository*, New Series (November 1797), pp. 574–575.
[74] *The Monthly Anthology and Boston Review*, II (April 1805), 182.
[75] *The Port Folio*, IV, no. 18 (May 5, 1804), 139.
[76] *The Works of William Smith*, I (Philadelphia, 1803), 9n, in the funeral oration delivered in memory of General Montgomery, February 19, 1776.

*Oratory*. Adams explained that the powers of language in all the tongues with which he was acquainted recognized "only three degrees of comparison; a positive, a comparative, and a superlative." "But climax," he said, ever sought "for a fourth"; and of "this grandeur of imagination," which stretched "beyond the bounds of ordinary possibility," the most frequent examples could be found "in the daring and sublime genius of Milton." As an instance of this "fourth degree" of comparison Adams cited the well-known picture of Moloch in *Paradise Lost*, asking whether anything stronger than this could be uttered. No, language alone could not achieve the effect Milton desired. But the imagination could "conceive in the indistinctness of generalities something worse"; and Milton had "supposed" it "to complete the character of Moloch." [77] Perhaps the effect Milton had achieved through the method Adams explained led Benjamin Pardee to ask whether anyone could read the description of Heaven and Hell in *Paradise Lost* "without the greatest anxiety, astonishment and adoration." [78] But whatever the basis of Pardee's query, Milton's secret had now been revealed, and that regularly to students at Harvard, who after 1805 heard John Quincy Adams speak from his chair as Boylston Professor of Rhetoric and Oratory.

The image of Milton the consummate artist appeared so often during the early Republic that Americans made him a touchstone of judgment and a model for poets. The patriotic fervor that had inspired Timothy Dwight's *The Conquest of Canäan* and Joel Barlow's *The Vision of Columbus* had now somewhat subsided, but Americans still yearned to create a great literature and still spoke of Revolutionary effusions with considerable respect, seeing in them a manifestation of early American genius. Poems of this sort so far outdistanced in scope

---

[77] *Lectures on Rhetoric and Oratory* (Cambridge, 1810), II, 127–128.
[78] *Two Orations, and Poetry on Different Subjects* (Plattsburgh, 1810), pp. 32–33.

and design anything Americans had been able to write to the present that they invited comparisons with epics of an earlier day, particularly with *Paradise Lost*. Thus John Whittler equated Samuel Butler's *Hudibras* with John Trumbull's *M'Fingal* and *Paradise Lost* with *The Conquest of Canäan*.[79] *The Columbian Phenix and Boston Review* picked up Whittler's comparisons and developed them in hyperbolic detail, making only one important exception. That Trumbull "shone" like a star in the dawn of the Revolution and that with Timothy Dwight America had emerged from "Egyptian darkness" could be readily conceded. That *M'Fingal* could be compared with *Hudibras* and *The Conquest of Canäan* with *Joan of Arc* could be further admitted. But was Dwight comparable to Milton? Decidedly not. *The Conquest of Canäan* might be favorably compared with any modern epic, except *Paradise Lost*.[80]

The practice of assessing American epics by reference to *Paradise Lost* drew a plaintive note from Charles Jared Ingersoll, that acute observer of American and English society. Time alone would determine whether Joel Barlow should take his seat in Parnassus alongside Homer, Virgil, and Milton, he declared. He was certain, however, that the design of *The Columbiad*, the final revision of Barlow's earlier work, afforded a broader basis for sublimity than any other poem except *Paradise Lost*. Yet, he asked with some justice, was it fair to "condemn" an American poet because he fell "short of Milton"? [81] Perhaps it was not. But his question implied how often American critics presented Milton as a touchstone of excellence, how often *Paradise Lost* served as a model for epic language and form.

Such comparisons naturally led Americans to call on Milton

[79] *The United States Magazine*, I, no. 1 (April 1794), 17–19.
[80] *The Columbian Phenix and Boston Review* (April 1800), pp. 226–228.
[81] *Inchiquin, The Jesuit's Letters* (New York, 1810), pp. 82, 85, 93.

to heighten the style of their verse. Before the eighteenth century closed the practice had become so common that John Blair Linn ridiculed it in a satirical poem. As an inherent Romantic, particularly in his early career, Linn saw the dangers of unimaginative discipleship, and hence warned the young American "Compositor" to beware invoking Homer and Milton, since to do so would stifle original genius. Linn himself had idolized Milton, placing him even above Homer and Virgil, but he saw that imitation of even perfection could produce artificial posturing, in illustration of which he wrote some supposed lines of a callow American poet:

> O come, ye muses, with a laurel crown,
> Pour, O Parnassus, pour your torrents down!
> Blow ye poetic zephyrs gently blow,
> Ye heavenly choirs, O strike in accents slow;
> Ye gods immortal, swell the present lay,
> O Homer, Milton, hearken when I pray.[82]

Yet such satire on the practice of invoking the great of the past had little effect on American poets: the neoclassical doctrine of imitation still prevailed. In his "Profiles of Eminent Men," J. M. Sewell asked Milton's muse to inspire his "lays"; [83] and in "The Patriot" Nathaniel Topliff called not on Milton alone but also on Shakespeare, Dryden, and Pope.[84] American poets turned to many authors for guidance to fame, but they asked Milton for singular help, particularly if they wished to write epic verse.

Americans of the early Republic created the complex image of Milton out of specific needs of the time. Scholars called on him to support learning and wisdom; ministers, to witness Christian belief; critics and poets to clarify values and tastes

---

[82] *Miscellaneous Works, Prose and Poetical* (New York, 1795), pp. 18–19.

[83] *Miscellaneous Poems, with Several Specimens from the Author's Manuscript Version of the Poems of Ossian* (Portsmouth, 1801), p. 262.

[84] *Poems, Moral, Descriptive, and Political* (Boston 1809), p. 8.

and to strengthen an ambitious American literature. Reiteration of Milton's greatness from so many quarters of the American community so exalted his name that he became a popular idol and a symbol of authority. Charles Prentiss, commenting on Milton's poetic power, declared that Milton possessed "such a nobleness and independence of expression that every sentiment seems an hero, commanding his little company of words, ever ready and suitable." [85] But if Milton's art lent to his sayings a potential currency, investing them with a relevance and an urgent command, his popular image of greatness confirmed their validity and gave them a vogue. As *The Monthly Anthology* said: "So delicate were his perceptions of taste, so exuberant was his fertility of fancy, so enlarged were the faculties of his mind, and so extensive the range of his erudition," that it would be "hazardous to deny" what his "sentiment" established. [86] Far from hazarding a denial, Americans invoked Milton for divers purposes on countless occasions, finding authority in what he had said.

[85] *A Collection of Fugitive Essays, in Prose and Verse*, no. XI, p. 24.
[86] *The Monthly Anthology and Boston Review*, IV (September 1807), 489–492.

# Colonial Days

Copies of Milton appeared in the Colonies long before his image became great and complex. As early as 1664 Increase Mather recorded that his library shelved *An Apology for Smectymnuus, The Reason of Church Government,* and the *Pro Populo Anglicano Defensio.* By the turn of the century, as might be expected, college and city corporations had secured larger collections. About 1698 or shortly thereafter the Corporation of the City of New York purchased for its library the *Artis Logicae, The Doctrine and Discipline of Divorce,* the *Pro Se Defensio,* and the 1669 edition of *Paradise Lost,* a selection indicative, as were the items in Mather's collection, of an early interest in Milton's prose. But acquisitions soon widened to include Milton's poetry as well, particularly in centers of culture and learning, where men turned their attention to the study of literature. By 1714 Yale possessed not only a "Complete Collection" of Milton's prose but also "Paradise Lost and all Poetical Works"; and, through the generosity of Thomas Hollis the Elder, Harvard received the nucleus of what was to become for some time the most extensive collection of Milton on the American continent. To such college holdings may be added a fair number of Milton volumes in the New York Society Library and the Library Company of Philadelphia, all of which suggest that by the early years of the eighteenth century Milton had become an established name wherever books were assembled.[1] His reputation apparently grew less from general hearsay than from first-hand acquaintance.[2]

As libraries in America increased, booksellers began to supply a public demand for his works. By 1683 the Boston merchant John Usher had received *The History of Britain* and in 1685 ordered three copies of the *Artis Logicae*, one year after his invoice showed that he had purchased four volumes of *Paradise Lost*. Such enterprise foreshadowed announcements to come. On May 25, 1738, *The Pennsylvania Gazette* advertised *Paradise Lost*, and in 1744 the *South Carolina Gazette* printed a notice of sale for the same poem, accompanied by Joseph Addison's notes.[3] On September 19 and 26, as well as on October 3, 1743, *The Boston Evening Post* advertised "Milton*'s Paradise Lost and regain'd*," and on January 1 and 8, 1750, announced the importation of many philosophical and theological books, including both of Milton's long poems.[4] *The Boston Evening Post* became so interested in making Milton known to Americans that it not only advertised his works, but on May 7, 1750, reprinted an extract from *The London Magazine*, which had brought to the "notice of the publick," among many things, the fact that Milton had served as Secretary of Foreign Tongues to the Council of State of the

[1] See Leon Howard, "Early American Copies of Milton," *The Huntington Library Bulletin*, No. 7 (April 1935), pp. 169–179; and Thomas Goddard Wright, *Literary Culture in Early New England 1620–1730* (New Haven, 1920), pp. 180–186.

[2] For a discussion of libraries in New England, see Samuel Eliot Morison, *The Intellectual Life of Colonial New England* (Ithaca, Great Seal Books Edition, 1956), pp. 133–151. For information on printing and bookselling, see pp. 113–132.

[3] See Leon Howard, "Early American Copies of Milton," *The Huntington Library Bulletin*, no. 7 (April 1935), pp. 169–179.

[4] *The Boston Evening Post*, nos. 424, 425, 426. See also no. 751 (January 1, 1750); no. 752 (January 8, 1750). For other references to Milton, chiefly excerpts from English journals, see no. 237 (February 18, 1740); no. 380 (November 15, 1742); no. 399 (March 28, 1743).

Commonwealth Government.[5] Such information was "peculiarly proper" to bring out at midcentury, *The Boston Evening Post* declared; it could also have been profitable.

Almanacs soon followed the path marked out by newspapers and magazines. In 1760 and 1761 *Father Abraham's Almanac* listed among many items just imported and ready for sale *Paradise Lost* and *Paradise Regained*;[6] and in 1765 *The Virginia Almanack* placed on the market at the printing office in Williamsburg "a *Collection of the most esteemed modern* B O O K S ," among which appeared "Milton's poetical Works: Containing Paradise lost; Paradise regained; Samson Agonistes; Comus, a Mask; and all his other Poems."[7] Advertisements of Milton's works increased apace as the century unrolled.

But more importantly Americans revealed in their diaries and journals that they not only possessed copies of Milton but read them. The Reverend Thomas Buckingham of Hartford carried with him on the 1711 expedition against Crown Point the Bible, a psalm book, and *Comus*.[8] William Byrd of Westover recorded in his *Secret Diary* on fifteen separate occasions from February 23 through March 22, 1712, an intense session with Milton in both Latin and English.[9] At the age of twenty-one Benjamin Franklin assembled under his several "Articles of Belief and Acts of Religion" a rubric of prayers excerpted from *Paradise Lost*, which he called Milton's Hymn to the Creator,[10] and later recommended to the Trustees of the Philadelphia Academy for study in the Sixth Class selections from the best English authors, such as Tillotson, Milton, Locke,

---

[5] *The Boston Evening Post*, no. 769 (May 7, 1750).
[6] *Father Abraham's Almanac* (Philadelphia, 1760 and 1761).
[7] *The Virginia Almanack* (Williamsburg, 1765).
[8] Thomas Goddard Wright, *op. cit.*, p. 195.
[9] *The Secret Diary of William Byrd of Westover 1709–1712*, eds. Louis B. Wright and Marion Tinling (Richmond, 1941), pp. 490–504.
[10] *The Works of Benjamin Franklin* (New York, 1904), I, 322–325.

Addison, Pope, and Swift.[11] Americans of perception and taste knew Milton well—well enough to record their reaction to what he said and to recommend him for the consideration of others. Such testimony, along with notices in newspapers and magazines and almanacs, suggests that Milton was read and appreciated from Massachusetts to the Carolinas, that his phenomenal fame, though partially imported from England, was largely an indigenous growth, nurtured by Americans reading American-sold books on American soil. Colonial activity in making Milton available set the stage for American response.

## I I

Tradition holds that Milton made his first imprint on America in the liberal settlement of Rhode Island. In *Areopagitica,* so runs the legend, Milton had Roger Williams in mind as one of the revolutionaries actively searching for truth, and impressed upon him in that noble oration several arguments for toleration and for freedom of conscience. From this tradition sprang the story that Milton, through Williams, helped shape the liberal divorce laws of Rhode Island. Now Williams did preside over the Rhode Island court which, in 1655, passed a law including incompatibility as grounds for divorce. And Milton had earlier argued in *The Doctrine and Discipline of*

[11] *The Works of the Late Dr. Benjamin Franklin* (New York, [1793]), II, 131–139. Scholars have made extravagant claims for Milton's influence on Franklin, but some of them are quite tenuous. See, for example, Verner Winslow Crane, *Benjamin Franklin Englishman and American* (Baltimore, 1936), p. 38, who saw Milton, Newton, Shaftesbury, Mandeville, Sir William Petty, Locke, and Sidney as Franklin's spiritual godfathers. See also Thomas Woody, *Educational Views of Benjamin Franklin* (New York, 1931, pp. 150, 156, 171, 175–177, 179), for the effect of Milton on Franklin's "Proposals to the Education of Youth In Pennsylvania"; and Malcolm R. Eiselen, *Franklin's Political Theories* (New York, 1928, p. 5), who said that "Most of Franklin's political ideas may be found in the writings of Locke and Milton." Stuart Sherman, in his essay on Franklin in *The Cambridge History of American Literature* (New York, 1936), I, 105–106 took a more moderate position.

*Divorce* that husband and wife could be legally separated, should their minds prove to be "contrary." Furthermore, in 1652 Williams had openly approved some of Milton's positions in the current dispute over liberty of conscience. In view of such close affiliations, what would be more logical than to suspect that Williams had found some of his arguments for divorce in Milton, and that these arguments had become legalized in the Rhode Island statute?[12] If such an influence could be established Milton's earliest imprint in America would be worthy of careful analysis, but unfortunately little truth resides in such a fascinating conjecture. The friendship between Roger Williams and Milton has been more than exaggerated,[13] and the Rhode Island statute contains nothing tangible to indicate the presence of Milton's thought, even at second hand.

Not Roger Williams but Cotton Mather appears to have been the first American to leave a clear record of Milton's impress. That this imprint should come from *Paradise Lost* seems somewhat strange—even ironic. For Mather failed to mention Milton in his own discussion of poetry, and with other Americans of the time his interest lay in Milton's logic and in his controversial tracts. But in his *Magnalia Christi Americana* Mather paraphrased three times not from Milton's prose but from *Paradise Lost,* once in order to enlarge his own exposition and twice to heighten particular scenes. The passage he em-

[12] See, for example, James Ernst, *Roger Williams: New England Firebrand* (New York, 1932), pp. 99, 225–233; and Samuel Hugh Brockunier, *The Irrepressible Democrat* (New York, 1940), p. 231. The legend could have started with Moses Coit Tyler, *A History of American Literature* (Student's Edition, New York, [1897]), I, 251–252. Here Tyler simply stated that Williams spoke to Parliament in noble Miltonic accents in the introduction to his *Queries of Highest Consideration.* See also pp. 253–254 for comparisons between *The Bloudy Tenent of Persecution for Cause of Conscience* and *Areopagitica.*

[13] See George R. Potter, "Roger Williams and John Milton," *Rhode Island Historical Society Collections,* XIII (October 1920), 113–129. Potter's discussion of the correspondence between Williams and Mrs. Anne Sadlier, which contained references to Milton, should be particularly noted.

ployed to augment his own discourse appeared in the biography of Sir William Phips, when, speaking of the perplexities of Indian warfare, Mather stated that neither an army greater than Xerxes' nor Tamerlaine himself could have easily conquered New England's wily enemies. The English themselves had found that "they were like to make no Weapons reach their Enswamped Adversaries." A predicament so grave called for a solution Mather remembered in *Paradise Lost:* only "Mr. *Milton,*" he declared, "could have shown them how

> *To have pluckt up the Hills with all their Load,*
> *Rocks, Waters, Woods, and by their shaggy tops,*
> *Up-lifting, bore them in their Hands, therewith*
> *The Rebel Host to've over-whelm'd . . ."* [14]

By directing attention to the way God's hosts had routed the rebel angels, Mather dramatized the difficulties of overcoming the Indians and at the same time associated New England's struggles with the great war in Heaven, which Milton had presented in Book VI of *Paradise Lost.*

Mather stressed this association later in the *Magnalia.* Diverse "Nations of *Europeans*" in "diverse Colonies bordering upon one another" had furnished the Indians with guns, he declared; and this reminded him of Satan's scheme to find new weapons to combat the forces of God:

> *. . . Tools, pregnant with Infernal Flame,*
> *Which into Hollow Engines, long and round,*
> *Thick-Ramm'd at th'other Bore, with Touch of Fire*
> *Dilated and Infuriate, doth send forth*
> *From far with Thund'ring Noise among their Foes*

[14] *Magnalia Christi Americana: Or The Ecclesiastical History of New-England, From Its First Planting in the Year 1620, unto the Year of Our Lord, 1698* (London, 1702), Book II, p. 47. For an interesting discussion of the function of Mather's allusions and quotations, see William R. Manierre, II, "Cotton Mather and the Biographical Parallel," *American Quarterly,* XIII (1961), 153–160. Mather did not drag learned trappings into the *Magnalia* by force, Manierre argued, but placed them at strategic points to magnify his subject.

*Such Implements of Mischief, as to dash*
*To Pieces and or'whelm whatever stands*
*Adverse. . . .*[15]

Seen against the transcendental background of the struggle between Evil and Good, New England's conflict with the Indians here assumed cosmic significance: God's chosen on earth had simply enacted in time the eternal fight against the forces of Satan.

One "desperate Action" in that conflict reflected so clearly God's plan for New England that, as Mather admitted, he could "scarce forbear" turning again to "the Colours in the *Sixth Book* of *Milton.*" The skirmish to which he referred had claimed seven hundred Indian warriors, as well as three hundred more who afterward died, together with "Old Men, Women, Children, *Sans* Number." In contrast to this great slaughter about eighty-five Englishmen died and only one hundred and fifty lay wounded. Such a wonderful providence of God's ways to his chosen could best be described by reference to the rout of the rebel angels:

*And now their Mightiest quell'd, the Battel swerv'd,*
*With many an Inrode gor'd; deformed Rout*
*Enter'd, and foul Disorder; all the Ground*
*With shiver'd Armour strown, and on a heap,*
*Salvage and Sagamore lay overturn'd,*
*And Fiery, Foaming Blacks; what stood recoil'd*
*Oerwearied, and with Panick Fear surpris'd.*[16]

Even as Satan and his apostates had blenched before the might of the Heavenly Host, so had the Indians met defeat at the hands of the English. The simile was not only apt, enhancing Mather's vigorous narrative; it interpreted New England's

[15] *Magnalia Christi Americana,* Book VII, p. 44.
[16] *Magnalia Christi Americana,* Book VII, pp. 49–50. Samuel Eliot Morison chose the description of the Great Swamp Fight, including the paraphrase from *Paradise Lost,* to illustrate Mather's historical imagination and style. See *The Intellectual Life of Colonial New England,* pp. 186–188.

battles with *"unknown Numbers of Devils in Flesh"* in terms of transcendent reality. Only archetypal action in Heaven could properly assess the bitter struggles to establish God's kingdom on earth.

Yet to say that Mather's adaptations of Milton constitute a substantial debt would force the evidence out of proportion. Mather quoted often from classical authors, and studded his ecclesiastical history of New England with so many references that to list them all would be endless. In the vastness of his project his three citations from Milton are all but lost. But they are instructive in revealing Mather's art of narration, and they point to reasons why Milton later achieved his great reputation. For Mather had found Milton's scenes not only pictorially effective but transcendentally significant: existential activity could be read and adjudged in terms of their spiritual truth.

But through the first half of the eighteenth century relatively few Americans showed Mather's insight or followed his practice. Thousands of pages in pamphlets and books disclose no references to Milton at all, let alone use of his lines to achieve special rhetorical or metaphysical effects. In the first few decades of the century, however, American magazines introduced from time to time short excerpts from Milton not so much to enhance a narration or to sharpen a moral perception as to dramatize an implicit argument.

One of the first so to do was *The New England Courant*, published by James Franklin. In 1722 Franklin printed a letter-essay on the "most Malignant and baneful Evil" of pride, which had brought, he reminded his readers by citing Isaiah, the fall of the rebel angels. Since Isaiah's account of this event in the Christian story seemed to be insufficiently vivid, Franklin turned to the picture of Satan at the beginning of *Paradise Lost*—to the image of the *"Infernal Spirit"* dwelling in Hell, bound *"In Adamantine Chains and penal Fire."*

To dramatize the result of pride in man, Franklin alluded to Milton's picture of Adam and Eve in the Garden, implying a contrast between "the blissful Shades of *Eden*" and the miserable state of mankind after the Fall.[17] The result of original sin as pictured in *Paradise Lost* served to dramatize numerous arguments. To stress the virtue of temperance, Nathanael Ames recalled the lazar house the Angel Michael had disclosed to Adam;[18] to advance the sale of *Every Man His Own Doctor*, William Parks referred to the same scene in *The Maryland Gazette*.[19]

Such scattered references in this early period indicate little more than that Americans knew Milton and occasionally recognized the relevance of what he had said to a wide variety of human experience. No discernible pattern of influence outside the poetic community had yet developed. But during this time Americans began to respond to one of the most heartwarming and magical scenes in *Paradise Lost*—the vision of connubial bliss in the Garden of Eden. An essay on love in *The New England Courant* for 1723 began with Milton's lines describing the conjugal caresses of Adam, followed by the question, "*O! When meet now/ Such Pairs, in Love and mutual Honour join'd?*" The essay itself bewailed the rarity of such unions in modern times, a condition which also called for reference to Isaac Watts's poem, *Few Happy Matches*.[20] But what seemed to have captured the essayist most was Milton's idyllic picture, a vision so charming that *The Pennsylvania Gazette* called it to mind again by citing the hymn, "Hail! Wedded Love."[21] An article on marriage in *The American Magazine*, asserting

---

[17] No. 48 (June 25–July 2, 1722), p. [1].

[18] *An Astronomical Diary, Or An Almanack For the Year of Our Lord Christ 1744* (Boston, 1744).

[19] See Elizabeth Christine Cook, *Literary Influences in Colonial Newspapers 1704–1750* (New York, 1912), p. 173.

[20] No. 123 (December 2–December 9, 1723), p. [1].

[21] Cook, *op. cit.*, p. 104.

that it may be "the safer Way not to endeavour to bring that high and philosophical Strain of Notions into Practice, so much espoused by *Milton* and others, of having a Wife sutable only to the Genius of a wise and learned Husband," [22] misinterpreted Milton's position and at the same time ran athwart a growing sensibility of the day. For before long the picture of Adam and Eve would supplant the story of Ruth or of the good wife or Proverbs as a model of nuptial perfection,[23] at least in popular journals, where Milton spoke on the mysteries of love with greater authority than Scriptural judges or kings.

## III

The authority of Milton spread far enough in the first half of the eighteenth century to affect the sermons of a few prominent New England clergymen.[24] He had not yet become an advertised author for the well-stocked minister's library, nor taken the place of such widely quoted theologians as Luther and Calvin, or of moralists like Beza and Grotius, or even of more recent popular writers such as Algernon Sidney, Richard Baxter, or John Tillotson. But except for Isaac Watts among modern poets he was the most often referred to, and in addition to furnishing ministers with significant ideas he began to affect their visual imagination as perhaps no other one man.

Among the first American ministers so affected was Benjamin Colman, a long-time preacher in Brattle Street, Boston, and one of the most prolific pastors of early eighteenth-century New England. Graceful if not profound in thought, learned

---

[22] *The American Magazine* (October 1745), pp. 446–448. For other random references to Milton at this time, see Cook, *op. cit.*, pp. 104, 114, 203, 257.

[23] For a comment on how Milton's hymn expressed the Puritan ideal of love and marriage in New England, see Morison, *The Intellectual Life of Colonial New England*, p. 10.

[24] For an interesting account of the relation between Puritan thought and literary theory and practice, see Kenneth B. Murdock, *Literature & Theology in Colonial New England* (Cambridge, Mass., 1949).

but not pedantic, he displayed his considerable knowledge by references to Seneca and Cato, to Tillotson, Baxter, Richard Steele, and "Mr. Milton," to mention a few of the many authors he had read. *Paradise Lost* became a part of his spiritual vision, furnishing him with a language to expound doctrine and with images to dramatize Biblical events.

In *A Discourse on the Incomprehensibleness of God* preached in Boston in 1714 Colman turned to *Paradise Lost* to describe the metaphysical mystery of the Divine Being. In the early days of the Church, this mystery had absorbed Justin Martyr, Lactantius, and Tertullian, who had partially resolved the enigma by likening God to the sun and to its rays of streaming light.[25] But Colman wished to present, in accordance with his proposition, not so much a clarification as the depth of the mystery, and hence found Milton's cryptic description of God in his invocation to Book III of *Paradise Lost* particularly helpful. If "the creatures be unsearchable," Colman declared in his *Discourse*, "much more is the creator incomprehensible. If such dazling wisdom and perfection shine forth in the things that are made, what then is the light wherein God dwells? whom no man hath seen nor can see?" Such questions out of the way, Colman further darkened the mystery of God by loosely paraphrasing part of Milton's difficult invocation to light, to which he appended the physical enigma of rays streaming endlessly from an eternal sun. He explained that light was the "first and most wondrous work of God . . . like the first-born it doth of all bodies most resemble its great parent, the father of light and glory"—information that led him to expostulate, in Milton's words, "Ethereal Stream! thy fountain who can tell? Before the sun, before the heavens thou wert." No wonder, Colman went on, that pagans bowed to the

---

[25] See William B. Hunter, Jr., "Holy Light in *Paradise Lost*," *The Rice Institute Pamphlet*, XLVI (January 1960), 1–14, for an illuminating study of the problem.

sun: the mystery of its origin and operation, even in view of current scientific speculation, made such worship the most excusable of pagan idolatries! But the metaphysical, not the physical mystery of God and light, fascinated Colman most; and he wanted it known that in this main interest "Mr. Milton" had been a source of his thought.[26]

The metaphysical mystery Colman presented his Boston congregation proved so fascinating that he returned to it again in *A Brief Dissertation on the Three First Chapters of Genesis*, a series of lectures taken from sermons preached earlier on the creation, the life of Adam and Eve, and the Fall. The purpose of this series, Colman explained, was to answer Deists and infidels who would subject all experience to the iron dictates of reason. In partial refutation to this narrow approach to experience he recalled how the mystery of creation had been described by the angels, by Milton, and by Mr. Matthew Henry, whose *Method for Prayer* Colman particularly admired. To explain the enigma of creation Colman again paraphrased, or at least made use of, the invocation to light at the beginning of Book III of *Paradise Lost*. "God is *light*," he declared. "So He represents Himself unto us, because Light is the *first-born* of the Visible Creation". . . . The angels cried, "*Hail, Holy Light!* . . . Our *Milton* learn'd it of Them in his Darkness. And so our late Angel of a Man, Mr. Henry in his Exposition."

Such an exploration into the mystery of creation allowed Colman to comment on how God reveals truth. He explained that "GOD is the *Father of Light, from Whom every good and perfect gift comes down; and with Him there is no Variableness, nor Shadow of Change*"—a position that forced him to conclude that "in the *New Creation* Light is the *first* Thing

---

[26] *A Discourse on the Incomprehensibleness of God: in Four Sermons, Preached at the Lecture in Boston, A.D. 1714* (Northhampton, 1804), Sermon the Second, pp. 57–58 and note.

formed. GOD *gives the Light of the Knowledge* of his more Spiritual *Glory, in the Face of* J E S U S  C H R I S T ." [27] Colman here not only reasserted the mystery of creation as a partial refutation to the rational arguments of Deists; he reaffirmed the validity of revelation itself, the very gift for which Milton had asked in his invocation to Book III. In one sense, the revelation of *Paradise Lost,* as later Americans never wearied of saying, refuted the arguments of infidels and freethinkers as no other discourse could.

Colman's interest in metaphysical mysteries, however, was not persistent nor was his analysis of them profound. He turned more often to the exegesis of Biblical stories, where his talent in captivating an audience best shone. This talent revealed itself especially in *A Brief Dissertation on the Three First Chapters of Genesis,* a subject requiring a picture of Adam and Eve in the Garden, which he drew less from Scriptural details than from Book IV of *Paradise Lost.* In this book Milton had described the happy rural seat in which Adam and Eve led their innocent lives. Some "Trees wept odorous Gumms and Balme"; others bore "fruit burnisht with Golden Rinde." "Flours of all hue" spread over the valley of Eden; and nearby, in the cool recesses of a shady grot or cave, the "mantling vine" put forth her "purple Grape."

In this paradise of trees and flowers, "murmuring waters" descended the sloped hill into a crystal lake, birds choired their songs, and the whole air breathed the smell of field and grove. Such a delicious spot was the home of Adam and Eve, who walked about in "naked Majestie" and "seemd Lords of all." Here "to thir Supper Fruits they fell." Here they held high conversation about the tree of knowledge, their own creation, and the nature of man. Here they strolled hand in hand to the bower of nuptial bliss and under the open sky worshipped

[27] *A Brief Dissertation on the Three First Chapters of Genesis* (Boston, 1735), p. 8.

God, the Creator of all. Secure in their understanding of each other and of their place in the Garden, they embraced, while roses rained petals on their uncovered limbs. O blest pair, sleep on! exclaimed Milton, putting his final strokes on the nuptial scene. O, if they could only know that they would be happiest if they sought "no happier state, and know to know no more."

Colman presented precisely this picture in his *Brief Dissertation*. Perhaps even earlier, when he was visiting in England, Milton's vision had begun to possess his own mind, for during his long stay in that country he had strengthened his ties with literary and religious liberals who had undoubtedly found inspiration in the Milton tradition. At any rate, in his biography of Colman, Ebenezer Turell told the story of Colman's meeting there Mrs. Elizabeth Singer, a young lady of poetic aspirations, whose father showed his American guest his daughter's sylvan retreat and asked, after their mutual friend Mr. Rogers had already made the request, that he say a few words in its praise. Colman graciously complied in a few undistinguished lines describing Eve in the Garden, musing among "*Eden's Streams, and Banks, and tow'ring Groves.*" [28]

In his *Brief Dissertation* Colman expanded this Miltonic outline into a colorful picture filled with details supplied from Book IV of *Paradise Lost*. In Eden "*Adam* and *Eve walk'd* together, contemplated and discoursed, eat and worship'd. . . . The *Birds* sang in the Branches, the *Trees* were laden with painted *Fruit*, the *Plants* were covered with *Flowers* of the sweetest Odour, and *Streams* of pure Water ran by the green shady Walks." So salubrious was this "*Paradisaic* State" —the "*Air* without, and *Wisdom* within"—that our "Parents needed no *Covering. The man and his Wife were naked, and were not ashamed.*" The "Purity" and "Wisdom" of God so

---

[28] *The Life and Character of The Reverend Colman, D.D.* (Boston, 1749), pp. 35–36.

dwelt within them that "they could have nothing to blush at." Indeed, Adam and Eve lived in a "State of Innocence and moral Perfection," and this "was the *better*, the Superiour Part of Paradise." For "more than all its delicious Fruits to the Eye or Palate, or than the perfum'd serene Air to their Nostrils," was the "Paradise *within Themselves*" Adam and Eve enjoyed.

To the undoubted satisfaction of his congregation Colman rounded out his vision by saying that such a state of perfection lay within the grasp of every wise and good man who had the "Grace of God" within him.[29] Whether this last touch came from the Angel Michael's explanation of the *felix culpa* in Book XII of *Paradise Lost* is open to doubt. Michael had told Adam that through God's grace he could achieve a "paradise within," happier far than the Eden he once knew. But the doctrine of the happy Fall was as old as Christianity itself and except for the phrase "paradise within" could hardly be called Miltonic. The vision of Eden that Colman presented to the spiritual eyes of his flock, however, unquestionably sprang from the picture Milton had drawn. Colman indeed was one of the earliest Americans to exemplify the process by which *Paradise Lost* was to become "not so much a secondary Book of Genesis as a substitute for the original—at least as far as the pictorial imagination was concerned." [30] By the nineteenth century Milton's picture of Paradise had become so much a part of the American mind that some of its details could be seen in American primitive painting.[31]

In the meantime, Joseph Bellamy turned to Milton to

[29] *A Brief Dissertation on the Three First Chapters of Genesis*, pp. 31–32.
[30] See Perry Miller, *Errand into the Wilderness* (Cambridge, Mass., 1956), p. 220. See the *Publications of the Colonial Society of Massachusetts*, Vol. XVI, Harvard College Records (Boston, 1925), II, 466–467, for an account of Hollis, Colman, and the dispositions of some copies of Milton's poetical works.
[31] Perry Miller, "The Garden of Eden and the Deacon's Meadow," *American Heritage*, VII (December 1955), 55–61, 102.

dramatize several problems of doctrine. An able and forceful preacher, considered by his contemporaries and followers one of the most distinguished writers of his time, Bellamy associated himself with Jonathan Edwards in the Great Awakening and became obsessed by the depravity of man and the power of God. Edwards himself thought highly of Milton, whose "inimitable excellencies," he said, could be appreciated only by an uncommon power of mind. Bellamy seemed to possess such intellectual power. At the least, he appreciated Milton enough to quote at length from *Paradise Lost* in two of his sermons, both of which exuded the fervor of the Great Awakening.

The first he preached in Goshen in 1753 under the title *The Great Evil of Sin As It is Committed Against God*. Here in his main rubric on "Doctrine" he set out to prove how different sin is from what passes for such in an *"apostate rebellious World."* The great evil of sin, Bellamy argued, is that it is injurious to man, yet few people, being the apostates they are, realize this truth. Ironically, Bellamy went on, even rebels against rightful sovereigns on earth fail to understand that the deeds which they think are heroic and call by the name of virtue are in fact selfish and sinful. Such an observation reminded Bellamy of Milton's apostate angels and led him to state in a note that man's worldly actions could be compared to Milton's presentation of the Great Consultation in Book II of *Paradise Lost*, where Satan, after volunteering to seduce mankind, received the plaudits of the *"infernal Crew*, as paying a publick Honour to his V I R T U E . ' ' [32] False values in Hell, seen in the speeches of the apostates, assessed man's general defection as well as the political scene in mid-century America. As the Colonies moved closer to open rebellion, the Infernal Council served as a prototype of evil councils among men.

[32] *The Great Evil of Sin As It is Committed Against God* (Boston, 1753), pp. 23–26. See particularly notes on pp. 25–26.

But mid-century issues of government interested Bellamy less than the hopeless condition of man. To stress this position he called on St. Matthew and Milton, who had spoken of divisions among men and of the apparent solidarity among the forces of Satan. Milton had written beautifully to this very point, Bellamy explained, citing the lines in *Paradise Lost* where Milton had lamented concord among devils and enmity and strife among men. Such lines allowed Bellamy to press, but with only a shred of justification, one of the central doctrines of the Great Awakening—the total depravity of man.

Even social or political unity among men was illusory, Bellamy argued. "And yet the little Appearance of *publick Love* and *publick Spirit* there is among Mankind, altho' not so well united among themselves as *Devils* be, is by some *Writers* wonderfully applauded, as *true Virtue,* and used as an unanswerable Argument, to prove that Mankind *naturally* have, in a Measure, that *moral image* of God, which 'tis acknowledged the *Devils* have totally lost: and that notwithstanding we are represented in Scripture as being *dead in Sin,* (Eph. iii.1)— *by Nature Children of Wrath;* (ver. 3)—*Enemies to God;* (Rom. v.10)—*Enmity against him.* (Rom. viii.7)." [33] Such a defense of old Calvinist doctrine neither accurately interpreted Milton's view of the Fall, which allowed man to retain a "measure" of the image of God, nor conceded a whit to the new moralism, which had already captivated a large segment of the American clergy. But Bellamy's misreading of Milton should cause no surprise; Scripture at times has notoriously lent itself to variant meanings. Of importance is that Bellamy placed the authority of Milton and of Scripture side by side.

Bellamy returned to the depravity of man in a sermon on *The Wisdom of God in the Permission of Sin* and again called on Milton and Scripture to assess the human condition. The gap between man and God was infinite, he maintained. The

[33] *ibid.,* pp. 23–26.

plain fact was that man, since the Fall, had shown his true character in his enmity both to God and to his own kind. To substantiate man's enmity toward God, Bellamy quoted from the seventh chapter of Acts; to show his enmity toward man, he cited the third chapter of Titus and reproduced, so that his congregation could visualize the core of his argument, Milton's clear-eyed view of humanity:

> Who live in Hatred, Enmity and Strife
> Among themselves, and levy cruel Wars,
> Wasting the Earth, each other to destroy:
> As if (which might induce us to accord)
> Man had not hellish Foes enough besides,
> That Day and Night for his Destruction wait.

Such a picture forced Bellamy to conclude that man had been so obstinate in his ways that no "external Means" had ever been able to "reclaim" him, that he had become so "alienated from God" that no "Arguments" could persuade him to be reconciled with his Maker. Ever since the Fall, notwithstanding "all the outward Means" which man had used, the world had remained very much what it had been, even Christian nations being "little better, if so good," as some heathen.[34] Only the down-reaching arm of Grace, regenerating the individual, was the answer to man's ills; for nations as nations, Bellamy implied, could do little, perhaps nothing, to ameliorate the human condition. The optimism of the Enlightenment found no congenial niche in his mind.

Yet however much Bellamy misread Milton, the central argument he adduced from him was not entirely alien to the great vision of future events the Angel Michael unrolled for Adam in Book XI of *Paradise Lost*. Milton had here shown nations rising and falling to no purpose; even the rainbow

---

[34] *Sermons Upon the Following Subjects, Viz. The Divinity of Jesus Christ. The Millennium. The Wisdom of God, in the Permission of Sin* (Boston, 1758), p. 201.

after the Flood had proved to be but an illusion. Such a vision —or at least the device of opening man's eyes to the future— was a generation later to inspire Joel Barlow and Timothy Dwight, who tried unsuccessfully to accommodate Milton's language and symbols to the prospect of a New World Millennium. But if Bellamy understood better than Barlow or Dwight Milton's picture of fallen man as portrayed in Book XI, he failed to grasp Milton's whole vision and furthermore omitted entirely Milton's earlier hopes of reforming England through the agencies of Church and State. Alone among ministers at mid-century to show an interest in Milton the political reformer was Jonathan Mayhew, whose arguments for freedom stirred up angry protests and replies as the nation moved inexorably toward the Boston Tea Party and Paul Revere's ride.[35]

Jonathan Mayhew, as pastor of West Church in Boston, nourished his flock not so much on Calvinistic doctrine as upon a practical Christianity, oriented specifically toward America's developing conflict with England. This hardly means that he left theological or moral problems untouched. As preachers are wont, he sometimes frightened his congregation with visions of sin, and to do so he occasionally found Milton helpful. In his sermon *Upon the Necessity of Yielding a Practical Obedience to the Gospel*, he described the unhappiness of wicked men as comparable to the privation of Milton's apostates: "Farthest from him is best"; [36] and in his disquisition *Of the True Value, Use and End of Life* he twice quoted from *Paradise Lost*, once to intensify grief and once to picture the

---

[35] See Alice M. Baldwin, *The New England Clergy and the American Revolution* (Durham, 1928), for the best account of the authorities and arguments used to prepare the American mind for the Revolution. Milton by no means led the list of authorities, but New England clergymen referred to him with some regularity.

[36] *Sermons* (Boston, 1755), pp. 93–94 and note.

vices of mankind since the Fall.[37] Moreover, in a series of eight sermons on *Christian Sobriety* preached for the special benefit of young men attending West Church, he quoted from Scripture and Milton to depict the eternal tortures of the wicked in Hell. The "dismal region" described in the text of his sermon sprang as much from Book I of *Paradise Lost* as from the second chapter of Titus.[38]

But the sermons that brought Mayhew most fame centered more in pressing political issues than in moral or theological problems. Well versed in the history of seventeenth-century England, Whiggish and Independent in his opinions, he preached with the fervor of a political reformer the heritage of English freedom as codified in the Revolutionary Settlement of 1689. Charles Chauncy, in his funeral sermon on Mayhew, quite rightly observed that he "was eminently a friend to liberty both civil and religious"; and he noted further, with equal acuity, that few had written "more copiously, more elegantly, or more forceably upon this interesting point." [39] In response to the request of his congregation at West Church, Mayhew himself, in the year of his death, had preached a vigorous sermon entitled *The Snare Broken*, in which he had rejoiced with his fellow Americans at the repeal

---

[37] *ibid.*, pp. 470–471 and notes.

[38] *Christian Sobriety: Being Eight Sermons on Titus II. 6* (Boston, 1763), Sermon VIII, pp. 305–306 and note.

[39] *A Discourse Occasioned by the Death of the Reverend Jonathan Mayhew* (Boston, 1766), p. 27 and note. Mayhew's love of truth found expression in a Harvard commencement poem, delivered in 1792 by Robert T. Paine:

> Truth gave his mind electric's subtle spring,
> A Chatham's lightening, and a Milton's wing.

See Alden Bradford, *Memoir of the Life and Writings of Rev. Jonathan Mayhew, D.D.* (Boston, 1838), p. 450. For a brief discussion of the career of Jonathan Mayhew, with occasional references to Milton's influence on his political views, see Moses Coit Tyler, *The Literary History of the American Revolution 1763–1783* (New York, New Printing, 1957), I, 121–140.

of the Stamp Act. Toward the end of his sermon he asked permission to indulge in a bit of autobiography in order to explain further his notions of freedom. In the days of his youth, he informed his listeners, he had been initiated into "the doctrines of civil liberty" as they had been "taught by such men as Plato, Demosthenes, Cicero and other renowned persons among the ancients," as well as by men "such as Sidney and Milton, Locke and Hoadley, among the moderns." He had liked these authors because they seemed "rational." Furthermore, through his study of Scripture he had learned that "where the Spirit of the Lord is, there is liberty," which had made him conclude that "freedom was a great blessing." Such notions of freedom as he had learned in his youth and had cherished in manhood, he could not relinquish after middle age, he confessed; and this was one reason he rejoiced at the repeal of the Stamp Act.[40]

Yet *The Snare Broken* failed to arouse the controversy the sermons of his prime manhood engendered. Its importance lies chiefly in its reiteration of Mayhew's views and in his spelling out the main sources of his thought on civil and religious freedom. Of greater intrinsic significance are *The Right and Duty of Private Judgment Asserted, Objections Considered*, and *A Discourse Concerning Unlimited Submission and Non-Resistance to the Higher Powers*. The last called out several sharp letters and essays in *The Boston Evening Post;* all three show clear marks of Milton's language and thought.

In *The Right and Duty of Private Judgment Asserted* Mayhew addressed himself to religious freedom, a subject which by mid-eighteenth century had received so much attention that almost nothing new could be said. But as America moved toward open conflict with England and ultimately to a

---

[40] *The Snare Broken. A Thanksgiving-Discourse, Preached at the Desire of the West Church in Boston, N.E., Friday May 23, 1766* (Boston, 1766), pp. 35–36.

separation of Church and State, Mayhew felt compelled to reassert the old propositions. To do so effectively he turned to one of the most eloquent orations of all time on toleration and freedom of conscience—*Areopagitica.*

Mayhew could not bring himself to copy verbatim from Milton, a practice followed in England by Charles Blount in the preceding century.[41] He could, however, paraphrase loosely a number of arguments, and sometimes came so close to Milton that he must have had *Areopagitica* in mind as he refreshed the ancient yet ever-pertinent proposals. Like Milton, Mayhew declared that God had endowed man with reason, that duty required man to exercise this divine gift, and that only by using his freedom to choose and to sift information could virtue and truth be attained. Mayhew made no attempt to follow Milton's intricate structure, but a few parallels will show how similarly they spoke on main issues:

| *Areopagitica* | *The Right and Duty* |
|---|---|
| I conceive therefore, that when God did enlarge the universall diet of mans body, saving ever the rules of temperance, he then also, as before, left arbitrary the dyeting and repasting of our minds; as wherein every mature man might have to exercise his owne leading capacity. How great a vertue is temperance, how much of moment through the whole life of man? yet God committs the managing so great a trust, without particular Law or prescription, wholly to the demeanour of every grown man. And therefore when he himself tabl'd the Jews from heaven, that | It appears, then, that all who any ways discourage freedom of inquiry and judgment in religious matters, are, so far forth as they are guilty of this, encroachers upon the natural rights of mankind; that they set up their own authority in opposition to that of almighty God; and that they are enemies to truth, and the Gospel of Jesus Christ. They are encroachers upon the natural rights of mankind, because it is the natural right and privilege of every man to make the best use he can of his own intellectual faculties—They set up their own authority in opposition |

[41] George F. Sensabaugh, *That Grand Whig, Milton* (Stanford, 1952), pp. 58–61, 155–162.

*Areopagitica* (cont.)

Omer which was every mans daily portion of Manna, is computed to have bin more then might have well suffic'd the heartiest feeder thrice as many meals. For those actions which enter into a man, rather then issue out of him, and therefore defile not, God uses not to captivat under a perpetuall childhood of prescription, but trusts him with the gift of reason to be his own chooser (IV, 309–310).[42]

Since therefore the knowledge and survay of vice is in this world so necessary to the constituting of human vertue, and the scanning of error to the confirmation of truth, how can we more safely, and with lesse danger scout into the regions of sin and falsity then by reading all manner of tractats, and hearing all manner of reason? (IV, 311–312)

*The Right and Duty* (cont.)

to that of almighty God, because God has not only given us liberty to examine and judge for ourselves; but expressly required us to do it . . . While other tyrants enslave the bodies of men, these throw their chains and fetters upon the mind, which (as the *Jews* said of themselves), was *born free;* and which ought not to be *in bondage to any man:* but only to the *Father of Spirits* . . . If a man has a right to judge for himself, certainly no other has a right to judge for him: And to attempt it, is to strike at the most valuable interest of a man considered as a reasonable creature (57–58).

They are enemies to truth, and the gospel of Jesus Christ; because free examination is the way to truth, and the gospel in particular, gains ground the faster, the more its doctrines and evidences are examined (58).[43]

To claim that these passages argue for freedom of inquiry on the same grounds would be false and misleading. Milton's structure is built on the Renaissance principle of temperance; Mayhew's on the eighteenth-century concept of natural right. But their arguments cluster in like patterns, their words are tantalizingly similar, and their conclusions about the right and

[42] *The Works of John Milton* (New York, Columbia University Press Edition, 1931). All references to Milton will be to this edition.
[43] *Seven Sermons Upon the Following Subjects* (Boston, 1749), Sermon III. The last sentence here has been moved from the middle of the paragraph to the end.

duty of man to use reason in the search for truth are identical. Furthermore, Milton's image that the golden rule in theology is the same as that in arithmetic parallels Mayhew's extended account of the similarity between the rule of science and religion.

Even clearer parallels of argument and phrase appear in *Objections Considered*, a sequel to Mayhew's earlier sermon. In developing this discourse Mayhew spoke again of the similarity between religious and scientific inquiry, and condensed into inferior yet fairly vigorous prose some of Milton's greatest arguments and figures, such as the eagle facing the sun. A few more passages will demonstrate Mayhew's procedure:

| *Areopagitica* | *Objections Considered* |
| --- | --- |
| . . . Mr. *Selden*, whose volume of naturall & national laws proves, not only by great autorities brought together, but by exquisite reasons and theorems almost mathematically demonstrative, that all opinions, yea errors, known, read, and collated, are of main service & assistance toward the speedy attainment of what is truest (IV, 309). . . . Well knows he who uses to consider, that our faith and knowledge thrives by exercise. (IV, 333) . . . For if we be sure we are in the right, and doe not hold the truth guiltily, . . . what can be more fair, then when a man judicious, learned, and of a conscience, . . . publish to the world what his opinion is, what his reasons, and wherefore that which is now thought cannot be sound (IV, | Free examination, weighing arguments *for*, and *against*, with impartiality, is the way to find the truth. Who imagines that free inquiry into philosophical subjects, has any tendency to lead men into a wrong idea of the natural world? No one was ever so infatuated as to assert this. And it is in all respects as improbable, that free inquiry into religious subjects should lead us into wrong notions concerning the moral world. One would think that a man who had received his religious principles upon mature and deliberate consideration, and so had in his own mind rational arguments to support them, could not have the least apprehension of their suffering any thing by being thoroughly scanned and examined to the bottom. Error and imposture |

| *Areopagitica* (cont.) | *Objections Considered* (cont.) |
|---|---|
| 336). . . . Methinks I see her as an Eagle . . . kindling her un-dazl'd eyes at the full midday beam, . . . while the whole noise of timorous and flocking birds, with those also that love the twi-light, flutter about, amaz'd at what she means, and in their envious gabble would prognosticat a year of sects and schisms (IV, 344). | fly from the light, like the *owl* and *bat:* But truth and honesty, like the noble *eagle*, face the sun. The cause of error and superstition may suffer by a critical examination; its security is to lurk in the dark: But the true religion flourishes the more, the more people exercise their right of private judgment (p. 71).[44] |

Mayhew's condensation of Milton's series of eloquent argu-ments suffers by such a comparison. Particularly unhappy is his transformation of fluttering birds of the twilight into owls and bats. But at other times in *Objections Considered* May-hew proved to be a more felicitous disciple. Milton's famous answer to the supporters of outward church unity, for example, he readily changed into vigorous prose. Milton, it will be re-called, had described fears and complaints among Christians over growing schisms and sects, and had argued that these very complainers, out of their ignorance and pride, should be blamed for disturbances then troubling the nation. The search for truth, not forced unity, could best bring harmony to the Christian community, he maintained. Mayhew presented the same complaints and gave the same answer, sometimes in Mil-ton's own words.

| *Areopagitica* | *Objections Considered* |
|---|---|
| There be who perpetually com-plain of schisms and sects, and make it such a calamity that any man dissents from their maxims. 'Tis their own pride and ignorance which causes the disturbing, who neither will hear with meeknes, | If all are left at liberty to chuse their own religion, and to enjoy it unmolested, we shall have unnu-merable *sects* springing up amongst us; which tends to *confusion*, and destroys the *peace* and *unity of the church* (74) . . . but directly the |

[44] *Seven Sermons Upon the Following Subjects*, Sermon IV.

*Areopagitica* (cont.)

nor can convince, yet all must be supprest which is not found in their *Syntagma.* They are the troublers, they are the dividers of unity, who neglect and permit not others to unite those dissever'd peeces which are yet wanting to the body of Truth. To be still searching what we know not, by what we know, still closing up truth to truth as we find it (for all her body is *homogeneal,* and proportionall) this is the golden rule in *Theology* as well as in *Arithmetick,* and makes up the best harmony in a Church; not the forc't and outward union of cold, and neutrall, and inwardly divided minds (IV, 339).

*Objections Considered* (cont.)

contrary. The confusion and disorder that have hitherto been in the church, have not arisen from christians exercising their own judgment, and worshipping God according to their consciences; (though in a manner somewhat different from others) but from the pride and insolence of those who deny their christian brethren this liberty; and who undertake to prescribe authoritatively to others what they shall believe, and how they shall worship. Were it not for the turbulent, domineering spirit of some Ecclesiasticks, who desire more power than Christ saw fit to intrust them with, there would be but little of that wrangling and discord which have hitherto disturbed the peace of the church (pp. 75–76).

Similar parallels could be adduced from *Areopagitica* and *Objections Considered,* but such a procedure would simply repeat a pattern which by now should be evident. Mayhew so felt the impress of Milton's rhetoric that when he preached on the central issues of toleration and freedom of inquiry he perforce recalled large segments of *Areopagitica,* sometimes in loose paraphrase, sometimes with surprising precision. Other voices from the past echo in Mayhew's political sermons, but in *The Right and Duty of Private Judgment Asserted* and in *Objections Considered* Milton's accents ring out loud and clear.

The same accents resound in Mayhew's discourse on *Unlimited Submission and Non-Resistance to the Higher Powers.*

a homily famous enough to be called the opening gun of the American Revolution. Directing his arguments against the doctrines of passive obedience and non-resistance, which the approach of January 30 and eulogies on Charles I brought to mind, he examined anew in the context of pre-Revolutionary America the old issues of individual freedom and magisterial power. The sensitivity of Americans to these particular issues at mid-century may be judged by the spate of letters and essays Mayhew's discourse brought out in *The Boston Evening Post.* Some praised the stand Mayhew took; some roundly condemned it. One demurrer in particular attempted to discredit some of his arguments by tracing their source to Bishop Hoadly's *Measures of Submission to the Civil Magistrate Considered.*[45] Such dependence cannot be denied. Mayhew himself would have been the first to admit that he had culled some of his views from the controversial bishop, as well as from other well-known authors, as he revealed to his congregation at West Church some sixteen years later. In his *Unlimited Submission and Non-Resistance to the Higher Powers* Mayhew indeed drew freely from the whole Western tradition of political thought. Nevertheless, parts of Mayhew's discourse echo so clearly specific sentences in both *The Tenure of Kings and Magistrates* and *The Ready and Easy Way to Establish a Free Commonwealth,* and some of his arguments follow so closely those in *Pro Populo Anglicano Defensio,* that his memory of Milton as this time would appear especially active and sharp.

Scholars have already noticed a number of obvious Miltonic reminiscences in this, Mayhew's most famous discourse. His

[45] No. 766 (April 16, 1750) and no. 767 (April 23, 1750). For other comments on the issue, see no. 758 (February 19, 1750); no. 759 (February 26, 1750); no. 761 (March 12, 1750); no. 762 (March 19, 1750); and no. 764 (April 2, 1750). Mayhew's sermon, as well as the sharp reaction to it, supports Carl Bridenbaugh's thesis that American fear of Anglican aggression in the New World contributed to the Revolution. See his *Mitre and Sceptre* (Oxford, 1962).

argument that some "have thought it warrantable and glorious to disobey the civil powers in certain circumstances," "to rise unanimously even against the sovereign himself, in order to redress their grievances," has recalled Milton's passage in *The Tenure of Kings and Magistrates*, which praised the wise and exemplary action of Parliament in exacting justice on a tyrannous king.[46] Moreover, Mayhew's assertion that "if we calmly consider the nature of the thing itself, nothing can well be imagined more directly contrary to common sense then to suppose that millions of people should be subjected to the arbitrary, precarious pleasure of one single man—who has naturally no superiority over them in point of authority—so that their estates, and everything that is valuable in life, and even their lives also, shall be absolutely at his disposal, if he happens to be wanton and capricious enough to demand them,"[47] recalls a similar passage in *The Ready and Easy Way to Establish a Free Commonwealth:* "Certainly then that people must needs be madd or strangely infatuated, that build the chief hope of thir common happiness or safetie on a single person: who if he happen to be good, can do no more then another man, if to be bad, hath in his hands to do more evil without check, then millions of other men."[48] Such similarities are typical.

But Mayhew's *Unlimited Submission and Non-Resistance to the Higher Powers* resembles most closely Milton's *Pro Populo Anglicano Defensio*. Even as Milton had in this tract excoriated Claudius Salmasius, who had argued for passive obedience in his defense of Charles I, so Mayhew scorned divines in America who preached passive obedience on the anniversary of the king's death. Furthermore, both Milton and Mayhew argued that resistance to tyrants was lawful by known

---

[46] See John Wingate Thornton, *The Pulpit of the American Revolution* (2nd edn., Boston, 1876), p. 62 and note.

[47] *ibid.*, p. 83 and note. Thornton points to a further similarity in *Pro Populo Anglicano Defensio*.

[48] *The Works of John Milton*, VI, 121.

ordinances, natural as well as divine; and both concluded with a portrait of Charles I, showing him to have been not simply inept but openly villainous. Such similarities lead to the suspicion that, of his acknowledged sources, Mayhew had turned to Milton for specific arguments to press his case against conservative American clergymen. Both the occasion and the purpose of his discourse would naturally send him to the greatest official defender of Oliver Cromwell's Commonwealth Government and of the action of John Bradshaw's High Court of Justice. In Milton's defense of the English people Mayhew could find all the ammunition he needed.

A closer examination of *Unlimited Submission and Non-Resistance to the Higher Powers* and *Pro Populo Anglicano Defensio* argues that this was Mayhew's very procedure. To Salmasius' commonplace argument that a king was like a father and was therefore no more to be resisted by his subjects than parental authority by children, Milton had answered that paternal and regal rule should not be confused and that even a father should be resisted, should his actions be tyrannous. Mayhew employed this "easy and familiar similitude" to enforce precisely the same view:

| *Pro Populo Anglicano Defensio* | *Unlimited Submission* |
| --- | --- |
| We bear with a father, as we do with a king, though he be harsh and severe; but we do not bear with even a father, if he be a tyrant. If a father murder his child, he shall suffer capital punishment; and why should not a king likewise be subject to the same most just law if he have destroyed the people his children? (VII, 45–47) | Suppose God requires a family of children to obey their father and not to resist him, and enforces his command with this argument, that the superintendence and care and authority of a just and kind parent will contribute to the happiness of the whole family . . . suppose this parent at length runs distracted, and attempts in his mad fit to cut all his children's throats. Now, in this case, is not the reason before assigned why these children |

*Unlimited Submission* (cont.)

should obey their parent while he
continued of a sound mind—
namely, their common good—a
reason equally conclusive for dis-
obeying and resisting him, since he
is become delirious and attempts
their ruin? [49]

Mayhew's expansion of Milton's concise image failed to strengthen his prose. Mayhew characteristically changed the syntax of his originals, or spoke more familiarly than his sources would warrant. Yet sometimes he followed his masters quite closely; and nowhere is this more evident than in his exegesis of St. Paul's Letter to the Romans, where he strung together Milton's exact words.

St. Paul's Letter to the Romans, beginning "Let every soul be subject unto the higher powers," had played a central role in nearly every serious analysis of individual freedom and magisterial power for more than a century. Defenders of the Divine Right of kings had referred to it in support of their argument for complete submission of subjects. Proponents of the theory of compact had found in it authority to rise up against a tyrannous ruler. That Milton had based a good part of his defense of the English people upon it, or that Mayhew should construct most of his sermon around it, should therefore cause little surprise. What is worthy of comment is that Mayhew should follow Milton so closely. Only a photographic memory or an open copy of *Pro Populo* could account for the phenomenon of the following passage:

| *Pro Populo Anglicano Defensio* | *Unlimited Submission* |
|---|---|
| "Whosoever . . . resisteth the power" the lawful power, that is, "resisteth the ordinance of God." | "Whosoever, therefore, resisteth the power, resisteth the ordinance of God; and they that shall resist |

[49] *The Pulpit of the American Revolution*, pp. 79–80.

*Pro Populo* (cont.)

*Unlimited Submission* (cont.)

This principle makes kings liable when they resist the laws and the Senate. But he that resists an unlawful power, or resists a person who goes about to overthrow and destroy a lawful one—does he resist the ordinance of God? In your right wits you would not say so, I trow. The next verse removes any uncertainty that the Apostle speaks here of a lawful power only; for lest anyone mistake, and thence go chasing stupid notions, it explains, by defining bounds and limitations, who are the officers that are the ministers of this power, and why he urges us to submit. "Rulers," says he, "are not a terror to good works, but to evil. . . . Do that which is good, and thou shalt have praise of the same: For he is the minister of God to thee for Good . . . He beareth not the sword in vain: for he is . . . a revenger to execute wrath upon him that doth evil." Who but the wicked denies, who but the wicked refuses, willingly to submit to such a power or its minister? And that not only to avoid "the wrath" and the stumbling block, and for fear of punishment, but even "for conscience sake."

Without magistrates and civil government there can be no commonwealth, no human society, no living in the world. But whatever power or whatever magistrate acts

shall receive to themselves damnation." Here the apostle argues that those who resist a reasonable and just authority, which is agreeable to the will of God, do really resist the will of God himself, and will, therefore, be punished by him. But how does this prove that those who resist a lawless, unreasonable power, which is contrary to the will of God, do therein resist the will and ordinance of God? Is resisting those who resist God's will the same thing with resisting God? Or shall those who do so "receive themselves to damnation"? For rulers are not a terror to good works, but to evil. Wilt thou then not be afraid of the power? Do that which is good, and thou shalt have praise of the same. For he is a minister of God to thee for good." . . . "But if thou do that which is evil, be afraid: for he is the minister of God, a revenger, to execute wrath upon him that doth evil." Here the apostle argues, from the nature and end of magistracy, that such as did evil, and such only, had reason to be afraid of the higher powers; it being part of their office to punish evil-doers, no less than to defend and encourage such as do well. . . .

Rulers have no authority from God to do mischief. They are not God's ordinance, or God's ministers, in any other sense than it is by his permission and providence

*Pro Populo* (cont.)

contrary to these precepts—neither the one nor the other is in any proper sense ordained of God. Neither to such a power nor to such a magistrate, therefore, is submission owed or commanded, nor are we forbidden to resist them with discretion, for we shall be resisting not the power nor the magistrate here excellently described, but a robber, a tyrant, a public enemy. If he notwithstanding to be called a magistrate just because he holds power, just because he may appear to be ordained by God for our punishment—in this sense the devil too shall be a magistrate! (VII, 175–177).

*Unlimited Submission* (cont.)

that they are exalted to bear the rule. . . . When once magistrates act contrary to their office, and the end of their institution—when they rob and ruin the public, instead of being guardians of its peace and welfare—they immediately cease to be the ordinance and ministers of God, and no more deserve that glorious character than common pirates and highwaymen . . . and such as are not, therefore, God's ministers, but the devils? [50]

To say that Mayhew's *Unlimited Submission and Non-Resistance to the Higher Powers* fired the opening gun in the American Revolution would be to exaggerate its importance. It was one among many such sermons preached on both sides of the Atlantic in opposition to Anglican insistence on recalling the death of Charles I—a liberal reply to High Churchmen in an ideological conflict reaching back several decades into the seventeenth century. Even the Revolutionary Settlement of 1689 could not keep Church and Dissent from debating the old issue of Divine Right on the day set aside to mourn the demise of the Martyr. But Mayhew's sermon unquestionably aroused comment, and it could have stiffened opinion against tyrannous acts of the Homeland, which subsequently caused

[50] *ibid.*, pp. 73, 74, 75, and 76. Mayhew's sentences have been rearranged to mesh with those in his apparent original. Thornton saw some parallels here to the *Defensio Secunda*, but those to the *Defensio Prima* are more precise and significant.

ᴄoncord farmers to make their historic stand. To say that through Mayhew, Milton himself helped crystallize views that later became to Americans self-evident truths would come close to what actually happened. The direct link between the Puritan Revolution and the American Revolution never became very important, but it was there. And whatever significance it later assumed owed largely to Milton.[51]

If clergymen outside New England knew Milton they left a scant record of what they had read. Even there, many divines failed to mention his name or to use him in any relevant context.[52] The Church Fathers and established philosophers and theologians dominated religious thought of the day; Milton and other poets trailed far behind on the list of authorities cited, even in the sermons of Benjamin Colman and Joseph Bellamy. But wherever Milton touched the minds of Colonial clergymen he left a mark of distinction: his imagery dramatized doctrine, his language strengthened and clarified argument. Most significantly, *Paradise Lost* and Scripture had begun to fuse in the clerical mind and Christianity itself had begun to take on new dimensions, having been shaped by the vast pictures Milton had drawn. Americans began to see from the pulpit the old Christian story in a new imagistic light.

[51] James Harrington also linked the two revolutions. See H. F. Russell Smith, *Harrington and His Oceana* (Cambridge, 1914). Caroline Robbins suggests that seventeenth-century revolutionary ideas came to America via the Commonwealthmen of the eighteenth century. See her *The Eighteenth-Century Commonwealthman* (Cambridge, Mass., 1959), pp. 378–386.

[52] Andrew Eliot did say, however, that he never wearied of the *Defensio Prima*, and that, though Milton should be read in Latin, his "sentiments" were "so just, and his attachment to liberty so firm, that he ought to be open to every Englishman." See the *Collections of the Massachusetts Historical Society*, IV, Series 4, 412–413. Lester Fred Zimmerman, in "Some Aspects of Milton's American Reputation to 1900" (Unpublished dissertation, the University of Wisconsin, 1950), found Milton parallels in a number of election sermons, but the similarities are general and tenuous. Samuel Davies of Virginia quoted Milton several times, though not significantly. See his *Sermons on Important Subjects*, III (Boston, 1811), 107, 274.

## I V

Milton moved easily from the religious life of the Colonies into the stream of American poetry. A good number of versifiers themselves belonged to the clergy, and religion and literature still walked hand in hand. Furthermore, the neoclassic doctrine of imitation sent poets to great men of the past with the Longinian hope that such an excursion would improve their own verse. Philip Pain in his *Daily Meditations* looked to the devotional poetry of George Herbert and Francis Quarles. Edward Taylor invoked the same meditational tradition in his distinguished collection of verse, only recently published.[53] Most Americans, however, eschewed the "metaphysical" style for the more regular manner of the principal Augustans; and almanacs quoted, as rhythmically as the moon changed its phases, from Dryden or Pope, or Isaac Watts or Edward Young or James Thomson.[54] *The Seasons* particularly, as its nature suggested, lent itself to quotation in such ubiquitous annals. Yet despite the weight of Augustan theory and practice, Milton affected American poetry more than any one English author. His syntax, language, imagery, and thought weave in and out of a large body of Colonial verse, and he sometimes dominated a few minor poets of the time.

To record every print Milton made on Colonial poetry would serve no intelligent purpose. Some of his influence has been pretty well traced through the tangle of early American verse, though a vast amount of poetry then published still

[53] See *The Poems of Edward Taylor*, ed. Donald E. Stanford (New Haven, 1960), Foreword by Louis L. Martz.

[54] See, for example, *The American Almanac* (Philadelphia) for 1722, 1724, and 1733; *The Virginia Almanack* (Williamsburg) for 1758; *An Almanack for the Year of Christian Account* for 1754; *An Almanack For the Year of Our Lord Christ, 1761*; *The Rhode Island Almanac* for 1763, 1764, 1765, 1766, and 1767; and *The New-England Almanack* (Providence) for 1768.

awaits careful assessment.[55] Nevertheless, a few well-known marks of Milton should be briefly recalled to show how widely he ranged and to reveal the variety of ways he entered into literature of the time. Such a procedure should indicate why American poets called on Milton so often, as well as point the direction his influence was taking.

Even a cursory glance at early American verse discovers the variety and range of his impress. Samuel Davies incorporated into his *Poem Wrote by a Clergyman in Virginia in a Storm of Wind and Rain* a number of Miltonic hierarchs, such as "Cherubs and Seraphs, Potentates and Thrones," whom he arrayed in "Glorious Light" before the majesty of God; and when he spoke of the souls of his flock, he rolled out, Milton-like, the exotic sounds of *Ophir* and *Peru*.[56] James Bowdoin turned Milton's hymn of nuptial love in Book IV of *Paradise Lost* into clanging heroic couplets for the purpose of celebrating the marriage of George III to Charlotte Sophia of Mecklenburg-Strelitz. Milton had opened his hymn with "Haile wedded Love," and had idealized family life, emphasizing the sharp contrast between bought sensual love and a true union of souls. Bowdoin believed that such sentiments described and enhanced the royal marriage in England:

> ALL-HAIL, connubial Love! whence copious flow
> Far greater joys than lawless love can know:
> Joys all sincere—to passion not confin'd—
> Resulting from an intercourse of mind:
> Not only joys that appetite inspires,
> But such as spring from friendship's nobler fires.
> True friendship dwells with thee, Connubial Love!
> And thou canst friendship's sacred fires improve.

[55] See Susanna Adeline Matteson, "The Influence of Milton on Early American Poetry up to 1800" (Unpublished Master's Thesis, Brown University, 1931), and Leon Howard, "The Influence of Milton on Colonial American Poetry," pp. 63–89.

[56] *A Poem Wrote by a Clergyman in Virginia in a Storm of Wind and Rain*, [1750], pp. 1–2.

From thee each love-inspiring name proceeds;
And in the breast the tend'rest motions breeds:
To B R U N S W I C K thou shalt give a father's name;
And with a father's love his breast inflame:
To C H A R L O T T E , the maternal—whence shall flow
The tender joys that only mothers know.[57]

Milton's hymn to wedded love had already called out an essay in *The Pennsylvania Gazette;* now it spoke in more strident tones for a graduate of Harvard who approved the marriage of England's new sovereign.

A group of heterogenous poems composed by an "American Gentleman" shows Milton's influence broadening to include imagery and narrative technique. The collection itself has little to recommend it, but *Man's Fall and Exaltation,* one of the most ambitious poems in the group, merits comment in that it followed so closely Milton's justification of God's ways to man. This poem presents many Miltonic phrases and scenes strung together in a narrative pattern reminiscent of unfolding events in *Paradise Lost,* though sometimes strange variations in sequence occur. Milton's dramatic study of flattery and pride in the temptation of Eve, for instance, was condensed into rapid heroic couplets. Eve's taking the fruit, the groaning earth, Satan's rhetoric, Adam's fondness for Eve—all appear; but in Milton's account the entry of Sin and Death into the world and the hissing applause of the Infernal Council occur later:

> Unable to resist th' alluring Charm,
> She took and eat—Earth felt the dread Alarm:
> Wild Horror stalk'd around; a sable Cloud
> O'erspread the Day; and Nature mourn'd aloud!
> E X U L T I N G , now, th' accused *Fiend* withdraws,
> And Hell, in Triumph, hiss'd a loud Applause.
> While *Sin* and *Death* with Giant-Strides advance,

---

[57] *Pietas et Gratulatio Collegii Cantabrigiensis Apud Novanglos* (Boston, 1761), pp. 102–103. Some of the poems in this collection mourn the old King; others praise the new.

And lowring Vengeance clouds the wide Expanse.
E V E , now, eccentric to her Orb of Bliss,
Expects the glorious *Metamorphosis.*
To A D A M the delicious Fruit conveys,
And all the *Serpent's* Rhetoric displays.
I N A P P R E H E N S I V E of the fatal Cheat,
Or fondly to partake his Consort's Fate;
The *sacred Morsel* from her Hand he took;
Earth groan'd a second Time, and Nature shook! [58]

Occasionally, Milton's stamp cut with even greater precision. Expressions such as ''C O E V A L with th' E T E R N A L M I N D,'' "Essence of L I G H T I N E F F A B L E,'' and "Thrones, Principalities, and Powers" almost match their originals. But more than any collection of phrases in *Man's Fall and Exaltation* the narrative imagery shows the extent of Miltonic influence. However violently the American Gentleman wrenched Milton's blank verse, he absorbed the vision of *Paradise Lost* and pictured the Fall and Redemption of Man as told in that poem. Like Benjamin Colman, he dramatized Christian doctrine by adding Miltonic colors and contours to the old Scriptural story.[59]

As Milton became better known he began to shape the syntax of heroic couplets. Poets apparently believed that Milton's distinctive word structure would elevate their effusions, even as would his language and imagery. One of the first Colonial poets to show this particular influence was Thomas Godfrey, who in two of his juvenile poems attempted to reach for sublimity by following Milton's patterned word order. Godfrey had shown elsewhere that he knew Milton well. His elegy on General Wolfe, for example, echoed *Lycidas* a number of times. Following the pastoral tradition, he turned General

---

[58] *Poems Moral and Divine, on the Following Subjects* (London, 1756), pp. 3–5, 14–15, 20.

[59] See George Cockings, *War: An Heroic Poem* (2nd. edn., Boston, 1762), p. 79, for an epic simile based on Milton's picturing of death. Cockings was an Englishman stationed in Boston.

Wolfe into the Shepherd Amintor, whose death inspired Damaetas and Lysidas to sing a funeral dirge. The elegy itself cannot be commended: it neither follows Milton's climactic structure nor elicits a haunting response. But it concludes with a couplet which brings to mind the last lines of *Lycidas:*

> So sung the Swains, 'til Phoebus' radiant light,
> Chac'd to her azure bed the Queen of Night.[60]

Such reminiscences suggest that Godfrey consciously imitated Milton's syntax to achieve special effects in the *Court of Fancy* and *The Assembly of Birds,* two juvenile poems obviously stemming from Chaucer. The famous image opening Book II of *Paradise Lost*—"High on a Throne of Royal State . . . Satan exalted sat"—so captured Godfrey's imagination that, hoping to elevate or to display wit in his own verse, he imposed Milton's word order on his own heroic couplets, with results somewhat less than sublime:

> High in the midst, rais'd on her rolling throne,
> Sublimely eminent bright F A N C Y shone.

> High on a shining seat with rubies grac'd,
> *Cupid,* the God of am'rous thoughts, was plac'd.[61]

The image of Satan sitting in proud eminence before the Infernal Council inspired Americans for nearly a century. Scarcely a picture of royalty, scarcely a throne scene or a conclave, escaped being cast into this Miltonic pattern. Milton had fixed the manner for presenting such stately affairs, and poets thought that by copying it they could dignify what they wanted to say.

Even so rapid a glance at fugitive verse of the day shows, however at random, the direction Miltonic influence was beginning to take. Milton's thought had undoubtedly moved into

[60] *Juvenile Poems on Various Subjects. With the Prince of Parthia, a Tragedy* (Philadelphia, 1765), p. 34.
[61] *ibid.,* pp. 52, 88.

the poetic community, perhaps as far as it had penetrated religious life of the age, but his language, imagery, and syntax left on belles-lettres marks more distinctive.[62] The prevalence of such marks suggests that Milton might have occasionally overpowered a few minor poets, and that these sometime disciples might show even more clearly where Miltonic poetry was headed. This, in fact, is actually what happened. No poet so affected could be called great, but some achieved fame in their day and their verse pointed directly to mood poetry of a later time and to the patriotic effusions of Hugh Henry Brackenridge and Philip Freneau, of John Trumbull, Joel Barlow, and Timothy Dwight. In this, they can be considered important, however slight their poetic achievements.

The first of these sometime Milton disciples was Richard Steere, whose *Daniel Catcher* appeared in 1682 and again in 1713, accompanied by several additional poems. Only a line or two in the earlier collection, such as "Terrour on his Brow," even faintly resembles Milton's typical language or phrasing, but two poems in the later edition argue that Steere knew the *Nativity Ode* and *Paradise Lost,* and that he consciously tried to achieve special poetic effects by following their separate styles.

Signs of *Paradise Lost* appear most clearly in a blank verse poem, *Earth's Felicities, Heaven's Allowances.* In presenting his picture of happiness on earth, Steere apparently had in mind Milton's vision of Eden: his "Silver *Streams,*" "Tap'stry green," and "*Birds* Enamel'd with their Divers *Plumes*" blend easily into Milton's idyllic scene. But more distinctively Miltonic is Steere's verse paragraph, with its piling up of sensuous

[62] For a number of reproductions and paraphrases of Milton's lines see *An Astronomical Diary, Or, An Almanack for the Year of Our Lord Christ 1746; An Almanack For the Year of Our Lord Christ, 1761;* and Leon Howard, "The Influence of Milton on Colonial American Poetry," pp. 63–89.

detail, often accompanied with information about exotic lands of origin or traffic, relevant but not always logically developed. His depiction of spices and odors displays a particularly Miltonic flourish:

> So, the *Olfactal* faculty's Supply'd,
> With Oderiferous, and Choice *perfumes*,
> Of *Myrrh*, of *Cassia*, and of *Bruised Spices*;
> Sweet Smelling *Gums*, from the Arabian Coast,
> Of our Domestick *Violets, Pinks, and Roses*;
> With Fragrant *Herbs, & Blossoms* of our *Gardens*.[63]

Such mellifluous sounds neither typify Steere's poem, nor add much to its worth. But his blank verse, his development of detail, and at times his line structure indicate clearly that through an imitation of *Paradise Lost* he was attempting to reach for sublimity.

More strikingly Miltonic was Steere's ode *Upon the Coelestial Embassy Perform'd by Angels*. Even a cursory reading of this poem—by far the best in the 1713 collection—brings to mind Milton's *Nativity Ode*. To argue that Steere slavishly followed Milton's intention and structure would exaggerate the real similarities these poems present. Steere neither showed the rout of the pagan gods, nor embellished his picture of the Nativity with metaphysical wit or classical allusion. His eyes focused squarely on the angels themselves as they descended to earth and arrived on Bethlehem's plains. Nevertheless, Steere caught something of Milton's spirit and tone. The peacefulness of the night, the guilt of the world, the angelic heralding of joy, the paradox of Christ in the manger—all quietly described in an unusual stanzaic form broken by a trimeter line and concluding with a hexameter—suggest at

---

[63] *The Daniel Catcher. The Life of the Prophet Daniel: In A Poem, to which is Added, Earth's Felicities, Heaven's Allowances, A Blank Poem. With Several Other Poems* (1713), pp. 56–57.

once that Steere had Milton before him when he composed his own poem. A typical stanza will illustrate the similarity of the two odes:

> But on a milder Errand these
> Are sent, an Embassy of Peace,
> Therefore they take a milder flame,
> And with their beams unpointed came;
> Having Commission from above,
> To Publish universal Love;
>   And being thus prepar'd,
> That mortals at Their sight might not be scar'd,
> Drest in their Trav'ling cloathes; Direct the way
> Unto *that distant place where their great Sov'reign lay*.[64]

Several paradoxes toward the end of the poem faintly recall Richard Crashaw's *Hymn* sung by the shepherds at the Nativity; but the nature of Steere's verse, like that of Milton's, is descriptive and leisurely narrative, not devotional. Both are indeed mannered in style. Had Steere followed Milton in no other poem,[65] *Upon the Coelestial Embassy Perform'd by Angels* would argue a minor discipleship.

Yet the style of Milton's *Nativity Ode* apparently appealed to few early Americans. The grand roll of *Paradise Lost* clearly interested them most, a fascination evidenced several times in Steere's volume of verse as well as in random echoes in the poetry of others. Among minor poets of the earlier period to feel the attraction of *Paradise Lost* most fully was James Ralph, to whom Milton was so real that he once felt compelled to paint his portrait in words. Perhaps Ralph should not be considered an American author: he published his three volumes of poetry and criticism four years after he left America for England, and is remembered for his vitriolic attacks

---

[64] *ibid.*, pp. 82–85.
[65] Of the six other poems in *The Daniel Catcher*, none shows Miltonic influence, and in *A Monumental Memorial of Marine Mercy* (1684) only faint echoes appear. See pp. 9–10.

upon Pope and for his political tracts addressed to English turmoils at mid-century. But historians usually place him in the annals of American literature, and even more than in Steere Milton lived in his verse.

Paradoxically, Ralph presented in his prefaces neoclassical views on the nature and function of poetry, but on the superiority of blank verse in narrative poems he entertained no critical doubt. In Milton's own words he campaigned to free poetry *"from the troublesome and modern bondage of* rhiming." [66] Blank verse could not be thought "less sonorous or musical," he exclaimed. No critic yet, "notwithstanding all the prejudice of custom," had imagined that Homer or Virgil or Milton "would have received an additional beauty from *rhime.*" But Ralph had to admit that no one had imitated Milton with "good grace." Milton's numbers were so "majestical" and his expressions so apt that those who had attempted to do so had run into an "affectation" of "antiquated words and phrases, rather than a lively and accurate method of designing and colouring like him." "Even Mr. *Phillips* himself," Ralph continued, "had succeeded better if he had not paid so strict a deference to *Milton*'s manner, and thereby neglected his own." [67] Such caveats, however, had little effect on Ralph himself. In his effort to demonstrate the vigor of blank verse he followed Milton so closely that his own lines take on the artificialities he so vigorously deplored. John Philips, ironically, had cast a Miltonic shilling more splendid than Ralph was ever to coin.

Yet among early American poets Ralph should not be lightly dismissed. If his interest in poetry outran his achievement, he nonetheless aimed for distinction, and this meant to him writing in blank verse, some of it imitative of Milton. Perhaps the

[66] *The Muses' Address to the King: An Ode.* See the title page. title page.
[67] *Night: A Poem. In Four Books,* pp. iii–viii.

sole stamp of Milton in *The Muses' Address to the King* appeared in a dedicatory poem to that collection, but the imprint is so light that it can be only felt, not analyzed in detail. That Ralph had Milton in mind through the entire volume, however, is evidenced by the appearance of Milton's words on the title page itself and by his high praise of Milton's genius and style in a poem describing a number of authors, including Spenser and Shakespeare.

Such impressions and references mean little in themselves: they assume significance only when correlated with Miltonic echoes in *Night: A Poem*, one of Ralph's pieces often thought to have been inspired by James Thomson's *Winter*. Whatever influence Thomson may have exerted, Ralph clearly believed that the language and imagery of *Paradise Lost* would elevate his verse and hence reminiscences in the poem are chiefly Miltonic. Consider, for example, Ralph's invocation:

> O thou, whose secret haunt is far remov'd
> From all the restless, glaring scenes of day,
> Sweet contemplation, daughter of the night!
> O deign thy favour to th' adventrous muse,
> And, on thy pow'rful pinions, safely guide
> Her daring progress thro' the darksom round.[68]

Ralph's "secret haunt," to be sure, is far removed from Milton's "secret Top" of Mount Oreb, and "Sweet contemplation" is quite different from the Holy Spirit of *Paradise Lost*. Yet like Milton, Ralph had asked for illumination, had called on light to guide him through darkness, and had invoked a power to lift him to adventurous and daring heights of poetic creation. But if, to judge from the dead level of most of Ralph's poem, Sweet Contemplation utterly failed him, the Holy Spirit still operative through Book IV of *Paradise Lost* offered him evident aid. For in numerous lines Ralph simply paraphrased Milton's famous picture of the arrival of night

[68] *ibid.*, p. 4.

in the Garden of Eden, a selection that was to become a favorite in American schools before the close of the century. "Now came still Eevning on," Milton had written; and as he added strokes to his picture of the deepening twilight, Hesperus appeared, shining in brilliance and leading the stars until that planet faded, while the moon,

> Rising in clouded Majestie, at length
> Apparent Queen unvaild her peerless light,
> And o'er the dark her Silver Mantle threw.

With the coming of night Adam and Eve retired; but before sleep overtook them Eve confided in Adam her love for him and spoke of her enjoyment in nature. The breath of morn was sweet, she said, and its rising was sweet, accompanied "With charm of earliest Birds." Ralph followed much of this scene in his own description of night, changing words here, shifting lines there, but sometimes copying phrases verbatim:

> Bright ,Vesper leads her peaceful wain, and rolls
> His radiant circlet up the starry vault,
> Or, o'er th' illumin'd earth, the friendly moon
> Streams down her grateful rays, and shines the queen of heav'n.
>
> .    .    .    .    .    .    .
>
> Or, when still evening o'er the sky returns,
> And, in their radiant orbs, the twinkling stars
> Prepare their circuits, . . .
>
> .    .    .    .    .    .    .
>
> At length the morning light illustrious dawns,
> Sweetly acclaim'd with charm of earliest birds.[69]

Ralph could not rest content simply to paraphrase the celebrated night piece of Milton. Like Godfrey and others who followed, he became enamoured of Milton's syntax, particularly with the construction which distinguished the opening

[69] *ibid.*, pp. 5–7, 13.

lines of Book II of *Paradise Lost*. Ralph's warning that poets copied Milton to their peril could hardly apply more appropriately than to his own verbal and syntactical imitation of Milton's colorful picture of Satan:

> High on a pompous throne, with glitt'ring gems
> Emblaz'd, the lordly tyrrant sits sublime.[70]

Perhaps Ralph wrought here more precisely than he had planned. In his refurbishing the pomp and grandeur of Pandemonium, he produced, as he said, a throne merely pompous, not royal.

Even in *Sawney* Ralph could not escape the dominating figure of Milton. In this satiric piece he dramatized his attack upon Pope with Miltonic symbols and imagery. The publication of *The Dunciad*, he believed, had marked Pope's fall from poetic grace, a fall so disastrous that it could best be defined by recalling Satan's anguished cry over his defeated compeer, Beelzebub: "*If Thou beest He—But O how fall'n! How chang'd!*" Even at this early date Ralph saw the power of Miltonic symbols. But more important than this was Ralph's recognition that the imagery of *Paradise Lost* could be employed to achieve special satirical effects: the golden scales Milton had pictured at the end of Book IV allowed Ralph to place Pope in the balance and find him wanting. Hand "me down great *Milton's* Scales," he called out, as he warmed to his task. Put Homer in one balance and Sawney in the other and observe the result! Ralph's scorn of heroic couplets, his championing of blank verse, and his hatred of Pope all could be dramatized and sharpened by reference to the great image in *Paradise Lost*:

> Blind *John* assist me—bless my Soul! the last
> Up flies and kicks the beam: How light! How vain!

[70] *ibid.*, p. 31.

How trifling! could the Wretch, in Rhime, pretend
To give us *Homer*, plain, majestick, great,
When *Milton*, his distinguish'd Son, who knew
His inmost soul, despis'd the *Lydian* Airs,
And, with a Grandeur equal to his Theme,
Delighted *Albion's* Sons? [71]

No one could say that Ralph's wit was subtle or rapier-like, but he left no doubt about his poetic position. Milton, he believed, had achieved true sublimity, and to raise his own verse he had occasionally copied his art, as had Steere and lesser, often anonymous, authors. What is distinctive about Ralph is not so much his consciousness of Milton or his imitation of his language and style as his recognition that the imagery of *Paradise Lost* could become an instrument of satire. Such a discovery was to bear later fruit.

After Steere and Ralph came Mather Byles, perhaps the most famous Milton disciple in Colonial times. Witty, urbane, and inordinately ambitious for literary fame, he carried on an abortive correspondence with Pope and Isaac Watts while he was creating a name for himself in *The New England Weekly Journal*, in which, as early as 1727, he published some of his poetry and prose. So famous had he become by the fifth decade of the century that the appearance of *Poems on Several Occasions* in 1744 and *Poems by Several Hands* in 1745 turned out to be major literary events of the day. His correspondence with Pope, who gracefully complimented him in a single reply, reveals neoclassical tastes and enthusiasms; and a good deal of his poetry, which received extravagant plaudits in New England, followed Augustan patterns and diction.[72] To find much

---

[71] *Sawney. An Heroic Poem. Occasion'd by the Dunciad*, pp. xii–xiii, 13.

[72] See *Poems on Several Occasions* (New York, 1940). Reproduced from the edition of 1744, with an introduction by C. Lennart Carlson. The introduction contains the best information about Byles's life, the dating of his poems, and his importance in the history of American literature.

of Milton in a man so obviously steeped in eighteenth-century tastes and so markedly differing from James Ralph in both theory and practice would seem paradoxical, yet Miltonic influence can be unhesitatingly traced through much of Byles's verse.

Such a paradox should not be interpreted to mean that Milton was Byles's chief poetic mentor. Byles's obvious admiration for Pope and Watts, evident in both his correspondence and poetry, shows that he was unable or unwilling to run counter to prevailing patterns of verse or standards of taste. As a sort of self-appointed poet laureate of New England, he produced a number of conventional religious pieces and celebrated contemporary people and events in familiar modes of the day. But Milton was much on his mind. In his first letter to Pope, dated October 7, 1727, he enclosed several verses published earlier in *The New England Weekly Journal,* one of which was entitled "Written in Milton's *Paradise Lost*" [73]—a piece he considered important enough to include in his *Poems on Several Occasions.* What impressed Byles most was Milton's power of description, a combination of harmony and force which could set forth equally the sublimities of the spiritual world and the simple beauties of nature. Somewhat timidly, though with more boldness as he progressed, Byles imitated both powers, revealing, as he did so, a growing tendency among American poets to turn to Milton for special pictorial effects.

In the first part of his imitation of *Paradise Lost* Byles strained for sublimity. Milton's genius had opened his eyes

---

[73] See Austin Warren, "To Mr. Pope: Epistles from America," PMLA, XLVIII (1933), 68–69. See also Arthur Wentworth Hamilton Eaton, *The Famous Mather Byles* (Boston, 1914), for further biographical details, and C. Lennart Carlson, "John Adams, Matthew Adams, Mather Byles, and the *New England Weekly Journal,*" *American Literature,* XII (1940), 347–348, for an account of how Americans shared the English literary tradition.

and ears to the terrors of Hell, making him see hideous spec-
ters and hear clanking chains; to achieve similar effects he
could do no better than follow Milton's effective techniques.
In consequence, Byles wrote most of his poem in blank verse;
and in his picture of Satan and Death he attempted to heighten
his scene by copying Milton's verse paragraph, his moving
caesura, and even several of his exact phrases:

> Here *Satan* rears his mighty Bulk on high,
> And tow'rs amid th' infernal Legions; fill'd
> With Pride, and dire Revenge; daring his Looks;
> Rage heaves his lab'ring Breast, and all around
> His fiery Eye-balls formidably roll,
> And dart destructive Flames; with dreadful Blaze
> The ruddy Ligh'ning rapid runs along,
> And guilds the gloomy Regions of Despair,
> With Streaks tremendous. Here assaults my Sight
> The gressly Monster *Death*, He onward stalks
> *With horrid Strides, Hell trembles as he treads;*
> On his fierce Front a bold defiance low'rs;
> Bent is his Brow, in his right Hand he shakes
> His quiv'ring Lance. How fell the Fiend appears
> In ev'ry Prospect, wrathful or serene?
> Pleas'd, *horrible he grins a gastly Smile;*
> And *Erebus* grows blacker as he Frowns.[74]

Byles could not even shift his scene from Hell to the plains
of Heaven without resorting to the device Milton had made
familiar in *Paradise Lost:* he called on the Heavenly Muse
to turn the vision away from Satan and Death to the mighty
armies embattled on high. Sketching the battle itself, condensed from Raphael's account told to Adam, so exhausted
Byles that his fainting muse folded her wings, "Unable to
sustain so strong a Flight." That such weariness set in is perhaps fortunate, for Byles's presentation of the great conflict
in Heaven no more achieved true sublimity than had his vision
of Hell. The panorama of celestial warfare served a much

[74] *Poems on Several Occasions*, pp. 26–27.

better purpose in his sermon on *The Glorious Rest of Heaven*, where he pictured to his congregation, as a part of a view opened up to the redeemed, the great Archangel *"Michael*, who drove down the rebel Angels thunder-struck from the Battlements of Heaven, into the deep Abyss of Damnation." [75] But of importance to the development of American poetry is the fact that Milton's image had stuck in his mind. Sublimity, Byles thought, lay in such scenes; the way to sublimity therefore lay in imitation of Milton.

If Milton could open to Byles the grand vistas of Heaven and Hell, his art could also unfold the "softer" vision of Adam and Eve in the Garden. Byles's purpose now was not to achieve grandeur but to charm the senses and melt the heart, as Milton had done so effectively in Book IV of *Paradise Lost*. To fulfill such an aim, Byles simply reproduced the main outlines of Milton's vision of paradise, with its mazy bowers and shadowy groves, its luxuriant flowers and singing birds, its purling brooks and embroidered banks—a scene crowned with an address to Adam and Eve:

> Hail, happy *Adam*, Heav'n adorns thy Soul,
> Full bless'd. And thou, immortal Mother, Hail!
> O heav'nly-fair, divinely-beauteous *Eve!*
> Thee to adorn what endless Charms conspire?
> Cælestial Coral blushes on thy Lips,
> No op'ning Rose glows with so bright a Bloom.
> Thy Breath abroad diffusive Odor spreads,
> A gay Carnation purples o'er thy Cheeks,
> While thy fair Eyes roll round their radiant Orbs,
> With winning Majesty, and nat'ral Art.
> Thy waving Tresses on thy Shoulders play,
> Flow loosely down, and wanton in the Wind.
> You, am'rous *Zephires*, kiss her snowy Breast,
> Flit softly by, and gently lift her Locks.[76]

[75] *A Sermon At the Thursday-Lecture in Boston, Jan[uary]3, 1744–45* (Boston, 1745), pp. 14–15.
[76] *Poems on Several Occasions*, p. 33.

Yet even here Byles's tender muse halted: as he came to the end of his poem he realized his failure to achieve Milton's effects. To be truthful, his paradise was artificial, his Adam unmanly, and his Eve lacked the seductive innocence with which Milton had endowed her. Even his lines had degenerated into an ineffective admixture of blank verse and heroic couplets. As Byles admitted, Milton's "mighty Numbers" had towered above his own "Sight," mocking his "low Musick." But Milton *had* pointed the way to sublimity and to scenes of charm and delight. Somehow, someone should be able to achieve through his idiom identical effects, though Byles in his heart knew he had been unsuccessful.

Byles attempted no more extended imitations of *Paradise Lost*. The rest of his verse followed conventional Augustan patterns and forms, with no distinctive variations or experimentations. But so strong was Milton's influence that even when Byles was most poetically modish marks of *Paradise Lost* often appear. He opened *The Comet*, for example, with "Descend *Urania*, and inspire my verse," [77] and *To the Memory of a Young Commander* with "Descend, immortal Muse, inspire my Song." [78] In *Eternity* he rejected trifling pastoral themes of love and declared that

A nobler Subject asks th' advent'rous Song;

. . . . . . .

And bid the Muse on soaring Pinions rise. [79]

But more noteworthy than such reminiscences was the way Byles metamorphosed Milton's imagery to serve his own poetic aims. He turned Milton's famous picture of Satan, burning "like a Comet" and shaking from his hair "Pestilence and

---

[77] *A Collection of Poems* (Boston, 1744), p. 14. C. Lennart Carlson claimed that *The Comet* is Byles's poem. See Carlson, *op. cit.*, p. vii, note.
[78] *Poems on Several Occasions*, p. 34.
[79] *ibid.*, p. 106.

Warr," into a description of a comet alone—a "ruddy wonder" of the western sky, rolling from star to star and alarming the poles, a "burning ruin" upon which nations gazed in dire terror, dreaming that its "sparkling hair" shook "famine, earthquake, pestilence and war." [80] Such a metamorphosis, however, hardly matched the change Byles imposed on the panorama of Satan's fall over the battlements of Heaven into the perdition of Hell. This grand image he utilized to condemn a profane compliment in a devout poem he had recently read. Even as Satan, he declared, had "left his heav'nly Song,"

> And mock'd his Maker with a Seraph's Tongue,
> MESSIAH, terrible in Wrath! arose,
> And hurl'd him down to Hell's tremendous Woes,
> Where Seas of Fire with roaring Storms resound,
> And endless Darkness spreads its brooding Horrors round,[81]

so should the evil lines of the poem be condemned to flames and destruction. Seldom had Byles moved more rapidly from the sublime to the ridiculous.

The image of Milton's apostate angel served Byles to better purpose in *Goliah's Defeat,* a religious poem of heroic aims. By making his giant of the Philistines look and talk like Satan as he strode over the burning marl prior to his address to his fallen compeers, Byles gave his personage a few commanding, if evil, characteristics. Goliah assumed stature when invested with Satan's physical and spiritual accoutrements:

> With hideous Strides he travers'd all the Ground,
> And o'er the Hills the Country view'd around
> His brawny Flesh, and his prodigious Bones,
> Bespoke him one of *Anak's* mighty Sons.
> Death and Defiance sat upon his Brow,
> Revenge and Hell his glaring Eye-balls show.
> Then his dire Hand uplifted to the Skies,
> Thunder his Voice, and Lightning in his Eyes,

[80] *A Collection of Poems,* pp. 14–17.
[81] *Poems on Several Occasions,* p. 16.

He cry'd aloud with such a dreadful Sound,
As shook the Heav'ns, and rent the trembling Ground.[82]

The address itself, which faintly resembled Satan's proud defiance of God, affected Israel's camp in much the same way the rebel angels reacted to the Messiah's might in Book VI of *Paradise Lost:*

> Behold, Concern and dire Amaze appear
> Thro' all the Host, when they his Accents hear,
> Shudd'ring Anxiety, and black Despair.
> Pale are their Faces, in their Hearts is dread,
> And panick Terror o'er the Field is spread.
> Ghastly Confusion reigns, and not a Knight
> Dares undertake to *think* upon the Fight.[83]

Byles claimed that he had written *Goliah's Defeat* after the manner of Lucan, but, until the arrival of David in Byles's account, the reminiscences are chiefly Miltonic.

Byles followed Milton so closely that the poet John Adams announced his discipleship in an encomiastic verse *To A Gentleman at the Sight of Some of His Poems.* Adams praised Byles for bringing accolade to American shores. Byles had, he said, so far ascended Parnassus that he could be compared to Horace, Isaac Watts, and Edmund Waller. But Adams saw Byles's greatest distinction in his imitations of *Paradise Lost* —in his presentation of "gay delightful scenes" in the Garden and in his descriptions of Satan and the battle in Heaven. Here Byles had mounted to Milton's "godlike heights," Adams declared, an appraisal attributable more to friendship than to perception or judgment. Yet it is significant to American poetry that Adams should praise the Miltonic element in Byles's verse, that he should declare that the swiftness and vigor of his numbers sprang from *Paradise Lost.* Adams also believed that through Milton poets could achieve special

[82] *ibid.,* pp. 18–19.
[83] *ibid.,* p. 19.

85

effects, though in his own verse relatively few marks of Milton occur.

Yet Adams was affected by Milton. Not so ambitious as Byles, nor so hungry for public acclaim, he wrote quietly on occasional topics and paraphrased Scripture. His admiration for Milton stopped just short of idolatry, or at least so it would seem, so high was his praise of the Miltonic element he found' in Byles's verse. In view of such a critical stance his own *Poems on Several Occasions* might be expected to show a few Miltonic touches. Like Byles, he became enamored of Milton's language and imagery and was unable to resist metamorphosing a striking figure or two in a most preposterous fashion. In his translation of Psalm 104, for example, he turned the famous picture of Satan condemned to captivity in Hell into a trope' damning the "threatening Billows," asking that they be

> In adamantine chains forever bound
> By Heav'n's Decree to sink below the Ground.[84]

In a poem on the death of Cotton Mather he succumbed to the Miltonic expression, "s a y Muse." [85] Such marks of Milton's imagery and style, however, are few.

But in his longest and most ambitious poem, *The Revelation of St. John the Divine*, he disclosed a habit of mind then becoming widespread in both the religious and poetic communities: he incorporated into his translation of Scripture some of the imagery of *Paradise Lost* for the express purpose of achieving special pictorial and dramatic effects. To St. John's apocalyptic vision of War, mounted on a white horse and bearing a bow and a crown, Adams added, for example, a Miltonic touch recalling the figure of Satan:

> When, rushing on my Sight,
> Arose a furious Steed array'd in White;

[84] *Poems on Several Occasions, Original and Translated* (Boston, 1745), p. 49.
[85] *ibid.*, p. 84.

> The Rider ghastly, fatal was his Bow,
> And Terror sat in Triumph on his Brow.[86]

And to St. John's cryptic story of the war in Heaven, telling of Michael's fight against that old Serpent called the Devil and Satan, whose defeat resulted in his being cast onto the earth together with all of his angels, Adams added, though in greatly condensed form, details from the more dramatic account of this action in Milton:

> Now War upon the Heav'nly Plain began,
> The Host with *Michael* blazing at their Van;
> While the fierce Dragon led his Angels on,
> Whose Rebel-Pow'rs at once were otherthrown:
> Eras'd from Heav'n, their shining Place was lost,
> Headlong he fell, and all his fainting Host:
> That ancient Serpent, who deceives the World,
> Was on the Earth in flaming Ruin hurl'd.[87]

Clearly Adams had here in mind Milton's vision of celestial warfare, but he could not, as had Milton, cast Satan into the bottomless reaches of Hell. The text of *Revelation* demanded that he be hurled to the earth. But Milton's obvious imprint on Adams' visual imagination, an effect similarly observed in Ralph and in Byles, validated the Augustan doctrine promulgated by Joseph Addison in the early part of the eighteenth century that the greatest poetry was pictorial. That the visions of *Paradise Lost* had begun to shape the imagination of American poets was in itself an argument for Milton's power and sublimity.

At mid-century Milton's influence among minor American poets began to spread into the realm of ideals and beliefs. In his *Philosophic Solitude*, William Livingston turned to *Paradise Lost* not so much to achieve special pictorial effects as to find expression for his feeling and thought. A poet by avoca-

---

[86] *ibid.*, p. 122.
[87] *ibid.*, pp. 138–139.

tion only, he left a law practice in New York for a pastoral retreat in New Jersey, where he hoped to live in accordance with his romantic dreams, but he became involved in political activity and during the Revolution was elected Governor of the state of his choice.[88] If he achieved distinction in prose, which argued the cause of liberty and truth, he scarcely rose to mediocrity in poetry, which articulated his philosophical views. Yet his *Philosophic Solitude* merits some comment; and since of the fifteen topics announced in "The Argument" of this poem seven include matter taken from or relevant to *Paradise Lost*, Livingston can be called a sometime Milton disciple.

Livingston's interest in philosophy did not mean that Milton's imagery failed to impress him. Like Adams and Byles, he drew from Milton's scene of celestial warfare to picture Satan's defeat on the plains of Heaven, making use of even more details than his predecessors had seen fit to employ. His narrative showing Michael in angelic conflict with Satan, the appearance of the Messiah, and the final doom of the rebels follows almost precisely Milton's account, though in greatly condensed form.[89] *Paradise Lost*, together with Dryden's *Hymn*, Pope's *Windsor Forest*, and Isaac Watts's devotional pieces, informs much of the language and imagery, as well as the tone, of Livingston's philosophical poem.

But Milton impressed Livingston most in the realm of feeling and thought. Under the topics "A Description of the Morning," "Hymn to the Sun," "Contemplation of the Heavens," "The Existence of God inferr'd from a view of the Beauty and Harmony of the Creation," and "Morning and Evening Devotion," Livingston presented segments from

[88] See Tyler, *A History of American Literature*, II, 218–223, for a sketch of Livingston and his accomplishments. See also *Literary History of the United States*, eds. Robert E. Spiller, Willard Thorp, Thomas H. Johnson, and Henry Seidel Canby (New York, 1959), pp. 94–95.

[89] *Philosophic Solitude: Or the Choice of a Rural Life. A Poem* (New York, 1747), pp. 32–33.

Books IV and V of *Paradise Lost*, often turning them into philosophical meditations on the nature of God and the world. He showed particular interest in Adam and Eve's morning hymn, beginning "These are thy glorious works, Parent of good"—a song that Milton had particularized from the Psalms and that was to remain a favorite of Americans for nearly a century.[90] This hymn, singing of the might and the goodness of God, of the sun and the moon and the stars, of light made from darkness, of Heaven and earth and all their inhabitants, furnished Livingston with precisely the sentiments he wished to express. In consequence, in order to articulate his own religious devotion, he simply paraphrased what Milton had said. Straitjacketed in heroic couplets, Adam and Eve's worship appears somewhat formal, but Livingston's sincerity cannot be denied:

> F A T H E R of *Light!* exhaustless source of good!
> Supreme, eternal, self-existent G o D !
> Before the beamy Sun dispens'd a ray,
> Flam'd in the azure vault, and gave the day;
> Before the glimmering Moon with borrow'd light
> Shone queen amid the silver host of night,
> High in the heav'ns, thou reign'd superior Lord,
> By suppliant angels worship'd and ador'd.

> .  .  .  .  .  .  .

> L ET T H E R E BE L I G H T , said God,—Light instant shone
> And from the orient burst the golden Sun;
> Heav'ns gazing hierarchies with glad surprize
> Saw the first morn invest the recent skies,
> And strait th' exulting troops thy throne surround
> With thousand thousand harps of heav'nly sound;
> Thrones, Powers, Dominions, (ever-shining trains!)
> Shouted thy praises in triumphant strains:
> *Great are thy Works,* they sing, and all around

[90] For a recent analysis of the meaning and power of this song, see Joseph H. Summers, *The Muse's Method* (Cambridge, 1962), pp. 74–86.

*Great are thy Works,* the echoing heav'ns resound.
Th' effulgent sun insufferably bright,
Is but a beam of thy o'erflowing light.

.     .     .     .     .     .     .

To this great God, alternately I'd pay
The ev'ning anthem, and the morning lay.[91]

Toward the end of *Philosophic Solitude* Livingston turned
to a consideration of marriage and love, finding, like James
Bowdoin, his ideals of nuptial companionship in the famous
marriage hymn of Book IV. Combining this hymn with the
narrative details which surround it, Livingston crystallized his
own views and at the same time popularized further a sentiment that was to become, by the turn of the century, a design
for connubial love. Eve herself would soon appear as a pattern
of wifely perfection, though Livingston only hinted at this
later development:

By love directed, I wou'd chuse a wife,
T' improve my bliss, and ease the load of life.
Hail *Wedlock!* hail, inviolable tye!
Perpetual fountain of domestic joy!
Love, friendship, honour, truth, and pure delight
Harmonious mingle in the nuptial rite.[92]

To this apostrophe Livingston added Milton's account of
Adam and Eve's nuptials in Eden, an event witnessed by
angels and blessed by God. Even nature rejoiced in their
union, showering their bower with roses and gladdening their
ears with bird-sung *"Hymenians."*

Such an adaptation of Milton's hymn could not be called
good poetry, but it affected two admirers of *Philosophic Solitude* enough to elicit verses of praise. One declared that Livingston's celebration of the nuptial tie had made him "pant"

[91] *Philosophic Solitude: Or the Choice of a Rural Life. A Poem,* pp.
24–26.
[92] *ibid.,* p. 38.

to "prove" Hymen's "rites"; the other declared that Livingston had moved his fancy to see the beauty and virtue of womanly charm.[93] Both might have been more effusive had they read Milton's original sentiments, which even at a poor second hand possessed enough power to arouse comment. Of importance, however, is not that such admirers responded so uncritically but that Livingston found in Milton ideals and beliefs which allowed him to articulate his own spiritual vision. Of importance, too, is that in pursuit of this vision he chose from *Paradise Lost* two hymns which soon became common American possessions. Perhaps Livingston himself contributed to their later popularity, though their intrinsic value alone could account for their being so widely accepted. More succinctly than Spenser, more dramatically than Isaac Watts, Milton expressed in his hymns Christian ideals of earthly and of Heavenly love.

The last sometime Milton disciple in Colonial America was Francis Hopkinson. Statesman, musician, and political satirist, Hopkinson was more strictly a Revolutionary than a colonial figure, for he achieved his considerable reputation after the break with England and became widely known for his popular ballad *The Battle of the Kegs*. But in his youth he admired Milton; and, what is significant for American poetry, his interest lay not so much in the grand style of *Paradise Lost* as in the lilting charm of *L'Allegro* and *Il Penseroso*. This is not to say that *Paradise Lost* left no marks on his early verse. In his commencement poem *Charity*, delivered at the College of Philadelphia on May 1, 1760, he spoke in his invocation of his "advent'rous lay" and addressed Charity herself in the familiar Miltonic manner, "Say, who is she that first in virtue's train?" [94] In a mocking poem praising dirt, entitled *Dirtilla*,

---

[93] *ibid.*, pp. vi–viii.

[94] *The Miscellaneous Essays and Occasional Writings of Francis Hopkinson, Esq.* (Philadelphia, 1792), III, in the section "Poems on Several Subjects," p. 56.

he invoked that "goddess sable clad" to aid his "daring muse" so that he could "rise with sooty wing" and sing a song "Ne're yet attempted by advent'rous bard." [95] But Hopkinson failed to sustain here, or elsewhere in this poem, the tone of burlesque he tried to achieve in the introductory lines. He lacked the talent to fashion humorous verse from the grand style of *Paradise Lost*, as James Ralph had done earlier and as John Trumbull was to do so effectively in *M'Fingal*.[96] His skill lay less in burlesquing heroic verse than in ridiculing events of the day, as in his rollicking *Battle of the Kegs*. Yet his interest in Milton was strong, particularly in 1757, when he imitated *L'Allegro* and *Il Penseroso*.

At this time Hopkinson began a vogue of imitating Milton's companion poems, both in whole and in part. Earlier, he had only echoed familiar meters and lines, as in his *Ode on Music*, a short poem inspired by the notes of a harpsichord. As the "sweet vibrating lyre" moved his soul, his mood turned to merriment, as had Milton's in *L'Allegro*:

> Neatly trip o'er the merry dance,
> And lightly touch, and swiftly glance;
> Let boundless transports laugh aloud,
> Sounds madly ramble mix and croud,
> 'Till all in one loud rapture rise,
> Spread thro' the air and reach the skies.[97]

But soon the tone shifted: something more solemn, more profound, affected his soul, producing lines reminiscent of *Il Penseroso*:

> But when you touch the solemn air,
> Oh! swell each note distinct and clear,

[95] *ibid.*, p. 114.

[96] See the *American Magazine and Historical Chronicle*, 1 (November 1743), 120–121, for the first attempt to burlesque *Paradise Lost*.

[97] *The American Magazine and Monthly Chronicle* (October 1757), pp. 44–45.

In ev'ry sound let sorrow sigh,
Languish soft, and sweetly die.[98]

Such changing moods, Hopkinson found, could best be expressed by following the rubrics Milton had already established.

So successful was this experiment, at least in his judgment, that Hopkinson turned to Milton several years later in his *Description of a Church*, a poem which attempted to capture the religious mood evoked by a visit to so holy a place. Solemnly, the poet moved between the "massy walls" of the Church with "monumental decorations hung." As his eye caught the high gilded organ, his imagination heard that instrument peal out full and clear, only to die away in a harmony so sweet that it sounded like chanting angels in flight. The reverie ended with an address to music and a desire to die with her, a conclusion reminiscent of the form if not the sentiment of the last lines of *Il Penseroso*. The "swelling arch" and the pealing organ here call up definite memories; and if Hopkinson was not thinking of Milton when he composed his own reverie, he nonetheless puts Milton in the mind of his readers.[99]

Yet that Hopkinson did have Milton in mind seems pretty clear. In November 1757, one month after the appearance of his *Ode on Music*,[100] he published in *The American Magazine* direct imitations of *L'Allegro* and *Il Penseroso*, two poems so patently based on Milton's that he even called his by the same names. He began his own *L'Allegro* with the familiar injunction, "HENCE *Melancholy*," though he avoided Milton's introductory rhetoric, varied meter, and in-

[98] *The American Magazine and Monthly Chronicle* (October 1757), pp. 44–45.
[99] *The Miscellaneous Essays and Occasional Writings of Francis Hopkinson, Esq.*, III, in the section "Poems on Several Subjects," pp. 59–60.
[100] *Ode on Music* was written in 1754.

tricate rhyme scheme. After a description of Mirth, he began his fancied journey through summer days, seeing sights and hearing sounds similar to those Milton had earlier presented. The "linnet's warbling lay" and the "lark's melodious song" charmed his tour, while far off, between two oaks, he spied the simple cottage of Darby and Joan, whose declining years rang with the merry songs of Phillis, their "hand-maid spruce and neat." From here, Hopkinson moved to the "friendly shade" of a tree, where an amorous swain eased away the tedious hours to the sound of his pipe, and later he beheld a "wily" shepherd baiting his hook by a stream. So passed the whole summer day, filled with "blythsome scenes and jocund ease." At this point in the poem Hopkinson betook himself to the city in winter, "Where mirth knows one continual round." Here he could lose himself in wine and good companionship, or could dance the night away amid the "sparkling throng," enthralled by music and beauty. Such joys—summer days in the country and winter nights in the city—so entranced Hopkinson that he, like Milton, could live forever with Mirth:

> If such thy pleasures, *smiling Joy!*
> Oh may'st thou e'er my mind employ;
> Dawn in my breast continual day,
> And chace dull sorrows far away.[101]

So obvious an imitation of subject, meter, rhyme, and structure of *L'Allegro* needs no further comment, other than to say that the closeness with which Hopkinson followed Milton allowed him to achieve a lightness of tone and a firmness of texture far beyond the powers his youthful talent at this time would permit. He had set about to depict a definite mood,

[101] *The American Magazine and Monthly Chronicle* (November 1757), pp. 84–86. Hopkinson revised extensively both his *L'Allegro* and *Il Penseroso* for publication later in his collected works.

and to fulfill his aim he found he could do no better than follow the path Milton had earlier pioneered.

To depict Melancholy Hopkinson followed an identical procedure. The opening lines of his own *Il Penseroso* will be sufficient to show how squarely he had focused his eyes on Milton's twin poem:

> V A N I S H mirth and vanish joy,
> Airy pleasures quickly cloy;
> Hence all ye bacchananian rout,
> And wine, and jest, and noisy shout,
> And quips, and cranks, and gay grimace,
> And wit that wears a double face,
> And ev'ry kind of jollity—
> For you have no delights for me.
>
> But welcome, welcome *Melancholy!*
> Thou goddess sage, demure and holy! [102]

Such fidelity to the language of Milton's *Il Penseroso*, however, failed to ensure a poem with the vigor or firmness of Hopkinson's first imitation; and neither of his verses possesses a tithe of the charm or shows a semblance of the seriousness of their originals. Yet as early attempts at light poetry they merit some praise, particularly when compared with most magazine verse of the time: they have a lilt and an ease seldom found in that early day, and they spurred a movement in mood poetry that affected American literature until the end of the century.

The varied and multiple ways Milton shaped the language, syntax, imagery, form, and thought of Colonial poets reveals a quickening yet dangerous impulse in the literary community. Americans clearly believed, as Longinus had argued centuries before and as neoclassic doctrine still maintained, that imita-

---

[102] *The American Magazine and Monthly Chronicle* (November 1757), pp. 86–88.

tion of greatness might produce greatness itself. They also believed, as Joseph Addison had declared in *The Spectator*, that highest poetic art lay in painting great pictures. On the eve of the Revolution in his *Poems on Several Occasions* Nathaniel Evans expressed such prevailing notions succinctly. Milton, he said, had followed the imagery and subject matter of Scripture, a procedure to which he owed much of his grandeur; and though few could climb Milton's heights, all should follow his *"illustrious example"* according *"to their ability,"* since anyone wishing to *"excel"* or to achieve anything *"laudable"* or *"great"* should *"look to a mark superior"* to his individual genius.[103] Evans himself looked to Milton and Scripture to elevate his own compositions; [104] hundreds of others turned to Pope, Young, and Gray. If the bulk of American writing shows that Augustan meter and forms overwhelmingly shaped verse of the time, *L'Allegro* and *Il Penseroso* had at least begun to inform a body of mood poetry, and *Paradise Lost* had given a language and imagery to more exalted effusions. At that moment such an impulse appeared to give life to American verse, or to lend it a certain kind of distinction; its dangers lay wrapped in the future.

[103] *Poems on Several Occasions, With Some other Compositions* (Philadelphia, 1772), p. 83.

[104] *ibid.*, pp. 38–41, 135. For a more complete analysis of Milton's influence on Evans, see Burton A. Milligan, "An Early American Imitator of Milton," *American Literature*, XI (1939), 200–206. Of the fifty-one poems in the volume, Milligan found six to be either paraphrases or imitations of Milton. See also Edgar Legare Pennington, "Nathaniel Evans: Some Notes on his Ministry," *Proceedings of the American Antiquarian Society*, L (1940), 91–97, for an account of Evans' life and of his debt to the tradition of Dryden and Pope; and *idem.*, *Nathaniel Evans A Poet of Colonial America* (Ocala, Florida, 1935), for an earlier study.

# THREE

# The Revolutionary Period

The Revolutionary period witnessed a deepening of Milton's imprint on American life and a wider scattering of his name over the land. Milton had not yet reached the peak of his fame, but forces converged during the conflict with England to make him better known from Massachusetts to the Carolinas. One of the most powerful was the freshly secularized textbook of grammar and rhetoric, which systematically presented passages from Milton's poetry for the instruction of youth in the civilizing arts of speaking and writing. A second was the appearance of new monthly journals, many of which filled their essays with lines from ancient and modern authors, among whom Milton was not the least quoted. A third was the War itself, which focused attention on political theorists in whose ranks Milton often appeared. In giving further currency to his name and works, such forces placed Milton in a position to speak with more authority than ever before.

Among numerous Americans at this time responding to Milton members of the literary community listened with closest attention. Spurred by the excitement of the Revolution, poets envisioned America as a Western utopia, as a land of freedom and plenty, where justice governed mankind. Such "prospect" poetry asked for a style commensurate with the grandeur and sweep of its theme, and this meant, for most authors, a turning to Milton, who for almost a half century, in their judgment at least, had pointed poets the way to sublimity. As a result, the first great surge to find an original voice to express New World experience produced some of the most imitative verse of the century.[1] But such an irony sprang not solely from the community of poets: popular opinion supported Milton's authoritative role everywhere.

## I I

Establishment of Milton as a popular authority owed much to a new kind of textbook which appeared in American schools about 1770. Before this time texts of grammar and rhetoric had depended for illustrative material primarily upon classical and Biblical quotations, or upon catechisms and rubrics of prayer. Such had been the practice of *The New England Primer*,[2] as well as of Nathaniel Strong's *England's Perfect Schoolmaster*,[3] George Fox's *Instructions for Right Spelling*,[4] and Thomas Dilworth's *A New Guide to the English Tongue*.[5] Only occasionally among early texts had English authors appeared. John White had cited Chaucer in *The Country Man's Conductor* [6] and John Houghton had reproduced two long passages from *Hamlet* in his *New Introduction to English Grammar*.[7] But not until the eve of the Revolution, except for *The Youth's Instructor in the English Tongue*,[8] did English authors begin to supplant the old standbys. Here, passages from Bacon, Herbert, Donne, Milton, and others illustrate points of grammar and usage; and shortly after the Revolu-

---

[1] For the eagerness of Dwight and others to create a national literature, see William B. Cairns, *British Criticisms of American Writings, 1783–1815*, in the *University of Wisconsin Studies in Language and Literature*, no. 1 (Madison, 1918), p. 7.

[2] Boston, 1727.

[3] Boston, 1704.

[4] Boston, 1743.

[5] Boston, 1770.

[6] Exeter, 1701.

[7] London, 1766.

[8] Boston, 1769. Evans lists printings of this text as early as 1731.

tion English authors began to predominate. New texts of this kind presented Milton as an authority on the correct and effective use of the English language, a procedure which brought many of his sayings and sentiments before a large captive audience and established his right to be heard.[9]

A glance at a few of the most popular texts of the day will reveal how widely Milton was used for instruction of this kind. Whether such texts were English or American in origin mattered little; the most popular in both countries appeared under American imprints and were adopted by American schools. One of the most prescriptive English texts to find its way to America was Robert Lowth's *A Short Introduction to English Grammar,* which after its publication in Philadelphia in 1775 gained wide recognition and remained a standard grammatical reference until well into the next century. Lowth made it clear in his preface that the principal design of any grammar was to teach students how to express themselves with propriety, that is, to give students enough information to judge "of every phrase and form of construction, whether it be right or not"; and the "plain way of doing this," he emphasized, was "to lay down rules, and to illustrate them by examples." [10] Such a procedure became common among grammarians of the day, with the result that lessons intrinsically dull sometimes sparkled with brilliant quotations.

In pursuit of his aim Lowth turned often to Milton, whose great reputation made him a "natural" for quotation and reference. To argue that English, though normally a language which distinguished between masculine and feminine by na-

---

[9] Catalogues, booklists, and almanacs extensively advertised Milton's works. See, for example, *The Connecticut Courant,* no. 305 (Tuesday, July 21, to Tuesday, July 28, 1772); *A Catalogue of New and Old Books in Arts, Sciences, and Entertainment* (Philadelphia, [1778]), entries 1476, 1741, 1742, 1954; Daniel George, *An Almanack for the Year of Our Lord 1782* (Newburyport).

[10] *A Short Introduction to English Grammar. With Critical Notes* (Philadelphia, 1775), p. viii.

ture, could in "the poetical and rhetorical style" convert nouns naturally neuter into masculine or feminine and thus make a personification more "forcibly marked," he cited several passages of poetry, one of which he excerpted from *Comus*, another from *Paradise Lost*.[11] To demonstrate that the "higher Poetry, which loves to consider every thing as bearing a personal character, frequently applies the personal possessive *whose* to inanimate beings," though such usage is normally wrong, he quoted the first three lines from *Paradise Lost*.[12] To illustrate that "will, possibility, liberty, obligation, &c. though expressed by the same verbs that are occasionally used as subjunctive auxiliaries, may belong to the indicative," he reproduced three more passages from Milton.[13] But the most interesting construction Lowth ruled as correct and found support for in Milton was "than whom," a locution in his time much discussed and now almost mandatory in speeches introducing politicians to candidacy for public office because of a presumed elevation its use confers on the occasion. No need exists to examine Lowth's argument; it is sufficient to say that, to support his position, he referred to Milton's description of "Beelzebub, *than whom*,/ Satan except, none higher sat." [14] Familiarity, if nothing else, would sanction such a construction for most early Americans.

Lowth admired Milton so much that he sometimes defended his usage from the criticism of his commentators and editors. In his discussion of the "case absolute," for example, he cited from *Paradise Lost* the idiom "*He descending*," remarking, as he approved the expression, that Milton's eighteenth-century editor Richard Bentley had erroneously emended the locution to make it read as a participle. Such an error, Lowth contended, sprang from Bentley's attempt to

[11] *ibid.*, p. 19, n.3.
[12] *ibid.*, pp. 24–25, n.8.
[13] *ibid.*, p. 32, n.8.
[14] *ibid.*, pp. 108–109.

force English "under the rules of a foreign language, with which it has little concern." [15] Lowth found Bentley so annoying that in his presentation of case and conjunctions he returned to the attack, charging that to change Milton's "such as *I*" to "such as me," as Bentley had done, showed a misunderstanding of English construction.[16] But to say that Lowth always found in Milton illustrations of proper grammar and syntax would be patently false. In accordance with the design of his book he excerpted several quotations from Milton and others to point out improprieties, demonstrating that even great authors sometimes could err. Such a practice so pleased Noah Webster that he incorporated some of Lowth's "Critical Notes" into an appendix to his *Institute of the English Language,* a patriotic text which queried, among other things, whether citations from English authors should establish correct usage on American soil.

Before Webster presented his views in Part II of his *Institute* Ralph Harrison issued his *Rudiments of English Grammar,* finding in Milton constructions which he sometimes condemned, sometimes condoned. To inform the uninitiated scholar how poetry differed from prose, he reproduced the first six lines of *Paradise Lost,* which he followed by a transposition of the introductory statement into a more "natural" order so as to point out differences in syntax. In a lesson on false construction he selected Milton's statement, "I have *chose,*" saying that here Milton had obviously fallen in error. But apparently Harrison found more in Milton to praise than to blame, for to illustrate the use of conjunctions he declared: "I think Milton *as* great a poet *as* Virgil." [17] Whether Webster could have subscribed to such a judgment, however, is doubtful: with almost devilish glee he pointed to errors in

[15] *ibid.,* pp. 78–79, n.8.
[16] *ibid.,* pp. 107–108, n.5.
[17] *Rudiments of English Grammar* (Wilmington, [1788]), pp. 59, 90, 41. The first edition appeared in 1777.

the works of great English authors, among whom Milton was one of the most prominent.

Such a procedure grew from Webster's desire to establish a pure American tongue, formulated more from principles arrived at by reference to everyday use than by reference to literary works of the masters. Two decades later he was to shift his position, finding at that time in Milton alone some of the most effective idioms in the whole reach of language. But in 1784, when he published Part II of his *Institute*, he stood solidly in the ranks of descriptive grammarians who delighted in revealing the errors of the respected and great. In consequence, he turned in his *Appendix* to what he called "Critical Notes by Dr. Lowth," a collection of remarks and examples culled from *A Short Introduction to English Grammar*. Here Lowth had asserted that some writers had used "ye" as the "objective case plural of the pronoun of the second person" very "improperly" and "ungrammatically," in illustration of which he cited lines from Shakespeare, Prior, and Milton. Webster copied both the assertion and the examples, as well as Lowth's critical comment: "Milton uses the same manner of expression in a few other places of his Paradise Lost, and more frequently in his Poems." Lowth had also asserted that "double comparatives and superlatives are improper," a position he illustrated with lines from a number of pieces, including *Il Penseroso*. Webster copied both the statement and illustration, adding, somewhat later, several more improprieties Lowth had excerpted from Milton, such as "He would *have spoke*" and "Words *interwove* with sighs found out their way." Other examples of improprieties and errors Webster copied from Lowth encompassed *Comus, Eikonoklastes, Paradise Regained*, and *Samson Agonistes* [18]—a selection representative enough to suggest that Webster wished

---

[18] *A Grammatical Institute of the English Language: Part Second* (Hartford, [1790]), pp. 81, 82, 85, 86.

to impress on American youth Milton's infelicities in grammar and syntax.

Such a querying of Milton's authority, however, apparently had little effect, least of all on Webster himself. Milton had spoken so forcefully, had manipulated the English language with such a telling effect, that he could not long be presented as an exemplar of linguistic ineptitude, even by so earnest a patriot as Webster. In his *Philosophical and Practical Grammar of the English Language,* published after the turn of the century, he found in Milton some of the happiest idioms mankind had ever been able to coin.

Long before this time Hugh Blair had presented much the same view in his *Lectures on Rhetoric and Belles Lettres.* Appearing under an American imprint as early as 1784, Blair's text became popular in New England colleges and universities, where it served generations of American students well into the nineteenth century. Blair quoted from Milton to exemplify "sublimity in objects" and "sublimity in writing" [19]—he stated indeed that "MILTON's great and distinguished excellence" *was* his "sublimity," in the achievement of which he perhaps excelled even Homer.[20] To Blair, Milton stood not only as one of the most sublime poets of all time but served as an authority *par excellence* to illustrate precise and effective uses of language.

To show how the "Structure of Sentences" could be enhanced by the use of words signifying their meaning by sound, Blair pointed to Milton's descriptions of the portals of Heaven and Hell. The "harsh thunder" of Hell's doors, he declared,

---

[19] *Lectures on Rhetoric and Belles Lettres* (Philadelphia, 1784), pp. 22, 30–31. Jedidiah Morse spoke of the "eloquent *Blair*" as being one of the instructors of Joshua Huntington, who, according to Morse, was pleased and edified by Blair's "pious discourses." See *A Sermon, Delivered May 18th. 1808, at the Ordination of the Rev. Joshua Huntington* (Boston, 1808), p. 29.
[20] *Lectures on Rhetoric and Belles Lettres,* p. 422.

contrasted sharply to the "harmonious sound" of Heaven's "ever-during gates" turning on their "golden hinges." [21] To present hyperbole growing out of the passions he cited Satan's famous soliloquy, saying that this moving meditation, however inflated, stemmed from profound emotion and hence expressed nothing but what was "natural and proper." [22] To illustrate "Personification" he referred to the passage describing Eve's Fall, where Milton had depicted the Mother of Mankind putting forth her "rash hand" to pluck the fruit forbidden by God—a scene so moving that Blair was forced to exclaim that no image, by any author, was "more striking" or had been "introduced on a more proper occasion." Blair became so enamored of the figure of Eve that he presented her later as an example of a "third and highest degree" of personification, that kind of trope in which inanimate objects are conceived not only as "feeling and acting, but as speaking to us, or hearing and listening when we address ourselves to them." This highest degree of personification Blair found in the "moving and tender" address Eve made to Paradise just before her expulsion, when she exclaimed: "Oh! unexpected stroke, worse than of death." This, Blair asserted, was "altogether the language of nature, and of female passion." [23] The validity of Milton's insight could hardly be more clearly asserted.

Blair never tired of pointing to Milton's mastery of language and trope, or flagged in praising the man and his works. To show how sense, not sound, should govern oral reading in classroom recitation, he cited lines from the invocation of *Paradise Lost*.[24] To illustrate descriptive poetry he referred to *L'Allegro* and *Il Penseroso*, which he claimed were above all

---

[21] *ibid.*, p. 116.
[22] *ibid.*, p. 140.
[23] *ibid.*, pp. 144–146.
[24] *ibid.*, p. 311.

odds the "richest and most remarkable" of their kind in the English language. In this latter poem, he declared, "there are no unmeaning general expressions; all is particular; all is picturesque; nothing forced or exaggerated." [25] Sometimes, to be sure, Milton fell "much below himself" in performance, but at other times he rose above every poet of the ancient or modern world.[26] Such exclamations of praise, accompanied by illustrations of effective language and figures, impressed upon American youth how great Milton was and strengthened his right to be heard.[27]

Yet "readers" and "speakers" more than grammars and rhetorics spread Milton's authority over the land. Milton's mastery in expressing feeling and thought sent compilers of such texts to *Paradise Lost,* from which they excerpted moving speeches and choice sentiments suitable for public delivery or classroom discussion. Such selections, in turn, served as a basis for instruction in speaking and reading. If the number of lessons so formulated offers a reliable guide, American schools must have resounded with Miltonic rhetoric, delivered to the accompaniment of professorial praise.

No text of the time deferred more to the authority of Milton than James Burgh's *The Art of Speaking,* an English text which appeared under an American imprint in 1775.[28] Popular in college and society libraries at Brown University by 1788, this book passed through numerous American editions and made a great impact on the elocutionary movement of the nineteenth century. Burgh addressed himself chiefly to

[25] *ibid.,* pp. 379–380.

[26] *ibid.,* p. 423.

[27] Timothy Dwight taught rhetoric from Blair's *Lectures* and in turn influenced American criticism. See Abe C. Ravitz, "Timothy Dwight: Professor of Rhetoric," *The New England Quarterly,* XXIX (1956), 63–72.

[28] English texts printed in America played an important part in the elocutionary movement in America. For a discussion of the influence of English books on American texts, see the *History of Speech Education in America,* ed. Karl R. Wallace (New York, 1954), pp. 80–104, 105–126.

the art of relating gesture and tone to subject matter, and to ensure this proper relationship he analyzed, in an introductory statement, the way bodily movement and tonal inflection combine with words to express human emotion. His presentation of *modesty* will illustrate his basic procedures: *"Modesty,"* he explained, "or submission, bends the body forward; *levels the eyes* to the breast, if not to the feet, of the superior character"—a stance to be accompanied, if the full effect was to be achieved, by a low voice, a submissive tone, and few words.[29]

In like manner Burgh described how *courage, boasting, pride*, and *authority* could be presented, to mention but a few of his many examples. How much Milton was on his mind as he formulated his instructions may be inferred from his comment on the qualifications of a "natural" speaker. Such a person needed an ear but not necessarily a musical ear, Burgh declared; he had indeed never heard Milton better read than by a gentleman who had so little discernment in music that the grinding of knives entertained him as much as Handel's organ.[30] So uncritical a statement inspires little confidence in Burgh's judgment, but his attempt to relate tone, gesture, and thought had brought to mind Milton, who furnished him with passages suited to his precise purpose, however artificial his procedures now seem.

An examination of Lesson XXIII on "Adoration" will show how Burgh relied upon Milton, as well as how young Americans learned to recite lines from *Paradise Lost*. Burgh first reproduced *"Milton's* Morning Hymn," which he accompanied with detailed instructions. This passage, it should be recalled, beginning "These are thy glorious works," William Livingston had paraphrased earlier. Now it became with all Milton's reverence for the created universe the core of a

---

[29] *The Art of Speaking* (Baltimore, 1804), p. 19.
[30] *ibid.*, p. 10. Burgh conceded in a note that Quintilian would have his orator by all means study music.

lesson on how to express adoration. In his rubrics of instruction Burgh insisted that the first line should be read with an expression of "Veneration"; and from here the speaker moved successively through "Admiration," "Veneration," "Love, with Veneration," "Sacred Rapture," "Admiration," "Lowly Submission," "Rapture," to "Profound Submission," with which the passage was brought to a close.

Such a succession of instructions, if they elicited the gestures and tones Burgh assigned them, must have produced a reading animated enough to satisfy the most ambitious young orator, but Burgh apparently believed them insufficient for expressing so important a sentiment. He therefore furnished further details for the part to be read with "Admiration," saying that the line beginning "Thou *Sun*" should be presented "a little more *ore rotundo*, or *full-mouthed*, than the foregoing, to image the stupendous greatness of a world of fire, equal as supposed by astronomers, to a million of earths." [31] Perhaps the image of the sun called out by young Americans following Burgh's instructions proved to be less astounding than the picture of the student himself, moving his body and modulating his voice as his lesson commanded. Yet however ridiculous such a scene appears now, Milton's hymn struck a responsive chord: it soon moved out of the classroom to become one of the most popular sayings of the time.

Burgh found Milton so useful in carrying out the aim of his text that he built eight more lessons upon passages from *Paradise Lost*. To examine them all with their attendant instructions would be tedious. But it is important to list them to show not only Burgh's taste in poetry, but also the speeches American students presumably made in oratorical contests or upon special literary occasions. Their titles, together with the moods to be expressed, read as follows:

[31] *ibid.*, pp. 87–89 and note 3.

1) Lesson XXXVIII: Anger. Threatening: *"Satan's speech to Death, stopping his passage through the gates of hell; with the answer."*

2) Lesson XXXIX: Deprecation. Recollection: *"The speech of Sin to Satan, to prevent an hostile encounter between the latter and Death; with the effect of her speech."*

3) Lesson XLI: Reflection. On Lost Happiness. Self-Condemnation. Horror. Desperation: *"Satan's Soliloquy."*

4) Lesson XLVIII: Joy. Trouble. Flattery. Daring. Fear. Romantic Imagination: *"EVE's Account of her troublesome Dream."*

5) Lesson LVI: Affection. Joy. Fear of Offending. Gratitude. *"A speech of ADAM to EVE."*

6) Lesson LXIX: Consultation: *"The Speech of SATAN, in his infernal palace of Pandæmonium, in which he proposes to the consideration of his angels, in what manner it would be proper to proceed, in consequence of their defeat, and fall."*

7) Lesson LXX: Fierceness. Desperation: *"The Speech of the fallen angel MOLOCH, exciting the infernal crew to renew the war against the Messiah."*

8) Lesson LXXI: Consideration. Dissuasion. Diffidence. *"The Speech of the fallen angel BELIAL, in answer to the foregoing."* [32]

Such choices reveal a taste for vivid imagery, for persuasive rhetoric, for psychological reality, and for supernatural event. Burgh here offered to American youth some of the most dramatic and sublime passages in *Paradise Lost*. That Americans later incorporated them into their sermons and pamphlets and poetry testifies to their effectiveness, as well as to a widening of Milton's authority. Perhaps neither Burgh nor his students knew at the time how successful his instructions had been.

Less effective but no doubt as popular was William Scott's *Lessons in Elocution*, which appeared on the American scene at least as early as 1786 and remained a standard reference until 1823. As a text, it offered little of Milton that American students could not find in either James Burgh or Hugh Blair.

---

[32] *ibid.*, pp. 123, 124, 126–128, 144–146, 162–163, 218–219, 219–221, 221–224.

To illustrate *emphasis* Scott quoted the famous line of Satan's speech, "Better reign in hell, than serve in heaven"; and under "Lessons in Reading" he reproduced the well-known night scene from Book IV of *Paradise Lost*, which James Ralph had paraphrased more than a half century earlier. In the same set of lessons Scott included *"Milton's Lamentation for the Loss of his Sight,"* beginning "Hail, holy light"; a good part of *L'Allegro*; and three selections from *Paradise Lost: "The Creation of the World,"* the *"Overthrow of the Rebel Angels,"* and *"Adam and Eve's Morning Hymn."* In addition to repeating the hymn Burgh had so carefully analyzed for gesture and tone, Scott placed under "Lessons in Speaking," as Burgh had before him, the addresses of Moloch and Belial in the Infernal Council. Finally, in an appendix, Scott illustrated "Suspension" and "Parenthesis" with lines from *Paradise Lost*.[33] So derivative a book lacked the force of *The Art of Speaking* or the precision of Blair's *Lectures,* which had appeared in England after Scott's text. But in its repetitiveness it spread Milton's name in America and helped invest his sayings with truth. All three English pedagogues simply played variations on an identical theme.

Such a story of Milton in early American schools hardly means that his authority overwhelmed pedagogues of the time. Many poets stood by Milton's side, some of the most popular being Shakespeare, Pope, Young, Thomson, and Gray, as well as numerous prose writers, old and new. Moreover, some texts omitted Milton entirely. But compilers of standard grammars and rhetorics, as yet chiefly English in origin, agreed in part with the Irish school principal Samuel Whyte, who changed the Duke of Buckingham's quatrain on Homer to support his assertion that Milton could "never be too much recommended":

[33] *Lessons in Elocution* (Stockbridge, 1808), pp. 51, 248–250, 259–260, 260–262, 264–265, 273–274, 274–275, 340–341, 341–343, 399, 401.

Read *Milton* once, and you can read no more;
For all Books else, appear so mean, so poor,
Verse will seem Prose; but still persist to read,
And *Milton* will be all the Books you need.[34]

This recommendation moved far beyond actual practice. But dependence upon Milton to support points of grammar and rhetoric, as well as pedagogic veneration for his sayings and sentiments, confirmed an already existing tradition of greatness and helped establish him as a popular authority. Where more likely than from American schools would spring the widespread conviction that *Milton dixit* was a voucher for truth?

## III

American acceptance of Milton's authority on a national scale had to await the last decade of the century. Yet in the Revolutionary period admirers so credited his dicta that patterns of influence began to emerge. Such patterns had been foreshadowed faintly during Colonial times in essays and sermons, as well as in imitations of *Paradise Lost*, but now they began to take on color and shape as they appeared in popular pamphlets and journals. No one now announced his discipleship of Milton, as had Jonathan Mayhew at mid-century; no one persistently referred to Milton's name or quoted extensively from his poetry or prose. Rather, Americans began to repeat Milton's sentiments in moral and religious contexts, finding that they expressed what they wanted to say. His words not only articulated their moral and spiritual convictions but helped confirm them in a hierarchy of eternal values.

[34] *Modern Education, Respecting Young Ladies as Well as Gentlemen* (Dublin, 1775), pp. 53–57. See also Russell K. Alspach, "A Dublin Milton Enthusiast," MLN, LVI (1941), 284–286.

To strengthen their values on marriage and love Americans occasionally turned to Milton's hymn on connubial bliss in Book IV of *Paradise Lost*. The idyllic picture of Adam and Eve in the Garden had already inspired essayists in *The New England Courant* and *The Pennsylvania Gazette*, and poets had transmuted the hymn itself into brassy heroic couplets. Now Milton's apostrophe to wedded love furnished the substance for meditations on marriage, or guided the language and imagery of native epithalamiums. Even William Livingston's version seemed good enough to reprint in *Father Abraham's Almanack*, where it appeared as A POEM IN PRAISE OF THE MARRIED STATE;[35] fortunately, however, most Americans found guidance in Milton's original lines.

One of the most dramatic uses of Milton's hymn appeared in Daniel George's *Almanack* for 1784 under the title *The Maid's Soliloquy*,[36] a performance which *The New Haven Gazette* repeated two years later with a short stage direction. The soliloquy itself followed Cato's famous meditation on Plato at the beginning of Act V of Addison's sententious tragedy. A maid entered, according to the version in *The New Haven Gazette*, with *Paradise Lost* in her hand, opened to the passage on wedded love. After reading the first line of the hymn she delivered a soliloquy on marriage in the manner of Cato ruminating on immortality in Addison's play:

> *Hail wedded Love! mysterious law!*
> *Our Maker Bids increase, who bids* abstain
> *But our destroyer, foe to God and Man!*
> It must be so; Milton, thou reasonest well,
> Else, why this pleasing hope, this fond desire,
> This longing after something unpossess'd;

[35] *Father Abraham's Almanack, for the Year of Our Lord, 1770* (Philadelphia), sig. D.

[36] *An Almanack, for the Year of our Lord Christ, 1784* (Boston).

Or whence this sacred dread and inward horror,
Of dying unespous'd? Why shrinks the soul
Back on itself, and startles at virginity? [37]

To such a question, the Maid had an immediate answer:
nature herself pointed to the alliance of marriage. And as she
mused on hopes and fears of the marital estate, she concluded
that both duty and interest bade her enter its happy domain,
since "the great end of nature's laws is bliss." Yet she was
disturbed that in wedlock woman must obey. She consoled
herself, however, that loss of liberty in marriage would be
gain in happiness and love, that indeed marriage would ultimately allow her to scorn infirmities and death, making her
"immortal in a filial race." Such ruminations on Milton's
hymn took the Maid far afield. Perhaps the two transposed
lines opening her meditations hold the clue to nearly all that
passed through her mind. But something of Milton's ideal of
companionship remained, something of his emphasis on the
spiritual values of love and on the purity of a relationship
ordained by God, or, to be more precise, by nature's God.
The Maid had to concede something to the philosophy of the
Enlightenment.

Milton's hymn to wedded love and his whole picture of
prelapsarian bliss sometimes shaped the imagery and values
of American epithalamiums. A subscriber to *The Pennsylvania
Magazine,* desirous of commending a friend upon his recent
marriage, asked that he be given the privilege of presenting
to the readers of that journal his poetical attempt to praise
connubial love. The poem he furnished for the occasion possessed no intrinsic worth; he indeed gave it no title. But in
the first part he pictured Adam and Eve in the Garden of
Eden as Milton had described them in *Paradise Lost.* The
two walked side by side in that happy place, Eve endearing

---

[37] *The New Haven Gazette and the Connecticut Magazine,* I, no. 30
(September 7, 1786), 233. Milton's lines, of course, have been transposed.

herself to Adam by meet conversation and by revealing each day some "newborn grace." From this Miltonic picture of Adam and Eve, the poem moved into an evaluation of married love, finding both its language and thought in the hymn to connubial bliss:

> Hail honour'd wedlock! sacred right!
> The crown of life is thine;
> The fountain thou of chaste delight
> To Adam's virtuous line.
> Despis'd by none but sordid souls,
> The fop and debauchee;
> Who reason drown in midnight bowls,
> Are wicked to be free.[38]

Here is Milton's contrast between true and false love, but it in no way matches his biting juxtaposition of chaste delights in marriage and the bought smiles of harlots, of the "Perpetual Fountain of Domestic sweets" and the casual fruition of courtly amours. Perishing lovers singing serenades at midnight balls had turned into unattractive drunken fops and debauchees. Yet Milton's values shaped the whole poem. The concluding stanzas returned to the innocent love of Adam and Eve and conferred on the bride and groom the happiness of that "first form'd pair." The very earth had furnished fruits for their nuptials, and Heaven itself had crowned their banquet with joy.

Milton's picture of Adam and Eve gave a similar impulse to *An Epithalamium* appearing in *The Massachusetts Magazine* for 1789. This poem took as its text several lines condensed from the last part of Book VIII of *Paradise Lost*, where Raphael had informed Adam of the nature and effect of true love. Love refines the thoughts and enlarges the heart, Raphael had said; it has its seat in reason and is the scale by

[38] *The Pennsylvania Magazine Or American Monthly Museum* (March 1776), pp. 145–146.

which to ascend to heavenly bliss. The Platonic concept Milton here had invoked informed a good part of *An Epithalamium*, but the language of the poem is more reminiscent of the wedding hymn of Book IV, as revealed in such lines as "Hail, happy pair" and *"Long happy live."* [39] Milton's hymn in truth was becoming so embedded in the American consciousness that it not only shaped poems on connubial love but also furnished, by its very idealism, an argument for divorce.

Such an argument so supported appeared in 1788 in *An Essay on Marriage,* a discourse addressed to the feelings of mankind and the first of its sort to be made public in America, its Preface declared. In the same year Benjamin Trumbull, speaking from his office as a minister in North Haven, had excoriated the liberal divorce laws of Connecticut, saying that for the good of society they ought to be tightened. As an example of how such a stiffening might work for the happiness of mankind he presented to the Consociation of the County of New Haven a page out of Milton's connubial life, implying, as he told the story, that Milton had shifted his views from the time he wrote his divorce tracts to his envisioning Adam and Eve in the Garden of Eden. "No man was ever more engaged in obtaining a divorce, or more loudly complained of his unhappiness in the conjugal relation, than the famous JOHN MILTON,'' he recalled; "yet as the laws of his country would admit of no divorce, he became reconciled to his wife, and lived happily with her ever afterwards." [40] Such a fortunate ending to so unhappy a beginning convinced Trumbull that, should the laws of Connecticut be strengthened, man and woman would benefit. For, he continued, if

[39] *The Massachusetts Magazine Or Monthly Museum of Knowledge and Rational Entertainment*, I, no. 2 (February 1789), 118.

[40] *An Appeal to the Public, Especially to the Learned, with Respect to the Unlawfulness of Divorces, In all Cases, Excepting those of Incontinency* (New Haven, 1788), pp. 42, note, and 53, note. Trumbull quoted from Book X of *Paradise Lost* the lines picturing Satan's announcement to the fallen angels of his triumph over Adam and Eve.

parties seeking divorce could be made to consider their plight over a long period of time, the sin and consequence of separation might be prevented.

But if Trumbull wished to make divorce more difficult by law, the author of *An Essay on Marriage* aimed to make separation more easy. Moved by his seeing a newspaper account of a suicide resulting from marital unhappiness, he felt compelled to argue, as Milton had earlier, that divorce should be declared legal simply to preserve the highest ideals of marriage and love. In his exordium he appealed to America's love of individual liberty, after which he moved rapidly to an examination of reasons for marital difficulties, such as unsuitable circumstances or differences in religious beliefs. In Chapter III, entitled *"Of the Lawfulness and Necessity of Divorce, and the Benefits Deriving Therefrom,"* he penetrated to the core of his discussion. He would not, he said, have it understood that his proposal for divorce lessened the solemnity or weakened the sacredness of marriage vows. Far from it. He would simply argue that a union of hearts should accompany a union of hands, since such a union alone ensured happiness. From spiritual affinity, as "streams flowing from a sweet, clear, and pure fountain," sprang true marital pleasure. Without such a conjoining all things would become "lifeless, insipid and disagreeable." Such a view of marriage reminded him of Milton, whose pen, he said, had been employed to vindicate the very cause he now espoused and whose sentiments on marital love he endorsed. To voice his precise views he reproduced the hymn from *Paradise Lost*, since for him no contradiction existed between Milton's earlier and later opinions. They simply showed different faces of the same coin.[41]

Before the Revolutionary period closed Eve herself began to emerge as a pattern of womanly perfection. Joseph Hunt-

---

[41] *An Essay on Marriage; Or The Lawfulness of Divorce, In Certain Cases, Considered. Addressed to the Feelings Of Mankind* (Philadelphia, 1788), p. 22.

ington of Connecticut implied as much in his defense of a Mrs. Fisk before an Ecclesiastical Council at Stockbridge when, in an allegory characterizing his client, he likened her to Eve, whose steps and gestures, Adam had said in *Paradise Lost*, showed grace, dignity, and love.[42] Joseph Lathrop informed an essay on "Female Honour" with Adam's description of Eve when she first appeared to his sight—a vision of woman so lovely, so modest and innocent, that Adam could only remark:

> Not obvious, not obtrusive, but retir'd,
> The more desirable, or to say all,
> Nature herself, though pure of sinful thought,
> Wrought in her so, that seeing me, she turn'd;
> I followed her, she what was honour knew.[43]

To Lathrop, Eve was a prototype of wifely perfection, a very model for American women to follow.

A casual essay "On the Pleasures Arising from an Union Between the Sexes" in *The Columbian Magazine* expressed precisely the pattern of marital perfection Milton had begun to impress on the sensibility of literate Americans. "The tender and passionate Milton," this essay asserted, placed such a high value on the intimate caresses of Adam and Eve that he represented Satan as turning aside jealously when he saw them exchanging embraces. "What exquisite force and beauty are there in this image!" the essay concluded. "The fondest lovers of antiquity may be challenged to produce its parallel in the most approved writers of any age or country." [44] The force of this image in American life would soon become evident.

---

[42] *A Plea Before the Venerable Ecclesiastical Council at Stockbridge in the Cause of Mrs. Fisk* (Norwich, 1780), p. 22.

[43] *A Miscellaneous Collection of Original Pieces: Political, Moral, and Entertaining* (Springfield, 1786), p. 163.

[44] *The Columbian Magazine Or Monthly Miscellany* (January 1787), p. 244.

As Americans fashioned from Milton a pattern of connubial bliss, they turned to his religious sentiments and imagery to strengthen their spiritual life. No one referred to Milton as often as had Benjamin Colman or Joseph Bellamy, nor had he become, at least by public announcement, a companion in ministerial libraries. But Milton allusions appeared in sermons and magazines,[45] and his hymn to the Creator in Book V of *Paradise Lost* was rapidly becoming a common possession. Religious Americans increasingly found comfort in what Milton had said.

In his *Mirror Representing Some Religious Characters of the Present Times* John Anderson revealed why Americans now turned to Milton for aids to belief. Anderson had first published his *Mirror* in England, but it appeared under a Philadelphia imprint in 1786 with a Preface declaring that its contents applied to the state of religion in America at that time. No need exists to examine the five different kinds of religious characters Anderson presented. Suffice it to say that he found Deism more fashionable than old-time Christianity. In short, Anderson found natural religion, that child of seventeenth-century science, more popular than supernatural theology. A belief in God through observation of nature had challenged the old view of a mysterious Deity, had begun to supplant the traditional concept of a Dispenser of inexplicable providence. Such a challenge called for a vigorous spokesman of ancient Christian belief, for a pattern, as Anderson observed, like the faithful Abdiel in *Paradise Lost*.[46]

Ironically, Milton furnished American Deists with as much

---

[45] See, for example, *The Pennsylvania Magazine Or American Monthly Museum* (October 1775), pp. 447–449, in a letter signed by D. B.; and *The United States Magazine* (October 1779), pp. 429–430, in a sermon by William Macfee. This same sermon appeared in *The American Museum Or Repository of Ancient and Modern Fugitive Pieces*, II (July 1787), 82–83.

[46] *A Mirror Representing Some Religious Characters of the Present Times* (Philadelphia, 1786), pp. 25–26.

spiritual grist as he supplied faithful Abdiels. "T. T. Philo-math" presented Milton's prospect of Eden in Book IV of *Paradise Lost* as evidence for deistic reflection in a discourse on spring. Prefatory to developing his argument, he spoke of the creation as "a perpetual feast to the mind of a good man": Providence had "imprinted so many smiles on nature" that it would be impossible for a man not "sunk in more gross and sensual delights" to survey beautiful and agreeable scenes "without several secret sensations of pleasure and inward satisfaction." This was precisely the feeling Philomath be-lieved Milton had described as "vernal delight" in his picture of Eden. So lovely was the landscape, with its blossoms and fruits, that even Satan had responded to the beauteous details spread before him.

So that he could respond more precisely to the beauties of spring Philomath recited several lines from the picture of Eden Milton had painted, and then continued his discourse. "Natural philosophy," he said, quickens a "true taste of the creation," rendering it "not only pleasing to the imagination but to the understanding" as well. But such a response to nature could not rest alone "in rural pastoral amusements, as the murmur of brooks and the melody of birds, in the shade of woods and groves, or the embroidery of meadows and fields." For a total response one had to consider "the several ends of Providence" which such beauty served, as well as "the wonders of Divine Wisdom which appear in the productions of several species of the vegetable world." Such ruminations could lead but to a single conclusion: observation of nature unquestionably heightened "the pleasure of the eye," but, what was more important, it raised such "a rational admiration in the soul" that it produced an elevation "little inferiour" to devotion.[47] God moved in rational rather than in mysterious ways his wonders to perform.

[47] *The Virginia Almanack for the Year of Our Lord God 1770* (Williamsburg), in an essay on "Spring."

Such a response to the beauty of spring would have surprised Milton, however much he contributed to it. His own
theology had followed the main Renaissance line: the rational
order of the universe could serve as evidence of God, but men
understood Him best through Divine revelation. God himself, not His creation, merited worship. But such a position
failed to deter Americans from using Milton's hymn to the
Creator to articulate their own deistic views. Benjamin Franklin had earlier reproduced this hymn under his "Articles of
Belief and Acts of Religion"; William Livingston had paraphrased it; James Burgh had presented it to American youth
as an exercise in "devotion"; and William Scott had repeated
it in his *Lessons in Elocution*. Now, Benjamin West reprinted
parts of it on the title page of his *North-American Calendar* [48]
and Samuel Stearns made it the poetical core of a dissertation
upon eclipses. Stearns began his discourse by recalling that the
"science of astronomy" had "deservedly claimed the superiour
attention and admiration of mankind." "The sublimity of this
science," he declared, "its excellence, and its utility, must interest the human mind in the cultivation of so important a
subject; and the more closely it is pursued, the more lively
do the sublime ideas it inculcates, animate the inquirer."

Calculation of the size of the earth and its distance from the
sun, a preliminary essential to any discourse on eclipses, so
elevated Stearns that he could express his feeling only through
the words of Milton's hymn to the Creator, which he paused
to recite before pursuing his reflection to its conclusion. In
this hymn Adam and Eve had seen the universal frame as the
creation of God, as declaring His "goodness beyond thought,
and Power Divine." But Stearns saw the creation as operating
by immutable, mechanical laws. The precision of this vast
world machine excited his mind, urging him to direct, in a
"solemn and awful" manner, his devotions toward "the su-

[48] *The North-American Calendar: Or, The Rhode-Island Almanack, For
the Year of Our Lord Christ 1785* (Providence).

preme, infinite and incomprehensible author of nature!" For from His hands "hath he powered numberless myriads of suns, with all their worlds revolving round them, in motions immensely rapid, yet calm, regular, and uniformly exact, each invariably keeping its path in the order prescribed by the eternal Fiat." [49] As a rational man, Stearns needed no revelation to posit the existence or to ask for the worship of God: to him, Christianity was in no way mysterious. Milton's great hymn of praise had become in his hands simply an instrument to express the rationality of his religious experience.

But faithful Abdiels no less than Deists could find in Milton articulation of religious views. The Reverend William Gordon, a pastor in Roxbury, called on Milton's imagery to impress his congregation with the reality of traditional doctrines. The old concept of man's Fall from grace and of his salvation through Christ, of the reward of the faithful and the punishment of sinners, had been attacked by "universalists" like Charles Chauncy, who had argued that all men would be eventually saved. Even the great battle on the plains of Heaven in which Satan had attempted to topple God's throne became to such moralists a myth without substance— the mere fiction of poets, claimed Chauncy, substantiating his position with a quotation from Samuel Clark.[50]

Such views horrified the Reverend Gordon. His training cried out for him to counter such a flabby concept of man's destiny, and to do so he called upon Milton. Universal salvation, he declared, was completely un-Scriptural. Truth might be ascertained in the dark regions of Hell, he admitted, conceding this much to the moralists; but sinners, once damned,

---

[49] *Thomas's Massachusetts, Connecticut, Rhode-Island, Newhampshire & Vermont Almanack* (Worcester, 1789).

[50] *The Mystery Hid from Ages and Generations, Made Manifest by the Gospel-Revelation* (London, 1784), pp. 180–181, note. See also *Divine Glory Brought to View in the Final Salvation of All Men* (Boston, 1783), for a letter on the same topic.

abode in the wrath of God and would never see life. Christ himself taught such doctrine, Gordon continued; and the "poet *Milton*" had given a far more Scriptural account of Hell than ever the moralists had, particularly when he had exclaimed:

> Regions of sorrow! doleful shades! where peace
> And rest can never dwell! hope never comes,
> That comes to all: but torture without end
> Still urges, and a fiery deluge, fed
> With ever-burning sulphur unconsum'd! [51]

The accuracy of Gordon's statement could be seriously questioned, however sound his interpretation of Milton. In truth, Milton had not so much given here a Scriptural account as his own imaginative version of the infernal regions. Gordon had simply equated the two, and when he wished to impress his parishioners with the reality of Hell he presented the more vivid picture. Such a habit of mind had been evidenced earlier in the century, and such a practice would become common before the century closed. Pictorial details from *Paradise Lost* increasingly dramatized and strengthened Christian faith and belief.

Milton's imprint on the moral and spiritual life of America during the Revolutionary period should be considered significant not so much in itself as in what had gone before and what was to follow. References to his works for the purpose of confirming an ideal or of strengthening a belief appear widely scattered in time and in place. But for the first time discernible patterns of quotation began to emerge, a phenomenon comparable, in a sense, to the patterns of language, imagery, and syntax Milton had imposed on Colonial poetry. Related senti-

[51] *The Doctrine of Final Universal Salvation Examined and Shewn to be Unscriptural: In Answer to a Pamphlet Entitled Salvation for all Men Illustrated and Vindicated as A Scripture Doctrine* (Boston, 1783), pp. 24–25.

ments began to cluster about the same topics, indicating, through their repetition, that Americans had found in Milton evaluations of experience that sharpened their moral and spiritual views. Such sentiments so patterned would soon become widespread in American life.

## IV

As the Revolution advanced, Milton's authority moved from the moral and religious life of the nation into the arena of political conflict. Colonial preachers had already felt the weight of his arguments. Jonathan Mayhew particularly had strengthened his thought on religious and civil freedom by reference to *Areopagitica* and *Pro Populo Anglicano Defensio*. Now, as smoldering resentment flamed against Britain, Americans called ever more urgently on past witnesses of the main European political tradition to testify in behalf of their cause.[52] To say that Milton stood foremost in this group would be far from the truth.[53] Perhaps Cicero and Polybius appeared as often in American polemics; and unquestionably James Harrington and John Locke led the ranks, followed closely by Algernon Sidney, Bishop Hoadly, and Montesquieu. But Milton served Americans on more than one front. His distinction lies not in offering them the most cogent argument for the contractual theory of government, which encompassed most political disputes of the day, but in giving them, through his imagery and vast learning, opportunities for a wide variety of tactical maneuvers.

One tactic becoming popular was to make the language and imagery of *Paradise Lost* speak to the general conflict. The struggle between Evil and Good as Milton had told it could

[52] See G. H. Guttridge, *English Whiggism and the American Revolution* (Berkeley, 1942).

[53] See Alfred Waites, *A Brief Account of John Milton and His Declaration of Independence* (Worcester, 1903), for an exaggerated account of Milton's influence.

dramatize numerous acts and events, or assess the whole War against a background of transcendent truth.[54] Benjamin Franklin damned the British "System of Politics"—that is, her policy of taxation—by saying that it put him in mind of "Milton's description of Chaos, where every Thing is inconsistent with, and contrary to every Thing."[55] Thomas Paine likened the breach between England and America to the enmity between Satan and God, an alienation so profound that, as Milton had "wisely" declared, never could "true reconcilement grow where wounds of deadly hate" had "pierced so deep."[56] Nathaniel Whitaker presented the same image in a discourse delivered at Salem to describe the hatred existing between Patriots and Tories, saying further that to expect anything good from America's enemies would be tantamount to hoping for "Satan's cordial friendship to mankind."[57] By now, Milton's images had begun to be recognized symbols which could argue affectively in disputes of the time.

Tories no less than Patriots understood the efficacy of such propagandist devices. Samuel Seabury prefaced his *View of the Controversy between Great-Britain and her Colonies* with Michael's query as he began his combat with Satan:

> how hast thou instill'd
> Thy *Malice* into *Thousands*, once *upright*
> And *faithful; now* prov'd *false?*

[54] See Philip Davidson, *Propaganda and the American Revolution 1763–1783* (Chapel Hill, 1941), for general information about methods of propaganda. See also Bruce Ingham Granger, *Political Satire in the American Revolution, 1763–1783* (Ithaca, 1960).

[55] *Benjamin Franklin's Letters to the Press 1758–1775,* ed. Verner W. Crane (Chapel Hill, 1950), p. 194.

[56] *Common Sense* (Philadelphia, 1776), p. 43. This part of Paine's *Common Sense* appeared in *The American Museum Or Repository of Ancient and Modern Fugitive Pieces,* I, no. 11 (February 1787), 105.

[57] *The Reward of Toryism. A Discourse on Judges V. 23. Delivered at the Tabernacle in Salem, May 1783* (Newburyport, 1783), pp. 23–24. This sermon appeared later in *An Antidote Against, and the Reward of, Toryism* (Salem, 1811), dedicated to George Washington.

Seabury plainly intended to fix upon Revolutionary Americans the stigma of evil, symbolized in Satan's revolt against God. The cause of England, by contrast, he saw as just and right, as represented in Michael's leadership of the loyal angelic host.[58] In his satiric poem *The American Times* Jonathan Odell adjudged the whole reach of Revolutionary activity in terms of *Paradise Lost*. Leaders of the American cause, like Jefferson and Washington, appeared in this poem in more or less Miltonic dress, or represented the sayings or actions of the fallen angels or of the offspring of Satan. William Livingston of New Jersey, for example, took on the characteristics of Milton's allegorical figure of Death:

> Whence, and what art thou, execrable form,
> Rough as a bear and roaring as a storm?
>
> . . . . . . . .
>
> Havoc, and spoil, and ruin are thy gain.

Perhaps more than anyone else of the time Odell saw that symbols taken from *Paradise Lost* could become weapons of choice in the battle for men's minds. To him, Milton's poem was truly prophetic, presenting in archetypal form the issues and conflicts then confronting the nation. Reference to its characters and scenes could therefore evaluate the whole Revolution in one panoramic sweep:

> O Poet, seated on the lofty throne,
> Forgive the bard who makes thy words his own;
> Surpriz'd I trace in thy prophetic page,

---

[58] *A View of the Controversy between Great-Britain and her Colonies* (New York, 1774), title page. See also *Peter Oliver's Origin & Progress of the American Rebellion*, ed. Douglass Adair and John A. Schutz (San Marino, 1961), pp. 36 and 93–94. Oliver, a professed Tory, damned James Otis by saying that he had adopted the maxim Milton had put into the mouth of one of his devils: "Better to reign in Hell than serve in Heaven"; and opened his discussion of the current practice of tarring and feathering by reference to a pandemonium of Milton's Fallen Angels.

The crimes, the follies of the present age;
Thy scenery, sayings, admirable man,
Pourtray our struggle with the dark Divan:
What Michael to the first arch-rebel said,
Well would rebuke the rebel army's head;
What Satan to th'angelic Prince replied,
Such are the words of Continental pride:
I swear by him, who rules the earth and sky,
The dread event shall equally apply;
That Clinton's warfare is the war of God,
And Washington shall feel the vengeful rod.[59]

Why Americans turned to Milton for "scenery" and "sayings" could hardly be phrased more succinctly. *Paradise Lost* still lived to unfold the deeper meanings of Revolutionary activity: its story and characters could interpret precisely events of the day, as well as assess them. A single image or symbol could damn or praise a man's actions, or reveal in a flash mundane existence in terms of transcendent reality.

But Milton's language and symbols argued more often for than against the American cause.[60] Josiah Quincy, Jr. found in Michael's lesson to Adam at the end of *Paradise Lost* a rallying cry against the Boston Port Bill, Britain's answer to the Boston Tea Party. Michael had here told Adam how the children of God would be protected with spiritual armor against the assaults of Satan and Death, giving them courage that would amaze their proudest enemies. Quincy turned this

---

[59] *The American Times: A Satire in Three Parts. In Which are Delineated the Characters of the Leaders of the American Rebellion* (London, 1780), pp. 3–4, 12. For a discussion of Odell as a Tory satirist, see Moses Coit Tyler, *The Literary History of the American Revolution 1763–1783* (New York, New Printing, 1957), II, 107–129.

[60] Milton's description of Death, "Grinnd horrible a gastly smile," became a common epithet. See, for example, *The United States Magazine* (June 1779), p. 265. For other examples of the political use of Milton's language or symbols, see *The United States Magazine* (January 1779), p. 27; Barnabas Binney, *An Oration Delivered on the Late Public Commencement at Rhode-Island College in Providence* (Boston, 1774), title page.

passage, along with selections from Lucan and Pope, into a shout of defiance against the actions of Parliament:

> What M A N can do against them, *not afraid*,
> *Though to* T H E  D E A T H; against such C R U E L T I E S
> With *inward consolation* recompenc'd:
> And oft supported so, *as shall amaze*
> Their  P R O U D E S T  P E R S E C U T O R S.[61]

*The Boston Gazette* picked up this cry, garbled it somewhat, and placed it beside the text of two retaliatory acts of the British Parliament, the first for the suppression of tumults, the second for regulating the government of Massachusetts Bay.[62] Oliver Noble of Newbury made the last lines of the passage a sort of text for a discourse commemorating the Boston Massacre, an event, he implied, that showed how the "Power and Oppression of STATE MINISTERS" could lead "to the Ruin and Destruction of GOD's People." [63] It mattered little that Myles Cooper, in *The Patriots of North-America*, declared that such discourses were but the spawn of Hell, "Abominable, inutterable, and worse/ Than fables yet have feign'd, or Fear Conceiv'd." [64] Milton's words had struck fire; and in their new context they contended with all the power of their old symbolic force that God had especially armored America against the Satanic actions of Parliament.

Yet during the Revolution such use of Milton was comparatively rare. For the present, Americans appeared more in-

---

[61] *Observations on the Act of Parliament Commonly Called the Boston Port-Bill* (Boston, 1774), title page. On p. 40 Quincy also referred to Milton's comment on "trained bands" in *Eikonoklastes*.

[62] Catherine Drinker Bowen, *John Adams and the American Revolution* (Boston, 1950), p. 442.

[63] *Some Strictures upon the Sacred Story Recorded in the Book of Esther, Shewing the Power and Oppression of State Ministers tending to the Ruin and Destruction of God's People: And the Remarkable Interpositions of Divine Providence, in Favour of the Oppressed* (Newburyport, 1775), title page.

[64] *The Patriots of North-America* (New York, 1775), pp. 6–7, 38n. Because of its Tory leanings, this sketch was attributed to Myles Cooper.

terested in proclaiming Milton a witness for liberty and in asking him to speak directly for the American cause. Writing for *The Boston Gazette,* an "Independent" cited the conclusion of *The Ready and Easy Way to Establish a Free Commonwealth* to show how precisely Milton's agonized cry in defense of the Good Old Cause was relevant to America's position in 1770. American backsliders in this crucial year, he said, should be reminded that their liberties might soon expire, that trade was not all, that unless they lifted themselves out of their lethargy, they might fall under the yoke of foreign and domestic slavery.[65] In short, Milton spoke to Revolutionary America as cogently as he had spoken to England on the eve of the Restoration. Such an identification of the Good Old Cause with American Revolutionary activity is important only in that it lends perspective to the political thrust of the seventeenth and eighteenth centuries. From Cicero and Polybius, from Harrington and Milton and Algernon Sidney, from Locke and Bishop Hoadly and Montesquieu sprang the seminal ideas that supported Americans in their struggle with England. No two revolutionaries understood this succession better than John Adams and Jefferson, both of whom turned to Milton to clarify specific issues in contest.

While he was still a young man, John Adams had undoubtedly become acquainted with Milton. Perhaps he first heard of him in the discourses of the Reverend Lemuel Briant, who quoted from Milton's prose in sermons addressed to the developing crisis with England.[66] Adams certainly knew and admired Milton's poetry as early as 1756, when he recorded in his diary that Milton's soul "was distended as wide as Creation," that he could "only gaze at him with astonishment,

---

[65] *The Boston Gazette and Country Journal* (March 12, 1770), no. 779.
[66] Catherine Drinker Bowen, *John Adams and the American Revolution,* p. 32.

without comprehending the vast Compass of his Capacity." [67]
Adams referred to Milton several times in his diary, and once,
while serving as moderator at a meeting in Faneuil Hall, he
rebuked his fellow Patriots by quoting from Milton's sonnet
*On the Detraction:*

> I did but prompt the age to quit their cloggs
> By the known rules of antient libertie,
> When strait a barbarous noise environs me
> Of Owls and Cuckoes, Asses, Apes and Doggs.[68]

The occasion of the rebuke was the raucous reception of
Josiah Quincy's proposal that all should join in alleviating
the hunger caused by the Boston Port Bill, and according to
legend Milton's biting words quieted and shamed the restless
assembly. Moreover, Adams occasionally mentioned Milton
in letters. Writing to James Warren about the unhappy state
of Boston in 1775, he said that he never thought about the
Junto there "without recollecting the infernal spirits in Milton after they had recovered from their first astonishment
arising from their fall from the battlements of heaven to the
sulphurous lake, not subdued, though confounded, and plotting a fresh assault on the skies." A brief selection from
Satan's clarion call to his fallen compeers in Book I of
*Paradise Lost* completed the image of the nefarious nature
of the Junto in Boston.[69]

Again, in a letter to Samuel Adams on October 18, 1790,
he wrote of the difficulties in defining *republican*, venturing
to suggest that his correspondent did not mean, when he spoke
of *republican form*, "the plan of Milton, Nedham, or Tur-

---

[67] *Diary and Autobiography of John Adams*, ed. L. H. Butterfield (Cambridge, 1961), I, 23. Entry for April 30, 1756.

[68] Bowen, *op. cit.*, p. 444.

[69] *The Works of John Adams, Second President of the United States*, ed.
Charles Francis Adams (Boston, 1856), IX, 354.

got." [70] Even in his last years, when the Republic had been safely established, he wrote Jefferson that he found much entertainment and instruction in Erastus, "whose disciples were Milton, Harrington, Selden, St. John, the Chief Justice, father of Bolingbroke, and others, the choicest spirits of their age." [71] From his early years to his death, Adams admired Milton and displayed an intimate knowledge of his poetry and prose.

Naturally, Adams showed most interest in Milton's political views during the period of the Revolution itself. In January 1776, after Adams had been caught up in the vortex of revolutionary activity, the North Carolina Provincial Assembly instructed its delegates to ask that he express his views on the form of government the Colonies should adopt if independence were proclaimed. Adams, in a lengthily candid reply, explained how the Colonies should build a government of laws, not of men. At the request of George Wythe, Adams wrote a similar letter for Virginia, which appeared under the title *Thoughts on Government*. Here for all Americans to see Adams listed his political mentors, and not the least important among them was Milton.

Adams began his *Thoughts on Government* with a refutation of Pope's oft-quoted couplet:

> For forms of government let fools contest,
> That which is best administered is best.

Such a statement was fallacious, Adams declared, and flattered tyrants besides. The form of government *was* important.

---

[70] *Four Letters: Being an Interesting Correspondence between Those Eminently Distinguished Characters, John Adams, Late President of the United States; And Samuel Adams, Late Governor of Massachusetts. On the Important Subject of Government* (Boston, 1802), p. 12.

[71] *Correspondence of John Adams and Thomas Jefferson*, ed. Paul Wilstach (Indianapolis, 1925), p. 70. Letter of July 18, 1813.

Adams then developed his concept of the best form of government: Divines and moral philosophers all agreed that happiness of the individual is the end of man; therefore that form which could give happiness "to the greatest number" in "the greatest degree" would be best. All sober inquirers into truth further agreed that the happiness and dignity of man consist in virtue. Would not then that form of government "whose principle and foundation is virtue" promote "the general happiness" more than any other form? The question answered itself, Adams felt.

But what form fulfilled such a requirement? At this juncture Adams turned to America's struggle with England and to political philosophers whose voices had often been heard. The "wretched condition" of America for the past decade or so had reminded him of the "principles and reasonings" of Sidney, Harrington, Locke, Milton, Nedham, Neville, Burnet, and Hoadly, men who, despite the "sneers of modern Englishmen," should convince any "candid mind" that the only good form of government was republican. The only valuable part of the British Constitution was republican "because the very definition of a Republic, is 'an Empire of Laws, and not of Men.' "

Having established this position and given its sources, Adams refined his views further: since a republic is the best form of government, "that particular arrangement of the powers of society, or in other words that form of government, which is best contrived to secure an impartial and exact execution of the laws, is the best of Republics." The details of Adams' proposed plan need not be presented here. One of his stated principles, however, is significant: "The dignity and stability of government in all its branches, the morals of the people and every blessing of society, depend so much upon an upright and skillful administration of justice, that the judicial power ought to be distinct from both the legislative and executive, and independent upon both, that so it may be a check upon both, as both should be checks upon that." [72]

Such arguments comprise the heart of Adams' proposal to George Wythe. Years later, after Adams had served his country as President, Levi Lincoln recognized the importance of what Adams had said about the source of his thoughts upon government. Reproducing the last part of Adams' letter to George Wythe, Lincoln wrote: "The above, and the quotations in my last, expressed not merely the sentiments of the late president, of 'Sydney, Harrington, Locke, Milton, Needham, Neville, Barney, and Hoadley.' They were," Lincoln asserted, "the sentiments of the Adamses, Bowdoin, Hawley, Livingston, Dickinson, Mason, Pendleton, Lee, Randolph, Rutledge, P. Henry, Madison, Jefferson, and Washington, and they were the sentiments of every American . . . the sentiments which you opposed to the claims of tyranny, which carried us through our revolution, gave to us our independence, and those republican governments, essential to its support." [73] If Adams claimed Milton as one of the sources of his views upon government, Lincoln saw him as one of the spiritual fathers of the Revolution itself.

Yet Adams' high admiration for Milton and his stated but intangible debt to his thought tell only part of the story. As the Constitution slowly took shape in American minds, Adams, as might be expected, looked more closely at the principles which had guided him through years of revolutionary activity. The results of this reappraisal he articulated in *A Defence of the Constitutions of Government of the United States of America*, a document which, among many readjustments of thought, put Milton under a more critical light. Why he

[72] *Thoughts on Government: Applicable to the Present State of the American Colonies* (Philadelphia, 1776), pp. 7–8, 21. The letter concluded with lines from Milton's sonnet *On the Detraction*, which Adams had spoken to the audience in Faneuil Hall at an earlier date.

[73] *Letters to the People. By a Farmer* (Salem, 1802), p. 93.

should change his opinion about Milton at this time can be readily explained. Before the Revolution was won, Patriots had cried mainly for freedom from tyranny. They therefore invoked authors who had notably opposed tyrants and had upheld the contractual theory of government. Since Milton had eloquently argued against all forms of intellectual and spiritual tyranny and had succinctly phrased the theory of compact Adams quite rightly listed him with Harrington, Sidney, and Locke, quite rightly called on his "principles and reasonings" to support the American cause. After the Revolution, however, a different situation prevailed. The emphasis now was not on asserting the rights of free men but on establishing the most effective machinery of government. The separation of powers so dear to Adams' heart, as embodied in the bicameral system of Massachusetts, ran into difficulties as early as 1786. Moreover, supporters of the unicameral system —notably Condorcet in France, Richard Price and Joseph Priestley in England, and Franklin and Thomas Paine in America—now arose to attack some of Adams' most cherished beliefs. Milton had earlier inspired Adams with his pulsing arguments for freedom; now he could offer no acceptable machinery of government either to answer his enemies or to support his revolutionary experience.

This is the reason why Adams now turned a critical eye upon Milton. So important was the American experiment to the political history of man that Adams felt duty-bound to disclose in a series of letters what "kind of reading and reasoning" had shaped the Constitution itself, what process of choice and rejection the Founding Fathers had followed to produce so noble a document. In this disclosure Adams mentioned Milton a number of times. In Letter L, a discussion of "Ancient Aristocratical Republics," Adams pointed to the continuity of political thought by saying that "Milton, Harrington, Sidney, were intimately acquainted with the ancients, and with Machiavel." But of chief interest is Letter LV, in which

Adams analyzed Locke, Milton, and Hume. Here, his disappointment in mere visionaries so overwhelmed him that hyperbole became his mode of expression. Even Plato or Thomas More, he declared, could at times be as wild as the ravers of Bedlam. Locke himself, the earlier patron saint of the Patriots, no longer spoke sense.

Such was the context of hostility that surrounded Adams' analysis of Milton's *The Ready and Easy Way to Establish A Free Commonwealth*. For Milton's greatness as a poet and for his character as a man, to be sure, Adams still had only praise. But a man "may spend his life in defence of liberty, and be at the same time one of the most irreproachable moral characters," yet when called upon "to frame a constitution of government" may demonstrate to the world "that he has reflected very little on the subject." In this specific task Milton had signally failed. What Adams objected to most was Milton's proposal for a perpetual senate of wise and good men. "Can you read, without shuddering, this wild reverie of the divine immortal Milton?" Adams asked. "Had Milton's scheme been adopted," Adams continued, England "would have either been a scene of revolutions, carnage, and horror, from that time to this, or the liberties of England would have been at this hour the liberties of Poland, or the island would have been a province of France." Such speculations so exercised Adams that he could only exclaim:

What! a single assembly to govern England? an assembly of senators for life too? What! did Milton's ideas of liberty and free government extend no further than exchanging one house of lords for another, and making it supreme and perpetual? What! Cromwell, Ireton, Lambert, Ludlow, Waller, and five hundred others, of all sects and parties, one quarter of them mad with enthusiasm, another with ambition, a third with avarice, and a fourth of them honest men, a perpetual council, to govern such a country! [74]

[74] *A Defence of the Constitutions of Government of the United States of America* (London printed, Boston reprinted, 1788), pp. 262, 295–300. In *Modern Chivalry*, ed. Claude M. Newlin (New York, 1937), p. 414,

As Adams speculated further on the immediate and ultimate results of such a mechanism of government his nervousness grew. The council would become "an oligarchy of decemvirs" on the first day of sitting, he declared; it would be instantly "torn with all the agitations of Venice, between the aristocracy and oligarchy, in the assembly itself." If by "ballots and rotations" and a "thousand other contrivances" the assembly could be combined, it would strip the "people of England of every shadow of liberty" and produce in the next generation a "lazy, haughty, ostentatious, group of palatines"; if the assembly fell into divisions, it would deluge "the nation in blood" until "one despot" would arise to rule over all.

Such a frightening vision of what might have happened in England had Milton's proposal struck fire sprang from Adams' profound political wisdom. Milton's scheme was an expedient, born of disillusionment in the Puritan Revolution and in fear of old Stuart tyrannies. Adams rightly assessed it. For Milton's strength lay not so much in specific proposals as in memorable cries for civil, domestic, and ecclesiastical freedom. Adams recognized that Milton was honest and that he was "a great friend of liberty"; he himself had fallen under the sway of Milton's persuasion in the early days of the War. But after the crucible of conflict, he and his fellow Americans had become far too enlightened "to be bubbled out of their liberties, even by such mighty names as Locke, Milton, Turgot, or Hume."

Americans now knew, Adams declared, that popular elections of one essential branch of the legislature frequently re-

---

Hugh Henry Brackenridge expressed the disenchantment of political theorists: "A mere philosopher is but a fool, in matters of business. Even in speculation, he sometimes, imagines nonsense. Sir Thomas More's Utopia has become proverbial; Harrington's Oceana has become a model for no government. Locke's Project was tried in South Carolina. It was found wanting. Imagination, and experiment are distinct things. There is such a thing as *practical sense*. Do we not see instances of this every day?"

peated could be the "only possible method of forming a free constitution, or of preserving the government of laws from the domination of men, or of preserving their lives, liberties, or properties in security." They also now knew, "though Locke and Milton did not, that when popular elections are given up, liberty and free government must be given up." [75]

In this manner Adams explained how the Constitution came into being. Taking here, rejecting there, the Founding Fathers created an instrument of government based on the most successful political experience of man and on the best thought of the past. If Adams himself, as one of those Fathers, rejected Milton's specific proposal, he responded to his impassioned call for intellectual and spiritual freedom. This response became part of his own political experience, and in such measure as he was moved Milton contributed to the Constitution of the United States.

The measure of Milton's imprint upon Thomas Jefferson can be taken with much greater precision, since Jefferson left an impressive record of reference to Milton's poetry and prose. Excerpts from his poetry appear in Jefferson's Commonplace Books, one of which was devoted to sayings of the philosophers and poets, the other chiefly to information taken from historians and legal authorities.[76] Extracts from his prose appear separately with notes on different matters, including citations from John Locke, the Third Earl of Shaftesbury, and others.[77] Taken together, these excerpts and notes reveal the enormous range of Jefferson's interests, and at the same time mark the forces which helped shape his mind. His curious in-

---

[75] *A Defence of the Constitutions of Government of the United States of America*, p. 298.

[76] See Gilbert Chinard, *The Commonplace Book of Thomas Jefferson* (Baltimore, 1926), p. 98; and *The Literary Bible of Thomas Jefferson* (Baltimore, 1928), pp. 134–140, 164–168.

[77] See *The Papers of Thomas Jefferson*, ed. Julian P. Boyd (Princeton, 1950), I, 539–558. See also *The Commonplace Book of Thomas Jefferson*, "Appendix."

tellect traveled extensively over the whole Western tradition, finding nourishment in its masters of law, literature, and philosophy. Any attempt to single out the effect of one personality on so capacious a mind should therefore be approached with unusual caution. Yet Jefferson, even in his youth, seems to have been particularly attracted to Milton, if excerpts from his poetry serve as an accurate gauge; and in crucial debates over the powers of Church and State in 1776 he turned to Milton's prose for arguments on specific issues of freedom.

What attracted Jefferson most in *Paradise Lost* was Milton's characterization of Satan and his presentation of the human condition. In common with other eighteenth-century readers of Milton, he focused a fascinated eye on the magnificence of Satan's speeches, on the almost human qualities of the apostate angel as he defied God and assessed his own fall. The great sweep of rhetoric in Satan's first call to his cohorts, his ringing challenge and plans for revenge—all so captured Jefferson's interest that he copied out many of the most telling lines. He apparently saw, as many other admirers of Milton then saw, heroic qualities in Satan's defiance of God and in his leadership of the apostates, who arose at his words and regrouped their strength in anticipation of joining battle against their implacable foes. But other scenes also charmed Jefferson. Adam and Eve in the Garden of Eden, their innocent nuptial love, their despair after the Fall—and particularly Adam's Hamlet-like query into the nature of death and his agonized cry at being deceived by the woman he loved —received respectful attention.

Scenes of human agony indeed so impressed Jefferson that he stressed similar insights into betrayal and suffering as depicted in *Samson Agonistes*. From this tragedy he recorded Samson's lament over his blindness, his pain at being deceived by Dalila, and his shame at being proverbed in the streets for a fool, as well as the Choral account of Dalila's final attempt to ensnare him. Apparently Jefferson believed that Milton had been unusually happy in presenting the nature and condition of man. Of one thing he was sure: Raphael's advice to Adam to eschew vain speculation was eminently sound. The core of the passage, which Jefferson reproduced in good part, expressed exactly his lifelong position.

Altogether, Jefferson excerpted forty-seven passages from *Paradise Lost* and *Samson Agonistes*—forty-eight, counting his quotation about the doctrine of Atonement in a footnote to his examination of criminal law.[78] Such passages reveal not simply Jefferson's interest in Milton; they imply, by their very selection, a set of values and an attitude of mind. Milton became a part of his intellectual equipment, however impossible it would be to adduce tangible evidence for such an assertion.

Yet Milton's effect on Jefferson—unlike his effect on Adams —need not be measured by the yardstick of general inferences. He drew directly from Milton's resources in the conflict over the disestablishment of the Church of England in Virginia in 1776, and since this was an important year of legislative activity, any influence Milton might have had at that time would be of a particular interest. How Jefferson used Milton during this period can be made clear after a glance at the struggle to disestablish the Church of England in Virginia and the part Jefferson played in it. The struggle, briefly, was the longstanding conflict of the Established Church and the Dissent over contributions and freedom of worship. The result of the struggle, on the plane of law, was legislation by the Virginia Assembly: (1) An Act for Exempting Dissenters from Contributing to the Anglican Church, passed in December of 1776; and (2) A Bill for Religious Freedom, passed in 1786. To this legislation, Jefferson made impressive contributions.

---

[78] See *The Literary Bible of Thomas Jefferson*, under "Milton." See also *The Commonplace Book of Thomas Jefferson*, p. 98.

Sometime before November 19, 1776, he drew up a "Rough Draft" of "Resolutions for Disestablishing the Church of England and for Repealing Laws Interfering with Freedom of Worship." [79] This "Rough Draft" no doubt served as a basis of discussion in a Committee on Religion, of which Jefferson was a member. Moreover, he was connected with the "Draft of a Bill for Exempting Dissenters from Contributing to the Support of the Church," though the exact part he played in forming this Bill has not been established.[80] Finally, he composed, perhaps as early as 1777, the famous Bill for Religious Freedom, which, as just noted, became law in 1786. No other man did more for the cause of religious freedom in Virginia than Jefferson.

Fortunately, Jefferson left an informative, though sketchy, record of this impressive period of legislative activity. Before he drew up the rough draft of his "Resolutions" he had read widely and made notes pertinent to the problem confronting the Assembly. These notes have been brought together under the following heads: "Lists of Acts of Parliament," "Notes on Acts of Parliament," "Notes on Locke and Shaftesbury," "Notes on Episcopacy," "Notes on Heresy," and "Miscellaneous Notes on Religion." [81] Some of these notes, as will be shortly shown, Jefferson incorporated into an "Outline of Argument in Support of His Resolutions," a document which apparently ordered his thinking during the struggle over the disestablishment of the Church of England and from which, in a sense, sprang his Bill for Religious Freedom.[82] So important is this document that, before its sources are analyzed, it needs to be examined in some detail.

---

[79] *The Papers of Thomas Jefferson*, I, 530.

[80] *ibid.*, I, 532–533.

[81] *ibid.*, I, 539–558. Exactly when these notes were taken is uncertain, but Jefferson apparently made them before he sketched his "Rough Draft." See the "Editorial Note."

[82] *ibid.*, I, 535–539. See also the "Editorial Note."

Jefferson seems to have divided his "Outline of Argument" into six main divisions, though the abbreviated nature of the document makes it difficult to ascertain the principal heads with any sense of assurance. If the numbers he occasionally placed by his arguments have any meaning, the main divisions may be arranged something like this:

I   Apostacy
II   Heresy
III   Recusancy
IV   Popery
V   Profaneness
VI   Contributions

Under each main division, except that of "Popery," Jefferson jotted down relevant details, often writing in cryptic form but nevertheless making his arguments clear. The amount of detail varies widely under each main head, but Section VI received the fullest treatment, since one of the greatest problems the Assembly faced was whether all citizens should contribute to an Establishment. In this section, Jefferson put down, among many things, observations on the justice of contributions, the theory of uniformity in religion, the purpose of an establishment, and the nature of liberty. This part of the "Outline" alone is a forceful argument for disestablishing the Church of England and for allowing not simply toleration but complete religious freedom.

A comparison of part of this "Outline" with some of the notes Jefferson took to prepare himself for his legislative activity will show at once how he used his reading to fill in the details of his argument. In his "Notes on Acts of Parliament," for example, appears the following information:

[1705] c. 6. if [any person] brought up in the Xn. relign. shall by
Arians.     writg. printg. teachg. or speakg. deny the being of a
Jews.       god, or the trinity, or shall assert there are more gods
than one, or deny the Xn. relign. to be true, or the old

& new test. to be of divine authority. 1st offce. disabled
to hold any office ecclesl. civl. or military. 2d. offence
disabled to sue, or be capable of gift or legacy & 3. years
imprisonmt. 1730. c. 2. to enforce the foregoing act. &
1744 c. 2. ditto. this act copd. from 9 & 10 W. 3.c.32.[83]

This information Jefferson incorporated, in condensed form,
into the first division of his "Outline":

*Apostacy.* act. 1705. c. 6.
>    1st. offce. disabd. to hold office.
>    2d. disabled to sue, incapb. of gift or legacy
>    3 three years imprismt. however conscients. ye Conversion.[84]

Again, in the same "Notes on Acts of Parliament," Jefferson
had recorded the following item:

>    1.E. 6. C. 1. Rast. 365.a. 'to deprave despise or
>    contemn the sacrament' imprisonmt. & fine ad
>    libitum repd by I. Mar. parl. I . . .[85]

In the "Outline" under Section III, Jefferson reduced this
item to the following statement:

>    *Sacramt.* 1.E. 6. c. 1.
>    to deprave it, imprismt. & fine ad libitum.[86]

These and other similarities establish without doubt the
relation between Jefferson's notes and his "Outline of Argument." [87] It would not be too much to say that Jefferson composed a good part of this important document from his notes,
that this document in turn ordered his thinking during the
"severe contests" over the disestablishment of the Church of
England, and that out of these contests came the famous Bill

[83] *The Papers of Thomas Jefferson*, I, 544.
[84] *ibid.*, I, 535.
[85] *ibid.*, I, 541.
[86] *ibid.*, I, 535.
[87] *ibid.*, I, 528. In the "Editorial Note" it is stated that a "cursory comparison of the notes" with the "Outline" is sufficient to show Jefferson's re-
liance on them.

for Religious Freedom. It now remains to see what notes Jefferson took from Milton, and whether he used them in formulating his "Outline of Argument."

Jefferson turned to Milton for his "Notes on Episcopacy," about half of which came from *Of Reformation in England* and *The Reason of Church-Government Urged,* two of Milton's early tracts on ecclesiastical freedom. Jefferson summarized the latter tract in part, recalling that Milton had stated the Anglican argument of the time touching on the relationship between Church and State. He put down, for example, Milton's analysis of Anglican contentions that Episcopal Church government alone was congenial with monarchy, a position which had been expressed in the slogan "no bishop, no king." Then, among other things, Jefferson went on to note that the Presbyterian spirit was "so congenial with friendly liberty, that the patriots after the restoration finding that the humour of people was running too strongly to exalt the prerogative of the crown, promoted the dissenting interest as a check and balance, & thus was produced the Toleration act." [88] When Jefferson jotted this down he perhaps had in mind the growing force of Presbyterianism in Virginia, which might prove helpful in bringing religious freedom to people long harassed with questionable laws. But what impressed him most in *The Reason of Church-Government Urged* was Milton's anticlericalism, his view that laymen possessed the right to hold opinions on matters of religion.

Jefferson found such a view so suitable to his purpose that he excerpted from this tract a number of pertinent phrases and arguments. Milton had argued that in early times laymen had actually taught Christian positions. Indeed, he went on, St. Peter gave the title of clergy to all God's people, and it was not until the time of Pope Higinus and succeeding prelates that this term was given to priests only. Furthermore,

[88] *ibid.,* I, 552.

Milton explained, when Origen was a layman he expounded the Scriptures in public and was defended for so doing by Alexander of Jerusalem and Theoctistus of Caesarea. In addition, Milton continued, the first Nicene Council called on the assistance of many lay people to resolve the problems before it. All this information Jefferson took down almost word for word. At the conclusion of each main citation he referred to the specific volume and page number of the edition of Milton's work from which he had copied.[89]

In *Of Reformation in England* Jefferson found additional arguments to support his cause, particularly in Milton's historical account of the Church during its early years of development. Milton had written this account in answer to the Anglican "Antiquarians," who had said that their kind of Establishment, with its hierarchy and succession of bishops, conformed to the organization of the Church in "pure" primitive times. Milton had countered this claim by contending that in the days of the primitive Christians bishops had been elected by the whole Church; and to back up this position he had cited the authority of Ignatius, who, in writing to the Philadelphians, had said that it belonged to them as to the Church of God to choose their bishops. Milton had then gone on to list other authorities supporting this view, noting particularly Cyprian; and he had concluded, with special reference to the Anglican Establishment of the time, that if a modern bishop were to be molded into a bishop like one in primitive times, he must be elected by the people, "undiocest, unrevenu'd, unlorded." Such information seemed to suit Jefferson precisely, for he took it down almost verbatim, again citing the volume and page numbers of the edition he followed.[90]

---

[89] *ibid.*, I, 552. For Milton's exact words, see *The Works of John Milton*, III, Part I, 257–258.

[90] *The Papers of Thomas Jefferson*, I, 553. See also *The Works of John Milton*, III, Part I, 15–19.

The notations from Milton suggest that Jefferson found in *The Reason of Church-Government Urged* and in *Of Reformation in England* at least two propositions which he thought would be of help in the contests over the disestablishment of the Church of England in Virginia. The first was that laymen possessed religious rights and privileges, as shown in primitive times, and the second was that bishops received their power by the authority and consent of the people. Both these arguments could have been very effective in the conflict over religious freedom, and it is quite possible that Jefferson used them from time to time in committee. But curiously, they fail to appear in the "Outline of Argument." What does appear in the "Outline" is not what he copied down in his "Notes on Episcopacy" but information found in the pages immediately following Milton's discussion of Primitive Christianity in *Of Reformation in England*. Here, apparently, Milton spoke so pointedly to the issues confronting the Virginia Assembly that Jefferson incorporated what he said into the text of the "Outline."

Milton indeed had presented in these pages arguments which played directly into Jefferson's hands. Milton had, to be sure, said that even in primitive times the Church showed corruption; but he had stressed, again and again, that decay set in with the establishment of Christianity as a state religion under Emperor Constantine. The most "virgin" times, Milton had contended, the period when the Church flourished with less taint than afterward, lay between Christ and Constantine, or during the first three hundred years of Christianity; but once the Christian faith became established by law, once it gained the support of civil authority, degeneration followed apace.

For Constantine, Milton had argued, "appointed certaine times for Fasts, and Feasts, built stately Churches, gave large Immunities to the Clergie, great Riches and Promotions to

*Bishops,*" all with the result that "the Church that before by insensible degrees welk't and impair'd, now with large steps went downe hill decaying." [91] And to those who had said that the times of Constantine were unsettled and that therefore the Church needed the strength of temporal authority, Milton had replied that he did not think the "Church a *Vine* in this respect," that is, that she could not "subsist without clasping about the Elme of worldly strength, and felicity, as if the heavenly City could not support it selfe without the props and buttresses of secular Authoritie." [92] In short, Milton had argued that the Church needed no secular crutch, and that, what was more, when it was given such props it immediately declined from its former purity.

This is exactly what Jefferson said in one section of the sixth division of his "Outline of Argument." It will be recalled that Jefferson was arguing in this division against contributions to an established religion, and that this in turn had led him into a discussion of church uniformity and religious freedom. As he came to the end of his argument, at least so far as the "Outline" is concerned, he noted that every man had a right to judge for himself in religion, that it was, furthermore, advantageous to religion itself to put all faiths on the same footing. Then he sketched, with his usual abbreviations, the following contention:

> Xty. florshd. 300. y. witht. establmt.
> soon as establd. *declind.* frm. *Purity*
> betrays wnt. confdce. in doctrnes. of chch. to suspct. yt.
> reasn. or intrinsck. xcllce. insfft. wtht. seculr. prop.[93]

This argument, in some ways, was the keystone of the structure Jefferson had reared in his "Outline." For in it he contended, with particular reference to the Anglican Estab-

[91] *The Works of John Milton,* III, Part I, 24–25.
[92] *ibid.,* pp. 22–23.
[93] *The Papers of Thomas Jefferson,* I, 539.

lishment in Virginia, that Christianity needed no help from civil authority to maintain itself or to keep itself pure, that indeed with an Establishment, as history had shown, Christianity had gone and would continue to go "downe hill decaying." For the inclusion of this sentiment in the "Outline of Argument" Jefferson had Milton to thank. The likeness of the arguments, the similarity of the words, and the proximity of the contention in *Of Reformation in England* to the pages from which Jefferson copied his "Notes on Episcopacy" can lead to no other conclusion.

The demonstrable debt Jefferson owed Milton, it must be admitted, is relatively slender. The section in the "Outline of Argument" attributable to *Of Reformation in England* comprises only a small item in a large list of contentions made preparatory to resolving only one part of a large legislative program which Jefferson developed through the stirring years of the American Revolution. But the fact remains that Jefferson did find Milton congenial and did make use of his works in some of the severest contests in which he was ever engaged; and out of the crucible of these contests came the Bill for Religious Freedom, a document second in importance to the Declaration of Independence alone. It is therefore safe to say that Milton, through Jefferson, contributed tangibly to the settlement of religious freedom in Virginia; and this contribution, in turn, established a clear and direct path from the Puritan to the American Revolution. The writer in *The Boston Gazette* who related the Good Old Cause with Revolutionary tumults in America spoke with more truth than he realized.

What is remarkable about Milton's imprint upon political disputes of the Revolution is not its depth but its breadth and variety. Yet a glance backward should make this phenomenon clear. The main principles upon which Americans based most of their arguments had already been established as self-evident truths. Even James Harrington and John Locke, whom Americans called on most often, simply lent a cooperative hand in reiterating positions of the main European tradition. Americans needed at this time not so much intellectual arguments for basic positions as emotional symbols and detailed information addressed to specific issues in contest. Milton supplied both, but the strength of his imagery soon prevailed over the relevance of most of his principles. For *Paradise Lost* would soon become a main arsenal of propagandist devices, furnishing Americans with images and symbols which could rhetorically if not logically argue a cause.

## V

During the Revolutionary period, Milton spoke with greatest authority in the literary community.[94] Patterns of imitation by now had been clearly established: his language, syntax, and imagery had become almost synonymous with exalted poetic expression. This inheritance now joined with an urgent national desire to express New World experience in sublime, immortal verse. American hopes for poetic achievement ran so strong that a patriot proposed that Congress establish an American poet laureateship, an office that would allow an ambitious author to "raise a new Parnassus on the Allegany mountains, and open a second Helicon at the source of the Potowmack"—an honor that would stimulate him to "rehearse" in "glorious numbers" the "rise and progress of the American Millennium." [95]

[94] For a recent discussion of the state of literature during the Revolution and the early Republic, see Russel Blaine Nye, *The Cultural Life of the New Nation* (New York, 1960), Chapter 11, "The Quest for a National Literature," pp. 235–267.

[95] See *The New Haven Gazette and the Connecticut Magazine*, I, no. 10 (April 20, 1786), 79–80, "Observations on the Present Situation and Future Prospects of this and the United States." This article is chiefly political, but its author paused long enough to propose the creation of a poet laureateship and to suggest that any one of the "Connecticut Triumvirate" might accept such an office.

Hard-headed Congressmen apparently looked at such a proposal with skeptical eyes. But unquestionably the Revolution spurred a literary movement of considerable importance, encompassing such respectable names as Hugh Henry Brackenridge and Philip Freneau, as well as John Trumbull, Joel Barlow, and Timothy Dwight. Never before had Americans so consciously attempted to create a distinct, national literature. No wonder, then, in view of such aims, that Americans should ask Milton to shape their expression, or that, having done so, his imprint should guide the course of their verse. Colonial experiments had convinced them that imitation of his manner and matter would assure a poem worthy not only of American greatness but of immortality as well. In their literary innocence they could only envision such happy results.

Minor poets of the Revolution no less than authors ambitious to celebrate the glories of the New World called on Milton to achieve special effects. Such poetasters revealed in miniature what more aspiring authors disclosed in more generous proportions—that consciousness of Milton pervaded the poetic community, that certain kinds of subject matter demanded Miltonic treatment and style. Sometimes openly, sometimes silently, they incorporated into their works Milton's language and idiom, or shaped their syntax according to Miltonic patterns or their poems according to Miltonic forms. Joseph Brown Ladd, for example, who for a while was almost as popular as Freneau, laced his translation of the Ossianic *Fingal* with words from *Paradise Lost*, a debt he publicly acknowledged in notes supplying the text of the lines from which he had pilfered.[96] In *The Country Meeting*, T[homas C.] J[ames] made similar open confessions.[97] Henry Pepper

---

[96] *The Poems of Arouet* (Charleston, S. C., 1786), pp. 34, 37, 41, 127–128. The poem *Retirement* (pp. 115–117) follows the tetrameter couplets of *Il Penseroso*. For an account of Ladd's popularity, see Lewis Leary, "The Writings of Joseph Brown Ladd, 1764–1785," *Bulletin of Bibliography*, XVIII (1945), 131–133.

[97] *The American Museum Or Repository*, I (January, 1787), p. 93.

began his *Juvenile Essays* with an invocation to Urania, followed by an address to God reminiscent of Milton's in *Paradise Lost:*

> Come rather Thou,
> Who sanctifi'st our hearts, O Spirit, pure!

And in a verse epistle to his friend Henry Mac-Neale Kennedy, his "Hail, holy Love!" sang of marriage in the familiar accents of the nuptial hymn Milton had addressed to Adam and Eve in Book IV.[98]

But even more pervasive among minor poets was the Miltonic image, the distinctive personages and vistas that had impressed themselves indelibly on the poetic consciousness of the age. Elijah Fitch confessed in his *Beauties of Religion* that he lacked Milton's genius; yet, to enhance an account of a battle, he recalled Satan's Pyrrhic return to the conclave of devils after the Fall.[99] Such memorable panoramas from *Paradise Lost,* impressed anew on Americans by reprints of English Miltonic verse,[100] had now become commonplace, as had also the bucolic landscapes in Milton's popular twin poems. An effusion succinctly entitled *Vacation,* from its opening irregular lines to its concluding tetrameter couplet, presented the precise form and much of the imagery of *Il Penseroso.*[101] Such eloquent testaments of Milton's penetration into the poetic life of Revolutionary America need little comment, other than to

---

[98] *Juvenile Essays; Or, A Collection of Poems* (Philadelphia, [1798]), pp. 1, 63. Since Pepper said he wrote these poems in his early youth, I have placed them in the Revolutionary period.

[99] *The Beauties of Religion. A Poem* (Providence, 1789), pp. 5–6, 72.

[100] *The Conflagration: A Poem on the Last Day* (Philadelphia, 1787), *passim.* Another edition appeared under a New York imprint in 1789.

[101] *The New Haven Gazette and the Connecticut Magazine,* III, no. 43 (October 30, 1788). The concluding couplet reads:

> These delights, vacation give
> And I with thee wil chuse to live.

say that minor poets carried on from Colonial times two main lines of Miltonic influence: the lilt of *L'Allegro* and *Il Penseroso* moved into occasional mood poetry, the grand style of *Paradise Lost* shaped the manner of subjects sublime. That poets attempting to "rehearse" in "glorious Numbers" the present and future greatness of America should turn to Milton's epic was therefore inevitable. Miltonic influence in them in fact rose to a flood tide, often quite overwhelming their very real talents in its rips and strong currents.

Among authors ambitious to sing of American greatness was Hugh Henry Brackenridge, though as a poet he left no work of importance.[102] During his youth, however, he joined with Philip Freneau and other patriots to celebrate in verse the glory of the "American Millennium." [103] What indeed is most important about Brackenridge's early poetic career is his contribution to "prospect" literature and his claim of being influenced by Milton. In *The Rising Glory of America*, a commencement vision composed in collaboration with Freneau, he saw a Homer and a Milton arising on the American strand; and three years later, in 1774, he contended that Milton was the source of his style. At this time he wrote *A Poem on Divine Revelation*, which he delivered as a commencement address at Princeton; and in a prefatory note he confessed that "imitation" of Milton could be "traced" through his entire exercise. Such a confession, he implied, served a dual purpose: it would obviate objections as to the source of the poem, and articulate his position that imitation of great originals

---

[102] His most important work was *Modern Chivalry*, in which he referred to Milton several times. See the edition of this work by Claude M. Newlin (New York, 1937), pp. 550–551, 681, 723.

[103] For a full discussion of "prospect" poetry and of other trends in American verse, see Mary Dexter Bates, "Columbia's Bards: A Study of American Verse from 1783 Through 1799" (Unpublished dissertation, Brown University, 1954). For an analysis of the continuity of the epic in America, see Roy Harvey Pearce, *The Continuity of American Poetry* (Princeton, 1961), Chapter 3, "The Long View: An American Epic."

would produce excellent writing, a principle he had found in Longinus.[104]

A reading of *A Poem on Divine Revelation* suggests that Brackenridge referred to Milton not so much to confess his literary dependence as to boast of his acquaintance with a celebrated bard. For his lengthy confession, as William Linn hinted, appeared to be wholly gratuitous, since the one clear mark of Milton in the entire poem lay in the word *"Erst."* [105] Yet Linn's skepticism was not solidly founded. Brackenridge *had* tried to catch the roll of Milton's blank verse, *had* tried to achieve some of his cadences by stringing together long lists of mellifluous names. If he failed to achieve the effect he intended, no one should deny him the attempt, or say that Milton was not on his mind when he composed, for example, the following lines:

> Fam'd Persia's mountains and rough Bactria's woods
> And Media's vales and Shinar's distant plain:
> The Lybian desert near Cyrene smiles
> And Ethiopia hails it to her shores.
> Arabia drinks the lustre of its ray
> Than fountain sweeter, or the cooling brook
> Which laves her burning sands; than stream long sought
> Through desert flowing and the scorched plain
> To Sheba's troop or Tema's caravan.[106]

Of importance here is not that Brackenridge failed to produce acceptable verse, but that he thought Milton's style suited the grandeur of the vision he saw. Consciousness of

---

[104] *A Poem on Divine Revelation; Being An Exercise Delivered at the Public Commencement at Nassau-Hall, September 28, 1774* (Philadelphia, 1774), Preface.

[105] See Claude Milton Newlin, *The Life and Writings of Hugh Henry Brackenridge* (Princeton, 1932), p. 32.

[106] *A Poem on Divine Revelation*, p. 7. Thomas P. Haviland pointed out this Miltonic passage, finding in addition to *Paradise Lost* echoes of the *Nativity Ode* and of *Lycidas* in Brackenridge's poem. See "The Miltonic Quality of Brackenridge's *Poem on Divine Revelation*," PMLA, LVI (1941), 588–592.

Milton and admiration for his style clung to Brackenridge through the early part of his life. In a sermon preached before the American Army a few days prior to the Battle of Brandywine, he quoted from Milton and divulged that he had been "touched" by the "magic sound" of his "harp"; [107] and somewhat later, as he viewed an island from the banks of the Alleghany, he envisioned a poet pouring "his magic numbers on this scene," a poet comparable to Homer or Milton, whom he considered to be the "father" of "modern bards." [108] Such admiration no doubt led him to echo *Comus* in his own *Masque* written at Warm Springs, Virginia. This *Masque*, honoring George Washington's visit to that small Virginia community, presented the Genius of the Woods, the spirits of rivers, and various naiads, all intent on the arrival of so great a personage. In announcing the occasion of the *Masque*, the Spirit of the Potomac sounded very much like the Attendant Spirit of *Comus* as he spoke of that "noble Peer of mickle trust and power," the Earl of Bridgewater:

> Go tell the naiads and the jocund deities,
> To cull their choicest flowers; a noble name,
> Has come this day to do them honour.
> That chief whose fame has oft been heard by them,
> In contest with Britannia's arms.[109]

The dance of the naiads, too, is reminiscent of the dances in *Comus;* and in a birthday ode honoring *The United States Magazine* Brackenridge echoed lines from *L'Allegro*.[110] But clearly the grand style of Milton attracted him most. "Miss Urany," he once said, was his "flame"; [111] and not until late maturity, as he implied in a letter to Jefferson, could he say

---

[107] *Gazette Publications* (Carlisle, 1806), pp. 125–132.
[108] *ibid.*, p. 13.
[109] *ibid.*, pp. 35–40.
[110] *ibid.*, p. 177–179.
[111] *The Life and Writings of Hugh Henry Brackenridge*, p. 33.

that Milton's muse no longer inspired him.[112] In the mean-time, however, "prospect" poetry flourished. What Bracken-ridge had hoped to accomplish through imitation of Milton, more talented poets attempted in more ambitious effusions. Failing to find expression for his particular genius in verse, he sensibly left prophetic visions to others and later sought fame in *Modern Chivalry*.

Even more affected by Milton and more contributory to epic efforts of the Revolutionary period was the early poetry of Philip Freneau, an author of importance in his day and still considered one of the fathers of American verse. Freneau had composed most of *The Rising Glory of America*, a poem which opened with the discovery of America, inquired into the origin of American Indians, sketched the struggles of early immigrants, and concluded with a vision of the present fame and future prospects of the land. Freneau's part in this poem can be pretty clearly determined by what he included in the 1786 edition of his works, and that part shows him deeply indebted to Milton for content and style.[113]

One of the distinctive marks of Milton's style in *Paradise Lost* was his verse paragraph, a series of unrhymed lines with variable caesuras and stops, ornamented by proper names freighted with memories and often mellifluous in sound. Fre-neau thought that such a style precisely suited his task, that such characteristics would lift his vision above commonplace poems and invest it with dignity and high purpose. Thus, as he pictured the landing of Columbus, he widened his pano-rama to include the story of Cortez, which he presented in a manner reminiscent of Milton:

[112] *ibid.*, p. 232.
[113] See *The Poems of Philip Freneau*, ed. Fred Lewis Pattee (Princeton, 1902), I, pp. 49–84, for a comparison of the text of 1772 and the text of 1809, the latter of which was based largely on the text of 1786. The text of 1772 has been used as the basis of the present analysis.

> But why, thus hap'ly found, should we resume
> The tale of Cortez, furious chief, ordain'd
> With Indian blood to dye the sands, and choak
> Fam'd Amazonia's stream with dead! Or why
> Once more revive the story old in fame,
> Of Atabilipa, by thirst of gold
> Depriv'd of life: which not Peru's rich ore,
> Nor Mexico's vast mines cou'd then redeem.[114]

Here is a clear imitation of the style of *Paradise Lost,* an attempt to evoke memories and to achieve epic effects through words designed to touch the ear as well as the mind. Such a manner pervaded a good part of *The Rising Glory of America.*

Freneau found Milton so helpful that, to fashion America's glorious future, he turned to the vision the Angel Michael had vouchsafed Adam in the latter books of *Paradise Lost.* The view of eternal bliss Adam had glimpsed, Freneau turned into an historical paradise, a time when joy would cover the earth, when men would see from a "fairer Pisgah" a new Canäan, of whose happiness Americans would be the first to partake. The vision William Bradford had already seen in his history *Of Plimoth Plantation* now abounded in Miltonic imagery. Such a Millennium would bring a new Eden, happier far than the one Adam had lost. No dangerous tree or deathful fruit would grow;

> no fierce disease
> No fevers, slow consumption, direful plague
> Death's ancient ministers,[115]

would affect mankind. Freed from second death, happy people would find repose. Even the lazar house which Michael had pictured for Adam would disappear from the earth—a scene so vividly presented, so painful to see, that Freneau

---

[114] *ibid.,* I, p. 52. Compare *Paradise Lost,* XI, 405ff.
[115] *The Poems of Philip Freneau,* I, 81.

could not refrain from presenting it later in *The House of
Night*,[116] where its loathsomeness animated an encounter with
death, a figure also drawn from *Paradise Lost*.[117] But significant to the development of epic poetry in America was Freneau's vision of a new world: after so fair a sight the step to
*The Conquest of Canäan* could not be postponed very much
longer.

The marks of *Paradise Lost* on *The Rising Glory of America* indicate but a tithe of the force Milton exterted on Freneau
during his early years of poetic activity. If Milton's influence
on Brackenridge was more claimed than real, his impress on
the early Freneau was more real than claimed. Nowhere can
this imprint be more clearly seen than in *The Power of Fancy*,
one of the happiest poems of Freneau's youth.[118] The poem
opened with a direct address to Fancy, after which Freneau
presented her lineage and a series of images to enliven her
character. Such an opening immediately suggests *L'Allegro* or
*Il Penseroso*; and as the poem progresses the similarities become even more evident. Unlike Milton, Freneau began with
tetrameter couplets; but like Milton he moved through a
period of time, describing scenes of interest as the journey unrolled.

Fancy's parentage, Freneau found in Jove's altar; the
mighty frame of the whole world was but a fancy of the

---

[116] *ibid.*, I, 218–219.

[117] See *The House of Night*, as it appeared in *The United States Magazine* (August 1779), p. 361, note to stanza 57.

[118] Harry Hayden Clark, in "The Literary Influences of Philip Freneau,"
*Studies in Philology*, XXII (January 1925), 1–33, finds the origin of Fre-
neau's poem in Warton's *Ode to Fancy*. But Moses Coit Tyler, in *The
Literary History of the American Revolution 1763–1783* (New Printing,
New York, 1957), I, 180, hears in it reminiscences "of the minor verse of
Milton"; and Thomas P. Haviland, in "A Measure for the Early Freneau's
Debt to Milton," PMLA, LV (1940), 1033–1040, sees its main source in
Milton. The literary influences on Freneau, of course, were many. See
Ruth Wentworth Brown, "Classical Echoes in the Poetry of Philip Freneau,"
*Classical Journal*, XLV (1949–1950), 29–34.

"Power divine." And as for the nature of Fancy herself: she appeared most clearly in men as she raised "Noble fabrics" in their minds. The lineage and nature of Fancy having now been established, Freneau was ready to demonstrate her power, which he revealed by walking with her through a day and a night. The first scene to come to their view recalls the dim religious light and the sound of the organ in *Il Penseroso,* that picture of reverence and awe which Hopkinson had already copied in his poem describing a church:

> Lo! she walks upon the moon,
> Listens to the chimy tune
> Of the bright, harmonious spheres,
> And the song of angels hears;
> Sees this earth a distant star,
> Pendant, floating in the air;
> Leads me to some lonely dome,
> Where Religion loves to come,
> Where the bride of Jesus dwells,
> And the deep ton'd organ swells
> In notes with lofty anthems join'd,
> Notes that half distract the mind.[119]

Freneau captured here the spirit of *Il Penseroso,* as well as its imagery and verse form, and, what is worth noting further, included an echo of Milton's "sphery chime" from *Comus* and a picture of the pendant world from *Paradise Lost.* As Freneau continued his journey with Fancy, he moved from the haunts of the shepherds to the far parts of the world, ending, while night yet brooded, in the lands of Sappho and Homer and Virgil. At this point, the scene changed abruptly, a shift similar to the change from day to night in *L'Allegro* or from night to day in *Il Penseroso.* Now Fancy bore Freneau away to the East "to meet the day," and after presenting such

---

[119] *The Poems of Philip Freneau,* I, 35–36. For the source of his picture of the pendant world, Freneau referred the reader to *Paradise Lost,* Book II, line 1052.

pleasures as light could provide, Freneau implored Fancy to walk with him alone:

Come, O come—perceived by none,
You and I will walk alone.[120]

Such similarities in meter, structure, and tone hardly argue that Milton and Freneau wrote their poems for the same purpose. Milton made his journeys to solve a personal problem, to evaluate two significant modes of experience; Freneau traveled with Fancy to show the transitoriness of human existence, a recurrent theme in much of his verse. If *The Power of Fancy* cannot be included among his best lyrics, it can be listed as one of the most skillfully executed poems of his youth, a fact directly attributable to the excellence of the model he followed.

Both *The Rising Glory of America* and *The Power of Fancy* strengthened tendencies in American poetry already evident. Great subjects demanded the style of *Paradise Lost;* the creation of moods asked for the lilting couplets of *L'Allegro* and *Il Penseroso.* As the Revolution moved inexorably toward open hostilities Freneau developed what Jonathan Odell stated later as one of his principles of satire: through the characters and plot of *Paradise Lost* current events could be lampooned and assessed. James Ralph had foreshadowed such a practice in his satirical poem *Sawney.* Now Freneau associated Milton's Satan with General Gage in a rollicking poem which appeared first under the title *A Voyage to Boston.*

This poem pictured a Traveler to Boston, who before he arrived in that city accepted a magic mantle from the Genius of North America—a mantle with the power of making its wearer invisible. So clothed and unseen, the Traveler arrived at General Gage's mansion, where a midnight consultation was in progress with Admiral Greaves, Lord Percy, General Bur-

---

[120] *ibid.,* I, 39.

goyne, and other enemies of American liberty. Earlier in the poem, Freneau had compared General Gage's conduct and temper with the cruelties of Cortez; now he presented him as the very personification of evil, a very Satan himself, who looked and spoke like Milton's apostate angel before the Infernal Council:

> High in the dome a dire assembly sat,
> A stupid council on affairs of state;
> To their dim lamps I urg'd my fearless way,
> And marching 'twixt their guards without delay,
> Step'd boldly in, and safely veil'd from view,
> Stood in the center of the black-guard crew.
>
> First, Gage was there—a mimic chair of state,
> Gage starts, rebounding from his ample seat,
> Swears thrice, and cries—'Ye furies, are we beat?
> Thrice are we drubb'd?—Pray gentles let me know,
> Whether it be the fault of fate or you?'
>
> He ceas'd, the anger flash'd from both his eyes,
> While Percy to his query thus replies.[121]

Following Lord Percy's speech, Admiral Greaves and General Burgoyne arose to deliver their views, a scene suggesting immediately the great speeches of Mammon, Moloch, and Belial; and before the poem closed the Traveler doffed his magic cloak, appeared before some patriots of Virginia, and heard a soldier express the hope that America and England would be reconciled before a wicked ministry forever made such a union impossible. The ministry was wicked indeed, and somewhat ridiculous as well. Freneau had to mention neither Milton nor the conclave of devils by name to present precisely this judgment. He needed only to cast his lines into Miltonic constructions and to use some of the imagery of *Paradise Lost* to call up the whole diabolical scene, to convey to his audience the combined evil and irony of plotting against God and the

---

[121] *ibid.*, I, 167–168. The 1775 version has served as the basis of the analysis.

right. Few instruments of satire could have been more effective.

Through Brackenridge and Freneau, Milton thus channeled the course of American poetry as the nation moved into its most intense period of literary activity prior to the Romantic Movement. Augustan standards still asked for heroic couplets; Pope, Blair, and Young still stood as models for hundreds of American poems. Furthermore, Brackenridge and Freneau soon dropped Milton from the front of their minds and sought individual styles. But during the ferment of the time Milton so dominated their "Millennium" verse that their efforts pointed straight to the practice of the Connecticut Wits. For a while, only Miltonic language and imagery appeared to be sufficiently vast to express visions of future peace and prosperity.

Yet only Barlow and Dwight produced serious imitations of *Paradise Lost*. In *M'Fingal* John Trumbull wrote mock heroic verse, however solemn the vision of American greatness with which the poem ended. Rather than celebrating New World experience in the grand style, he assessed current events through the fable and imagery of *Paradise Lost* in the satiric manner of Ralph, Freneau, and Odell. In the wit of this mock epic his interest in Milton matured, though he was never to push him far from the center of his poetic activity. In a commencement address delivered in New Haven in 1770 [122] Trumbull had spoken of *Paradise Lost* as being almost as much superior to Homer in "sublimity of conception" as it was in its "greatness" of subject; [123] and most of his life he clearly

---

[122] Even earlier, in 1768, Trumbull showed a knowledge of Milton in a manuscript poem in which he burlesqued barnyard love by reference to Adam and Eve as "good old Milton" had described them. See Alexander Cowie, *John Trumbull: Connecticut Wit* (Chapel Hill, N. C., 1936), pp. 44–45.

[123] See Clarence Arthur Brown, *The Achievement of American Criticism* (New York, 1954), p. 60.

preferred Milton above all other poets.[124] Other poetic forces of course converged on his mind. In his childhood he versified a number of Psalms, after having memorized Isaac Watts's *Divine Songs for Children;* and he seems to have experimented in the styles of Dryden, Pope, and James Thomson. Jonathan Swift and Samuel Butler, as well as Matthew Prior and Charles Churchill, put marks on his juvenile verse, but Milton made the strongest lasting impression.[125] Milton stood in his mind as a touchstone of excellence, as a model whom poets of the New World should follow.[126] As a measure of his admiration he presented in *The Progress of Dulness* the despisers of art as scoffing at the "deathless page" of the bard,[127] an observation which, in view of the context, should be regarded as the highest of compliments.

How fully Milton could dominate Trumbull may be seen in his *Ode to Sleep,* a poem memorable chiefly for its variety of Miltonic echoes. From the opening command "C O M E , gentle Sleep," to a couplet in the last stanza,

> Teach me, like thee, to feel and know
> Our humble station in this vale of woe,[128]

phrases and rhythms from the corpus of Milton's works haunt the poem. Surely, Trumbull's "gaudy eye of day" came from Milton's "Day's garish eie," or his "Mid shrieks and fiery shapes and deadly fantasies" from Milton's " 'Mongst horrid shapes, and shrieks, and sights unholy." Even as Milton had asked of the Holy Spirit, "what is low raise and support," so

---

[124] See Alexander Cowie, "John Trumbull as a Critic of Poetry," *The New England Quarterly,* XI (1938), 773-793.

[125] See Leon Howard, *The Connecticut Wits* (Chicago, 1943), pp. 37-78, for an excellent discussion of the literary influences on Trumbull. See also Kenneth J. Horton, "The Influence of John Milton on the Connecticut Wits" (Master's Thesis, University of Florida, 1940).

[126] *The Poetical Works of John Trumbull* (Hartford, 1820), II, 159.

[127] *ibid.,* II, 17.

[128] *ibid.,* II, 113-120.

Trumbull invoked the spirit of the Reverend Joseph Howe to "Raise" his "low thoughts"; and as Milton gave the injunction "Hence vain deluding joyes," so Trumbull implored

> Hence, false delusive dreams,
> Fantastic hopes and mortal passions vain! [129]

Familiar rhythms accompany such familiar expressions: some lines follow the tetrameter couplets of *L'Allegro* and *Il Penseroso*, others imitate the rhyme patterns of *Lycidas*. Perhaps no other poem of Trumbull's condensed more of Milton into so small a compass.

But *M'Fingal* was Trumbull's most significant Miltonic poem. Initially conceived as a simple satire on opposing Whig and Tory positions, it later grew into a mock epic, with all the conventional machinery of battles and visions. That Trumbull's main inspiration was Samuel Butler's *Hudibras* is of course well established. That he often called on the epic machinery of Homer and Virgil is incontestable. But he could not erase from his mind his knowledge of Milton and hence often recalled how he had used *Paradise Lost* and *Paradise Regained*.

Sometimes the reminder simply noted a phrase, such as " 'Gan thunder," which Trumbull rightly cited as coming from *Paradise Regained;* [130] at other times he singled out an expression, such as

> whose horrid hair
> Shakes forth the plagues of down and tar!

and invited a comparison with similar words in *Paradise Lost*.[131] In like manner Trumbull referred to Milton in notes when he spoke of "euphrasy" [132] and of dyeing the "trem-

---

[129] *ibid.*, II, 117.
[130] *ibid.*, I, 175 and note.
[131] *ibid.*, 165 and note.
[132] *ibid.*, 128 and note.

bling cheeks with pale." [133] But *Paradise Lost*, which he mentioned most often, furnished Trumbull with more than apt words and phrases; from its scenes he constructed elaborate tropes similar to those Milton himself had built from events in the *Iliad* or *Odyssey*. Honorius, for example, who in the mock epic defended the Whig cause, attacked Britain in latter days by likening her to an old woman past her climacteric in whom "Conceit and pride alone remain'd." Such a comparison could best be expanded by references to imagery in *Paradise Lost:*

> As Eve, when falling, was so modest
> To fancy she should grow a goddess;
> As madmen, straw who long have slept on,
> Style themselves Jupiter or Neptune:
> So Britain in her airs so flighty,
> Now took a whim to be Almighty.[134]

This simile must have seemed pat to many Americans, and the fact that the trope called to mind not simply Eve's delusion but also her Fall must have given further sharpness to the comparison. As Eve, so England.

Occasionally, Trumbull wove Milton's imagery through a whole episode. Prior to his presenting the mock heroic conflict between Whig and M'Fingal, he confessed that "the learned reader will readily observe the allusions in this scene, to the single combats of Paris and Menelaus in Homer, Æneas and the Turnus in Virgil, and Michael and Satan in Milton." [135] The fight which ensued echoed skirmishes in *Hudibras;* but the machinery of battle, as well as the clashing of swords, achieved a greater comic effect by being taken directly from well-known epic scenes, particularly from the angelic conflicts of *Paradise Lost*, whose grandeur contrasted sharply

[133] *ibid.*, 142 and note.
[134] *ibid.*, 14. A note informs the reader: "So says Milton."
[135] *ibid.*, 103–104n.

with the triviality of events in *M'Fingal*. Michael's finely tempered sword, for example, which had sliced through Satan's and had later given him pain, became a ridiculous spade in Whig's hands:

> The spade so temper'd from the sledge,
> Nor keen nor solid harm'd its edge,
> Now met it, from his arm of might,
> Descending with steep force to smite;
> The blade snapp'd short—and from his hand,
> With rust embrown'd the glittering sand.[136]

The spade prevailed over M'Fingal, sending him on a flight so precipitous that he appeared like "Old Satan struggling on through chaos"; and later it became the instrument to discharge "a blow / Tremendous on his rear below." [137] Even the Liberty Pole, upon which M'Fingal had been earlier raised, was likened to "Satan's walking-staff in Milton"; [138] and when he was hoisted to a pendant position, he reminded Trumbull of the round earth itself, hanging self-balanced on her center, as Milton had described the world in *Paradise Lost*:

> Then from the pole's sublimest top
> The active crew let down the rope,
> And once its other end in haste bind.
> And make it fast upon his waistband;
> Till like the earth, as stretch'd on tenter,
> He hung self-balanced on his centre.[139]

As Trumbull admitted, readers only "slightly versed in epic poem" would immediately recognize Milton's phrases, images, and epic devices in such episodes. The picture of Whig and M'Fingal grappling in battle, together with M'Fingal's humiliation on the Liberty Pole, would, when envisioned

[136] *ibid.*, 106.
[137] *ibid.*, 107.
[138] *ibid.*, 85.
[139] *ibid.*, 108.

against the titanic struggles and cosmic vistas of *Paradise Lost*, belittle the Tory position by rendering its adherents ridiculously ineffectual. Such of course was precisely Trumbull's intention; in his hands, Milton's transcendent scenes had become instruments of satire.[140]

Allusions to the imagery of *Paradise Lost* for the purpose of creating comic effects increased as the action of the mock epic unrolled. Canto IV opened with a sight of "Tory Pandemonium," where M'Fingal spoke words reminiscent of the anguished cry of Satan as he arose from the floor of Hell. Trumbull brought Milton's whole picture to mind: Satan's tarnished brightness, his sighs and tears, and his ringing exhortation to his fallen compeers emerge in sharp recollection. In contrast stood M'Fingal himself, streaked with tar and covered with remnants of feathers, attempting to rally his Tory companions. The grandeur was gone and only the comic remained, more comic because of the contrasting grandeur:

> Their chiefs all sitting round descried are,
> On kegs of ale and seats of cider;
> When first M ' F I N G A L , dimly seen,
> Rose solemn from the turnip-bin.
> Nor yet his form had wholly lost
> Th' original brightness it could boast,
> Nor less appear'd than Justice Quorum,
> In feather'd majesty before 'em.
> Adown his tar-streak'd visage, clear
> Fell glistening fast th' indignant tear,
> And thus his voice, in mournful wise,
> Pursued the prologue of his sighs.
> 　'Brethren and friends, the glorious band
> Of loyalty in rebel land![141]

---

[140] For a discussion of Trumbull's satirical method, see Max F. Schulz, "John Trumbull and Satirical Criticism of Literature," MLN, LXXIII (1958), 85–90. For evidence of Trumbull's love of poetic grandeur, see Alexander Cowie, "John Trumbull Glances at Fiction," *American Literature*, XII (1940), 69–73.

[141] *The Poetical Works of John Trumbull*, I, 122.

M'Fingal's address to his Tory companions comprised most of Canto IV and encompassed a vision of future events. M'Fingal had dreamed of his Tory friend Malcolm, he said; and Malcolm, who had barely escaped death by the noose, cried out that Whigs now had seized power and that the assembled Tories would do well to flee. To open his eyes to the "plagues" that awaited him and his friends Malcolm vouchsafed him a vision, M'Fingal went on. The two had ascended a ladder from whose height they saw the future unfold. Malcolm played the part of Michael in *Paradise Lost;* M'Fingal played Adam:

> As shown by great Archangel, Michael,
> Old Adam saw the world's whole sequel,
> And from the mount's extended space,
> The rising fortunes of his race:
> So from this stage shalt thou behold
> The war its coming scenes unfold,
> Raised by my arm to meet thine eye;
> My Adam, thou; thine Angel, I.[142]

Malcolm's vision pictured the conflicts of the Revolution itself. Since it showed defeats of the British, M'Fingal broke the narration occasionally with sighs of discouragement, even as Adam had complained to Michael in *Paradise Lost*. But Malcolm, like Michael, was implacable, though he attempted to cheer him by presenting ironically several "feats" of the British. He turned M'Fingal's eyes to the confines of an English prison, a place where famine, noxious food, and contagious plagues so scourged American captives that they were reduced to "moving skeletons" and died. Over this grim scene, like Death in *Paradise Lost*, the "haughty Loring" presided, thriving like a vampire on the blood of his victims, insulting "all their wants and pain" with "bitter taunt and scornful gibe." The scene appeared so horrible and death

---

[142] *The Poetical Works of John Trumbull*, I, 127.

stood so near that Trumbull likened it to the vision of the lazar house Michael had shown Adam:

> Distain'd around with rebel blood,
> Like Milton's Lazar house it stood,
> Where grim Despair presided Nurse,
> And Death was Regent of the house.[143]

Malcolm continued to unfold events of the War until his eyes became truly prophetic. He saw, as M'Fingal informed the assembled Tories before him, years of peace and prosperity unroll, a new country shining with promise through democracy and commerce, a veritable paradise on earth:

> And see, (sight hateful and tormenting!)
> This Rebel Empire, proud and vaunting,
> From anarchy shall change her crasis,
> And fix her pow'r on firmer basis;
> To glory, wealth and fame ascend,
> Her commerce wake, her realms extend;
>
> .   .   .   .   .   .   .
>
> Gay cities, tow'rs and columns rise,
> And dazzling temples meet the skies.[144]

For a moment the mock heroic mask dropped aside. Trumbull had presented the same eighteenth-century vision of progress that had fascinated Brackenridge and Freneau, a vison consonant with the hopes of revolutionary America but alien to the central thought of *Paradise Lost*. For Michael had concluded his glimpse of futurity with the hope of individual salvation, with the prospect of individual man achieving a paradise within through the down-reaching arm of God's grace. He had also implied, through his interpretation of events to the coming of Christ, that history was but the rise and fall of nations and tribes, that little could be done through

---

[143] *ibid.*, p. 144.
[144] *ibid.*, p. 174.

governmental machinery for the ultimate happiness of man. Such a view jarred sharply with the idea of progress and the optimistic vision of future American greatness in *M'Fingal*. *Paradise Lost* could serve as an instrument of satire; its language and scenes juxtaposed against current events could correct excesses of both Tory and Whig.[145] But serious use of Milton's symbols and values within the frame of the Enlightenment could produce poetic confusion.[146] If Trumbull was aware of the dangers his vision presented, he remained wittingly silent.

In *The Conquest of Canäan* Timothy Dwight compounded such dangers. Incredibly serious and theologically oriented, but fired with a sense of mission to advance the fine arts in the New World by writing a great poem,[147] Dwight looked to epics of an earlier day and to contemporary thought to fulfill his ambition. Virgil he knew in the original, and the *Iliad* and *Odyssey* in Alexander Pope's ever-ready translations. *Paradise Lost* was his constant companion. Surely here was an answer to his artistic problems.

As Dwight cast about for a subject and style commensurate with his ambition he hit on what he considered a happy solution: he would tell the story of Joshua and his heroic struggles to bring the Children of Israel into the land of Canäan, and he would model his narrative on what he thought was the most sublime of all epics, *Paradise Lost*.[148] That Americans often pictured themselves as Israelites claiming their heritage

---

[145] Trumbull lampooned Tory and Whig alike; though a Patriot, he was essentially a conservative. See Alexander Cowie, "John Trumbull as Revolutionist," *American Literature*, III (1931), 287–295.

[146] Trumbull favored the Old Divinity, despite his optimistic vision. See Bruce Ingham Granger, "John Trumbull and Religion," *American Literature*, XXIII (1951), 57–79.

[147] See *The Conquest of Canäan* (Hartford, 1785), the prefatory declaration, for Dwight's statement of his ambition.

[148] Leon Howard, *op. cit.*, has an excellent discussion of Dwight's literary background.

in a New Canäan was enough to satisfy Dwight's love for his country. All he needed to do was to tell his story in a style suited to the dignity of his intentions. Such a poem—elevated in language, vast in conception, and dignified in subject— would be truly epic and would ennoble not only Americans but mankind as well.[149]

The dangers Dwight encountered and the effects he achieved in telling the Old Testament story in Miltonic style with allusions to American life infused with ideals of the Enlightenment will be commented on later. Of importance first is to see how closely he followed *Paradise Lost*. In deference to prevailing poetic taste, he avoided Miltonic blank verse and cast his whole epic in heroic couplets; but this was one of the few concessions he made to Augustan poetic demands. Language, syntax, narrative machinery, character delineation, and scenes—all came from *Paradise Lost*.

Even a cursory reading reveals how many of Milton's characteristic words and how much of his syntax spring from the pages of *The Conquest of Canäan*. Milton was fond, for example, of saying "amaze" for "amazement," and so also was Dwight.[150] Such words, to which may be added expressions like "sweetness ineffable" [151] and "intermingled sighs," [152] only indicate the vast debt Dwight owed to Milton's charactertistic language; and along with such terminology Milton's syntax often appeared. The picture of Satan at the opening of Book II of *Paradise Lost*, which had so fascinated James Ralph and Freneau, impressed itself so deeply on Dwight that he could scarcely begin a graphic description

---

[149] See *The American Museum Or Repository*, v (June 1789), 564–567, for several of Dwight's comments on the epic and upon Milton. See also Clarence Arthur Brown, ed. *The Achievement of American Criticism*, pp. 62–65.

[150] *The Conquest of Canäan*, pp. 9, 77.

[151] *ibid.*, p. 88.

[152] *ibid.*, p. 159.

without following the word order of that famous scene. "High in the van exalted Irad strode" [153] and "High on her ramparts Gibeon's children rose" [154] exemplify a practice by now become common. Milton's distinctive language and syntax appear on page after page of the story of Joshua's struggles.

Dwight's imitation of Milton's diction and syntax is clear. But more significant was his following Milton's narrative technique, his reproducing in slightly changed order many graphic scenes essential to his unfolding story. Milton often pictured morning and evening to indicate the passage of time, sometimes lingering with such sensitivity on the scenes he presented that schoolmasters made them a part of their repertory for school recitations. The smell of morn was sweet in his nostrils, and eventide possessed special charms. The most loved evening scene appeared in Book IV of *Paradise Lost*, where Milton, preparatory to sending Adam and Eve to their nuptial bower, described the coming of night in the Garden of Eden. This picture indeed had so impressed James Ralph that he had incorporated it into his own poem called *Night*. Milton, it will be recalled, had begun by presenting "still Eevning," whose "Twilight gray / Had in her sober Liverie all things clad." Silence prevailed as bird and beast sought their couches and nests; and soon the heavens, led by Hesperus, glowed with stars, until the moon, rising in clouded majesty, at length "Apparent Queen unvaild her peerless light, / And o'er the dark her Silver Mantle threw."

Dwight indicated the passage of time in the same way, pausing even more often than Milton had paused to describe morning and evening, sometimes in Milton's own words. So close is his description of evening in Book IX of *The Conquest of Canäan* to Milton's famous picture that Dwight must have had his eyes on it when he composed his own scene. The

[153] *ibid.*, p. 142.
[154] *ibid.*, p. 282.

clothes metaphor, the spangled sky, the planets, the clouded moon, the silence, the retiring tribes—all are there, almost in the order of Milton's original:

> Now Night, in vestments rob'd, of cloudy die,
> With sable grandeur cloth'd the orient sky,
>
> .     .     .     .     .     .     .
>
> With magic hand, he becalm'd the solemn even,
> And drew day's curtain from the spangled heaven.
> At once the planets sail'd around the throne;
> At once ten thousand worlds in splendor shone:
> Behind her car, the moon's expanded eye
> Rose from a cloud, and look'd around the sky:
> Far up th' immense her train sublimely roll,
> And dance, in triumph, round the lucid pole.
> Faint shine the fields, beneath the shadowy ray:
> Slow fades the glimmering of the west away;
> To sleep the tribes retire; and not a sound
> Flows through the air, or murmurs on the ground.[155]

Milton and Dwight of course drew from classical models for the narrative technique of indicating time by reference to morning and evening; but the similarity of their scenes in language and structure suggests that Dwight had Milton in mind.

Further similarities will show how fully Dwight had succumbed to the spell of Milton's narrative technique. Milton's epic demanded, since it began in the midst of the action, an account of what had preceded the dramatic appearance of Satan in Hell. Milton hit upon the device of having God send to Eden the Angel Raphael, who was commissioned to unfold for Adam's instruction the fall of the apostate angels and the creation of the world. The great panorama unrolled through the conflict on the plains of Heaven and the Scriptural six days of creation.

[155] *ibid.*, p. 227.

Now Dwight's story also demanded an account of creation. The Gibeonites bowed to the sun; they therefore had to be informed of God and of His visible works. To perform this task Dwight brought into his story one of God's servants, Mina, who refused to worship the sun and who, upon the query of the Gibeonite king, unfolded the history of the universe down to the burial of Moses. The accounts of Raphael and of Mina hardly match in every detail, but some parts are close enough to establish that Dwight followed Milton, particularly in the narration of events of the fifth day, which described the creation of fish and fowl. Milton had achieved in this part of his story some of his happiest pictorial effects. The creeks began to swarm with fry innumerable, and shoals of fish glided "under the green Wave," or through groves of coral strayed, showing "to the Sun thir wav'd coats dropt with Gold." [156] Meanwhile, the sky filled with various fowls: the eagle, the stork, and the solemn nightingale, and unnamed smaller birds spread their painted wings in flight. Mina condensed Raphael's description but nevertheless rendered a faithful account in generalized terms:

> He spoke; and fishes fill'd the watry rounds,
> Swarm'd in the streams, and swam the Ocean's bounds;
> The green sea sparkled with unnumber'd dies,
> And varying beauty wav'd upon the skies.[157]

Even the order of description is the same in both accounts.

So compelling a story forced Dwight to imitate further: almost identical hymns of praise preface Mina's and Raphael's panorama of creation. Before Raphael's arrival in Eden, Adam and Eve, upon awakening from sleep, had sung a great song of morning devotion, praising the goodness of God for his infinite works. Such a song set the tone for the instruction which followed and became, as has already been noted, one of

[156] *Paradise Lost*, VII, 387ff.
[157] *The Conquest of Canäan*, p. 38.

the most quoted selections from *Paradise Lost* in early America. Dwight remembered this song and made it the Gibeonite hymn to the sun just before Mina began her instruction. In this position it, too, set the proper tone for the story which followed:

> O thou, whose bursting beams in glory rise,
> And sail, and brighten, thro' unbounded skies!
> The world's great Parent! heaven's exalted King?
> Sole Source of good! and life's eternal Spring!
> All hail, while cloath'd in beauty's endless ray,
> Thy face unclouded gives the new-born day! [158]

Even more similar than these two morning hymns is the picture of Adam and Eve in the Garden of Eden. Milton had presented a full account of their stature as seen through the eyes of Satan in Book IV of *Paradise Lost*. So that Adam would know more about himself and his mate, Milton allowed Raphael to fill in details of the idyllic pair at the end of his account of creation and again in his philosophical discourse on the nature of man in Book VIII. Of all the creatures of Eden, Milton had said, Adam and Eve appeared "Two of far nobler shape erect and tall," "For contemplation hee and valour formd," "For softness shee and sweet attractive Grace." Broad-shouldered, manly, large of forehead and sublime of eye, Adam, by his very nature, swayed Eve; but Eve in turn through her beauty and love drew Adam on with "sweet reluctant amorous delay." "So hand in hand they passd," Milton observed, "the lovliest pair / That ever since in loves imbraces met." [159]

Such an idyllic scene so captured Dwight's imagination that he concluded Mina's story of the creation with almost exactly the picture Milton had painted:

[158] *ibid.*, p. 30.
[159] *Paradise Lost*, IV, 288ff.

Then from his hand in silent glory came
A nobler form, and Man his destin'd name;
Erect, and tall, in solemn pomp he stood,
And living virtue in his visage glow'd.
Then too a fairer being shew'd her charms;
Young Beauty wanton'd in her snowy arms;

. . . . . . .

O pair divine! superior to your kind;
To virtue fashion'd, and for bliss design'd!
    He, born to rule, with calm, uplifted brow,
Look'd down majestic on the world below;—

. . . . . . .

    Her he endu'd with nature more refin'd,
A lovlier image, and a softer mind.
To her he gave to kindle sweet desire . . .
To her he gave with sweetness to obey . . .[160]

Dwight could not bring himself to say that Adam was made for God only, Eve for God in him. The Enlightenment had penetrated too deep for such a sentiment to be entertained by even the most pious. But Mina's instruction of the Gibeonites on the creation concluded with almost exactly what Milton had said.

If Milton's idyllic scenes could help Dwight to unfold his story, the vision of the Infernal Council could serve to dramatize the opening action. The plot of *The Conquest of Canäan* indeed began with a great consultation of the leaders of Israel for the purpose of determining a course of action after the death of Aram, one of their heroes. Should Israel continue the conquest of Canäan, or return to easy bondage in Egypt? This was the question put before the conclave of warriors; and one by one Hanniel, Joshua, and Caleb arose to present their positions. Dwight filled the debate with reminiscences of the great consultation in Book II of *Paradise Lost*, where

[160] *The Conquest of Canäan*, pp. 38–39.

the fallen angels arose to discuss a plan of action against God,
as well as with echoes from Satan's opening speeches in Book I
and from Satan's verbal conflict with the faithful Abdiel in
Book V. Satan-like, Hanniel addressed the assembly:

> Friends! Brethren! sires! or by what tenderer name
> Shall I address the heirs of Jacob's fame? [161]

As he spoke he combined Mammon's plea for the exploita-
tion of Hell and Belial's argument for peace, ending with an
apostrophe to Egypt very much like Satan's apostrophe to
Hell. When he finished, the assembly thundered applause;
and Joshua arose to refute an argument so unfriendly to the
execution of his commission from God. Curiously, Joshua
presented positions reminiscent of both Satan and Abdiel. Like
Satan after his midnight march to the North with a third of
Heaven's hosts, Joshua asked for the loyalty of the Israelites
in view of his former deeds and "midnight watchings." Like
Abdiel, he disclosed the falsity of his opponent's position and
confirmed his faith in God. Part of his reply is almost a replica
of Abdiel's famous answer:

> Far other end yon Chief ambitious eyes;
> Conceal'd by virtue's mask the danger lies.
> Unbrib'd, unaw'd, the honest task I claim,
> To burst the veil, and ward th' impending shame.
> Long vers'd in wiles, the lust of power his guide,
> He lulls our caution, and inflates our pride;
> With sense, that darts through man a searching view,
> With pride, that rest, or limits never knew,
> To deep designs mistrustless hearts he draws,
> With freedom soothes, and cheats with flatter'd laws;
> A crown to seize, the patriot's fire can claim,
> And mock with seeming zeal the fearful Name.[162]

Joshua's ringing answer to Hanniel stirred the Council to
action, for soon Caleb arose, looking like Satan and talking like

[161] *ibid.*, p. 6.
[162] *ibid.*, p. 16.

Moloch. "Deep thought sate musing on his furrow'd face" as he addressed the "listening throng," but his words brooked no ambiguity. "My voice impels to arms," he cried. So the Council parried and thrust, and so Joshua, Hanniel, and Caleb acted and spoke like Milton's angels. Only the Council in *The Conquest of Canäan* was not the Infernal Council, and Joshua and his peers were not evil. What Dwight gained in dramatic urgency by imitation of Milton he lost in poetic effectiveness. For all the symbols are wrong. Milton had so stamped his angels with specific varieties of evil or good and so motivated their arguments that any transfer of their language or looks to characters essentially unlike their prototypes could only produce moral, and hence poetic, confusion. Politicians of Dwight's day possessed a much surer instinct for appropriateness when they attributed to their enemies, not to their friends, the characteristics of Satan and his infernal crew.

Finally, Dwight turned to Milton for the now familiar device of presenting a view of the future, which unrolled through Book X of *The Conquest of Canäan*. His patriotism, as well as the precedent of Brackenridge, Freneau, and Trumbull, almost compelled him to allow Joshua a vision of things to come, a picture of the New Canäan inhabited by Americans of the New World; and Milton's technique suited his purpose precisely. He would instruct Joshua by an angel. Like Adam, Joshua expressed discouragement and bewailed his fate. Like Adam, Joshua was taken to a high hill to see the future unfold so that he could understand the Providence of God. Like Adam, Joshua was informed of Biblical history, and as the story pictured the entrance of Israel into the land of Canäan and the coming of the Messiah, it moved on to the New Canäan, the new promised land of America, the *"Glory of the Western Millennium"*:

> Far o'er yon azure main thy view extend,
> Where seas, and skies, in blue confusion blend,

Lo, there a mighty realm, by heaven design'd
The last retreat for poor, oppres'd mankind!

.  .  .  .  .  .  .

No dangers fright; no ills the course delay;
'Tis virtue prompts, and G O D directs the way.
Speed, speed, ye sons of truth! let Heaven befriend,
Let angels waft you, and let peace attend!
O smile thou sky serene! ye storms retire!
And airs of Eden every sail inspire! [163]

Dwight should have cut off his vision of futurity here. The
reign of Christ, the Day of Doom, and the final conflagration
of the world appear disappointing after so pleasant a visit in
so blest a land as America; and the belated lesson in astronomy, which copied Raphael's instruction to Adam in *Paradise
Lost,* is definitely anticlimactic. But the dramatic action continued. Refreshed in spirit by his vision, Joshua now turned
to the immediate task before him, the conquest of old Canäan.
The final battle, which presented scenes reminiscent of Christ's
defeat of Satan on the plains of Heaven, brought the action
to a close. With it ended one of the most promising, yet one
of the most unfortunate, imitations of Milton in early America. Dwight's taste for the grand and his hope to elevate mankind simply outran his talent, however much he was praised
in his day as a second Homer or Milton.[164] He failed to amal-
gamate the Old Testament story, Milton's symbols and style,

[163] *ibid.,* pp. 253–254.
[164] See *The American Magazine* (March 1788), pp. 265–266 for a commendatory poem "To the Author of the Conquest of Canaan." The *European
Magazine and London Review,* however, saw *The Conquest of Canäan* as
inferior to Homer and Milton, indeed, little superior to Blackmore, but at
least "decent and promising." See Cairns, *op. cit.,* pp. 34–35. For Noah
Webster's comment on English reviews of Dwight's poem see Theodore A.
Zunder, "Noah Webster and *The Conquest of Canäan,*" *American Literature,* I (1929), 200–202. For a handy reprint of Webster's patriotic defense
of Dwight, which appeared in the October issue of *The American Magazine,*
see *Literature of the Early Republic,* ed. Edwin H. Cady (Rinehart Edition,
New York, 1958), pp. 467–473.

and the ideals of the Enlightenment which animated the American dream. As a result *The Conquest of Canäan* stands as a monument to misled ambition and energy, as a signpost to the wrong turning American poetry took during the patriotic fervor of Revolutionary times.

Yet so intense was literary ferment during this period that no one saw any danger in what Dwight had done, least of all Joel Barlow, whose ambition to write an American epic haunted him for more than two decades. His *Vision of Columbus*, a long philosophical poem on the discovery of America, followed in the path of earlier "prospect" poetry and exhibited nearly all the difficulties of adapting the grand style to the ideals of the Enlightenment. Before completing this poem, Barlow had experimented with various styles in *The Prospect of Peace* and in *An Elegy on the Late Honourable Titus Hosmer, Esq.*, neither of which show very much talent, and in a few youthful lyrics he evidenced acquaintance with the "metaphysical" poets.[165] But most of his early poetry derived from the principal Augustans, notably from Dryden and Gray, whose manner and matter nevertheless failed to spur his growing ambition to write a long, narrative poem. He looked for a while at exploits of Cyrus the Great with the classics as his obvious pattern. Yet after composing a few lines on this subject his energy gave out, and, since Dwight and Milton had already preempted Biblical topics, he turned to Columbus and the New World, possibly holding in mind the *Lusiads* of Camoëns, who had extolled navigation and discovery. Whatever the source of his inspiration, he spent a quarter century of his life picturing the revolution Columbus had wrought; and for some of his syntax, imagery, and epic

---

[165] For a discussion of Barlow's early poetic career, see Leon Howard, *op. cit.*, pp. 133–165. See also Theodore A. Zunder, *The Early Days of Joel Barlow* (New Haven, 1934), and James Woodress, *A Yankee's Odyssey* (New York, 1958), *passim.*

machinery he turned to *Paradise Lost*, with results that can only be described as disastrous.[166]

Like many poets before him, Barlow followed Milton's syntax and imagery to delineate throne scenes and other royal occasions. Whether he envisioned Old World dynasties or the metallic opulence of the New mattered little: the famous picture of Satan presiding over Pandemonium guided his outline and furnished a structure. Consider, for example, the following scenes, picked at random from *The Vision of Columbus*:

> Fair on her throne, revolving distant fate,
> Imperial Katharine majestic sate,[167]

> There, robed in state, high on a golden throne,
> Mid suppliant kings, dread Montezuma shone.[168]

Such imitations force the conclusion that the style of *Paradise Lost*, however keen as an instrument of satire, could never enhance serious poetry. Delineation of royal scenes from Ralph's *Night* to *The Vision of Columbus* shows no improvement whatever. Yet Barlow felt compelled to follow the same tired construction, even in pictures of battle, as in, for example, "High in the front, imperial Capac strode," or "High in the frowning front, exalted shone." [169] Quite evidently Barlow believed that such syntax possessed a sort of poetic magic, that its use would automatically lift his poem from the commonplace to the epic grandeur of *Paradise Lost*. He still invoked the illusion that to follow Milton was to ensure poetic immortality.

---

[166] Contemporary critics, however, praised Barlow's epic. Even George Washington wrote that Barlow was honorably known in the Republic of Letters, though he read only portions of *The Vision of Columbus*. See Theodore A. Zunder, "Joel Barlow and George Washington," MLN, XLIV (1929), 254–256.

[167] *The Vision of Columbus* (Hartford, 1787), p. 182.

[168] *ibid.*, p. 59.

[169] *ibid.*, pp. 115, 167.

Such a hope impelled Barlow to pattern not only individual scenes but whole epic battles in the Miltonic manner. Barlow himself recognized how closely he had followed *Paradise Lost* when he likened the clash of arms on the American shore to the conflict between Satan and Michael on the ramparts of Heaven. As "on the plains of light," he said, "when Michael strove,/And swords of Cherubim to combat move," so unrolled the struggles for the New World. No Renaissance or eighteenth-century weapons appeared; all was grand, all was general:

> They tread the shore, the arduous conflict claim,
> Rise the tall mountains, like a rolling flame,
> Stretch their wide wings in circling onset far,
> And move to fight, as clouds of heaven at war.
> The smoke falls folding thro' the downward sky,
> And shrouds the mountains from the hero's eye;
> While on the burning top, in open day,
> The flashing swords, in fiery arches, play.[170]

Most of the campaigns of the New World, including the capture of General Burgoyne and the progress of General Greene, present gigantic figures wielding massy weapons in an etherial setting. Raphael's story of the warfare in Heaven had so crystallized Barlow's battle imagination that even skirmishes took on the appearance of titanic encounters.

More significantly, *Paradise Lost* helped to shape the structure of Barlow's philosophical poem. The action opened with the appearance of an angel to Columbus, who, lying in prison, regretted the day he had discovered the New World. The angel was none other than Milton's sociable Angel Raphael, who performed the function of Michael in vouchsafing a vision of future events to assuage the sorrow Columbus now felt for his having brought, as he believed, so much grief to mankind. So alike are the figures of Barlow's angel and Mil-

[170] *ibid.*, pp. 160–161.

ton's Raphael that a contemporary reviewer of *The Vision of Columbus* declared that Barlow must have had his eye on Book V of *Paradise Lost* when he composed his opening scene.[171] No observation could have been more accurate, as a comparison of the two figures will show. Descending through "Groves of Myrrhe, / And flouring Odours," Raphael had arrived at the door of Adam's bower as the sun "Shot down direct his fervid Raies." Two middle wings of "downie Gold" encircled "like a Starrie Zone his waste":

> Like *Maia's* son he stood,
> And shook his Plumes, that Heav'nly fragrance filld
> The circuit wide.[172]

The angel that descended to instruct Columbus could not have looked more like this figure:

> O'er all the dome, where solemn arches bend,
> The roofs unfold and streams of light descend;
> The growing splendor fill'd the astonish'd room,
> And gales etherial breathed a glad perfume;
> Mild in the midst a radiant seraph shone,
> Robed in the vestments of the rising sun;
> Tall rose his stature, youth's primeval grace
> Moved o'er his limbs and brighten'd in his face,
> His closing wings, in golden plumage drest,
> With gentle sweep came folding o'er his breast.[173]

But if the visiting seraph looked like Raphael, he performed the exact duty of Michael; and Columbus reacted precisely like Adam as scenes of carnage in the New World began to unroll.

"O Visions ill foreseen," Adam had lamented in *Paradise Lost*, after viewing the destruction of man in the Flood; better

---

[171] *The American Magazine* (April 1788), p. 335. This is a reprint of a notice in *The Critical Review* (January 1788). See also *The New Haven Gazette and the Connecticut Magazine*, III, no. 19 (May 15, 1788), p. [64].

[172] *Paradise Lost*, V, 275ff.

[173] *The Vision of Columbus*, p. 28.

had he lived "ignorant" of the future than by his foreknowl-
edge be tormented with visions of things to come. "O! hapless
day," cried Columbus in anguish, as he viewed the savagery
of Christian and heathen alike in the conquests that followed
in the wake of his voyage. Better had it been that the "lamp
of heaven" had never "mark'd the passage" across the Atlantic, had never "Taught eastern worlds these beauteous climes
to find, / Nor led those tygers forth to curse mankind." [174]
"Oh, hide me in the tomb," he implored, after seeing the
destruction of Peru. Why should he live "to view the impend-
ing doom"? [175] To check growing despair, the angel informed
Columbus that fairer days showed ahead and for a while he
was comforted; but his happiness, like Adam's at the appearance of the rainbow after the Flood, was illusory. Even the
Enlightenment, which witnessed a bold and free race growing
up in America, brought conflict and suffering.

After the establishment of a free race on the shores of
North America the angel brought his discourse to a lengthy
and a thoroughly confused close. First he reviewed for his
pupil the accomplishments of the Old and New Worlds; then
God himself seemed to reveal America's advancement in
science, painting, and literature. But Columbus was still puz-
zled why the progress of man in the sciences and arts had
been so agonizingly slow. The answer resembled that of
Raphael's, when Adam inquired about the secrets of the physical universe in Book VIII of *Paradise Lost*. To "thee 'tis
given," the Angel replied to Columbus, "To hold high con-
verse, and enquire of heaven"; but it was not in man's province to encompass truth at one sweep. Man must learn, the
Angel continued, that he must range through nature progres-
sively, that he must move toward "full perfection" by steps
gradual and slow.[176]

[174] *ibid.*, p. 63.
[175] *ibid.*, p. 130.
[176] *ibid.*, p. 216.

Here, loosely stated, was the eighteenth-century idea of progress, the idea of man's perfectibility through an historical process. The nativity of Christ, with its implication of God's grace, followed almost as a byproduct of a much larger and more significant vision. As the narrative picked up in Book IX an enlightened world came to view. Disease had been conquered; commerce had united the world; universal harmony prevailed. In answer to an earlier query of Columbus,

> Say, how shall truths like these to man be given?
> Or science find the limits mark'd by Heav'n? [177]

the Angel replied, in words reminiscent of Raphael's instruction to Adam:

> See worlds, and worlds, to Being's formless end,
> With all their hosts, on one dread Power depend,
> Seraphs and suns and systems round him rise,
> Live in his life and kindle from his eyes,
> His boundless love, his all-pervading soul
> Illume, sublime and harmonize the whole;
> Teaches the pride of man to fix its bound,
> In one small point of this amazing round;
> To shrink and rest, where Heaven has fix'd its fate,
> A line its space, a moment for its date;
> Instructs the heart a nobler joy to taste,
> And share its feelings with another's breast,
> Extend its warmest wish for all mankind,
> And catch the image of the Maker's mind;
> While mutual love commands all strife to cease,
> And earth join joyous in the songs of peace.[178]

The angel denied Columbus the actual sight of the Millennium, of man living in harmony with truth. Heaven neither permitted, nor could the angel show, "The unborn glories of that blissful day." All that could be revealed was the parliament of man, the federation of the world, with "One centred

---

[177] *ibid.*, p. 224.
[178] *ibid.*, pp. 253ff.

system, one all-ruling soul." [179] Columbus had to be satisfied with that. But he should not have been, for a more confusing vision of man and society would be difficult to imagine. Combining the concept of benevolence with observed cruelty in man, the love of God with faith in science, the idea of progress with man's limited knowledge, Barlow presented a vision entirely alien to that of Milton despite his use of Miltonic "machinery." An angel with all the accoutrements of Raphael and all the wisdom of Michael should have been clearer headed. *The Vision of Columbus* disappoints not so much because it poorly imitates so much of *Paradise Lost*, but because the very symbols of that epic lead to an expectation of something much greater, something much more profound. Milton had, through the instruction of Michael, asserted eternal Providence and justified the ways of God to man; Barlow's angel could only offer an amalgam of concepts, a hodgepodge unworthy so celestial a creature.[180] The old, heroic vision of man and his destiny could not be accommodated to the ideals of the Enlightenment.

The Miltonic impulse in epics of the Revolutionary period was of singular importance to the early history of serious American verse. Lesser effusions of the time often showed similar imprints: David Humphreys wrote a few lines reminiscent of the marriage hymn in *Paradise Lost*,[181] and *The Porcupine* burlesqued Eve's conversation with Satan prior to the

---

[179] For a discussion of Barlow's faith in America's republican experiment and in the cosmopolitan humanitarianism of the Enlightenment, see Robert F. Durden, "Joel Barlow in the French Revolution," *William and Mary Quarterly*, VIII (1951), 327–354. See also M. Ray Adams, "Joel Barlow, Political Romanticist," *American Literature*, IX (1937), 113–152.

[180] See Merton A. Christensen, "Deism in Joel Barlow's Early Work: Heterodox Passages in *The Vision of Columbus*," *American Literature*, XXVII (1956), 509–520, for a discussion of Barlow's thought.

[181] Humphreys also referred to Milton's Satan and echoed faintly his sonnets. See *The Miscellaneous Works* (New York, 1804), pp. 35, 198, 232–238.

Fall.[182] Such echoes, however, as well as imitations reaching
back as far as Mather Byles, show Miltonic impressions upon
only parcels of verse, or upon shorter poems designed to
achieve special immediate effects. Epic poets of the Revolution
aimed higher in that they seized upon Milton's manner with
the hope of creating a literature commensurate with their
vision of an American Millennium. In their attempt to achieve
greatness they imposed on their poetry an idiom suited to
neither the times nor their talents, stiffening their language
and syntax, congealing their imagery and verse forms. The
poems through which they hoped to celebrate New World
experience, as Homer had celebrated the glory of Greece and
Virgil the grandeur of Rome, succeeded only in presenting ill-
adapted figures pursuing unreal adventures in a factitious,
brocaded world. Only as an instrument of satire had the grand
manner ensured poetic effectiveness. Yet American poets
would not learn for some time to come that Milton in truth was
inimitable. The twin Miltonic impulses evident from Colonial
days moved through light and serious verse for a quarter century or more, producing husks so emptied of motivation and
meaning that even current response must have been mixed
with laughter.

[182] *The Porcupine, Alias the Hedge-Hog: Or, Fox Turned Preacher*
(Boston, 1784), pp. 36–39.

# The Early Republic

The first quarter century of the Republic saw Milton become a spokesman for literate Americans throughout the nation. Earlier, he had left his imprint on individuals of importance in their day, or had placed his mark on either the form or thought of single sermons or documents or poems. Now, he became a common possession. Speaking before the Massachusetts Charitable Mechanic Association, Benjamin Russell recalled the image of Satan's palace in the regions of the North to envision the mineral riches available to the ingenuity of man.[1] In an address to the American Antiquarian Society, Abiel Holmes described the field trips of the botanist by conjuring up the picture of the rugged terrain in the outskirts of Hell.[2] In a discourse before the Literary and Philosophical Society of New York, DeWitt Clinton argued that an intelligent principle governs the movements of birds by citing Milton on the migration of cranes.[3] The shape of a fig tree [4] or the crowing of a rooster at dawn,[5] a marine disaster [6] or the

---

[1] *An Address Delivered before the Massachusetts Charitable Mechanick Association, December 21, 1809* (Boston, 1810), p. 11.

[2] *An Address Delivered before the American Antiquarian Society* (Boston, 1814), pp. 14–15.

[3] *An Introductory Discourse* (New York, 1815), p. 46.

[4] Joseph Chandler, *The Young Gentleman and Lady's Museum* (Hallowell, 1811), p. 79.

[5] "Observations on the Notes of Birds," in *The American Museum Or Universal Magazine* (May 1791), p. 274.

[6] Benjamin Waterhouse, *A Journal of a Young Man of Massachusetts, Late a Surgeon on Board an American Privateer* (Boston, 1816), p. 125.

death of a friend,[7] thoughts on capital punishment [8] or on the Great Falls of the Connecticut [9]—all could be enhanced by reference to what Milton had said.

Yet such varied citations, however numerous, indicate only that Milton had become a household and a community name. More significantly, reference to his works now fell into recurring patterns clustered about topics of perennial interest such as love, religion, and politics; and he quite overwhelmed certain kinds of mood verse and epic expression. As an instrument to express how Americans thought and felt Milton possessed few rivals indeed.

## II

Nowhere was this instrument more assiduously polished or more highly praised for its effectiveness than in American schools. English authors of texts reprinted in America had already recommended Milton to the youth of the land. Now American pedagogues analyzed his poetry and prose, found both supremely expressive, and presented from them examples to illustrate the intellectual and affective uses of discourse. One of the first Americans to present Milton as a master of words was Lindley Murray, whose *English Grammar* became a standard work during the early years of the Republic and remained so for more than a half century.

Murray modeled his text after English grammars already in print.[10] To illustrate usage, for example, he quoted from authors of the present and past. But more than most earlier

---

[7] Elijah Parish, *An Eulogy on John Hubbard* (Hanover, 1810), p. 10.

[8] *The American Museum Or Universal Magazine* (February 1790), pp. 69–71, in an oration by a citizen of Maryland.

[9] *The Rural Magazine Or Vermont Repository* (December 1795), p. 614, in an article, "A Description of the Great Falls of Connecticut River."

[10] New texts by English authors also appeared in America, some of them heavily weighted with quotations from Milton. See, for example, G. Neville Ussher, *The Elements of English Grammar* (2nd. American edn. Exeter, 1796).

writers of texts he showed special interest in presenting effective devices in poetry, for which purpose he found Milton particularly helpful. He pointed out, through a careful analysis of selections from *Paradise Lost*, how Milton had achieved music through words, how he had magnified the figure of Satan through "an uncommon succession of long syllables," and how he had employed the abruptness of the caesura to impress the reader with the tragic loss of his sight.[11] Milton furnished Murray with examples of almost all the principles he chose to discuss. Like Dr. Johnson he believed that the Art of English Poetry could be learned from him alone.

But Murray not only showed American youth the devices through which Milton had achieved poetic eminence. In an appendix, under the heading "Of the Strength of a Sentence," he praised his prose and held up an excerpt as a model of excellence. What interested Murray most was the way Milton had strengthened his periods through a harmonious combination of sounds, in illustration of which he pointed to Milton's description of the ideal site for a school in *Of Education*. Everything about this picture conspired to promote harmony, Murray contended. Milton had chosen his words well, had picked expressions replete with liquids and soft sounds, such as *smooth*, *goodly*, and *charming*; and he had arranged them so artfully that were any one altered the melody of the whole sentence would suffer. Murray sensibly eschewed any reference to Milton's more thorny essays, centering attention in this most saguine piece of his prose; he knew that he could not press his contention beyond a few well-chosen lines. But Milton's *poetry—that* mine of riches never failed him. In the same appendix he presented two passages from *Paradise Lost* to illustrate "personification," and under "hyperbole" he re-

---

[11] *English Grammar, Adapted to the Different Classes of Learners* (New York, 1810), pp. 63, 68, 255–256. From the eighteenth edition, "enlarged and improved by the Author." The first edition appeared in 1795.

produced Satan's famous soliloquy beginning "Me miserable." Murray maintained that the extravagance here arose from love, terror, amazement, indignation, and grief, all of which had thrown Satan's mind into confusion. The resulting "picture of a mind agitated with rage and despair" therefore showed only what was wholly "natural and proper" for the occasion.[12]

Such excursions into rhetorical principles illustrated with references to Milton anticipated a fuller treatment of the subject by John Quincy Adams, who saw in Milton's language and syntax the iron sinews of English. In the meantime, grammarians continued to stress the propriety and power of Milton's constructions. In *The Thorough Scholar*, Daniel Adams explained the usage of "whose" and "than whom" by reference to lines from *Paradise Lost*, though he raised some doubt about the correctness of the latter expression.[13] Eldad Dewey opened *The American Instructor* with a passage from the same poem, asserting that it followed the order of Mr. Alexander's syntax and hence could serve to exercise students in grammatical rules. He likewise found that Milton could furnish him with lessons in parsing and in the study of words.[14] But the most interesting grammar to appear early in the nineteenth century matured from the researches of Noah Webster, who now, a quarter century after the publication of his *Grammatical Institutes*, presented Milton as one of the most effective masters of idiom in the history of English literature.

Webster called his new book *A Philosophical and Practical Grammar of the English Language*. His inquiry into the nature of English grammar, however, proved to be as much historical as philosophical, for to illustrate his contentions he

[12] *English Grammar*, pp. 311–312, 323, 328–329.
[13] (Leominster, 1803), pp. 55, 86–87.
[14] (Bennington, 1805), pp. [3], 8, 128–136.

turned to earlier masters of literature, in whom he found a primitive linguistic strength. Sometimes he supported Lindley Murray and Bishop Lowth in their attempts to justify idiom in the face of logical grammar. Sometimes he saw in the idiom more logic and strength than in the justification itself. Webster sanctioned, for example, the use of "whose" as a relative pronoun referring to *either* persons *or* things by calling attention to the declension of that word in "primitive" English,[15] a precedent which allowed him to praise Milton's expression "the tree whose mortal taste" not simply as effective poetically, as contemporary grammarians had asserted, but as effective because it was grammatically correct according to older linguistic patterns. Following the same procedure Webster pointed to other idioms that had made English a precise linguistic instrument, as seen, for instance, in the discriminating use of word pairs, such as *slow-slowly*. Milton knew how to employ such words idiomatically, Webster declared, citing as an example the line "Heaven opened *wide* her ever during gates." Such, he claimed, was not only one of the "most common" but one of the "most beautiful idioms" in English.[16]

So taken was Webster with Milton's use of this kind of idiom that to illustrate its effectiveness he cited two more lines from *Paradise Lost*. But other constructions caught his grammatical fancy as well. In a note on intransitive verbs he became so entranced with Milton's condensed predicates that to explain their precision and power he cited several startling examples,[17] one of which was "Grin a ghastly smile"—an expression widely quoted in the early Republic. Occasionally, Webster remarked that Milton had slipped into Latin idiom, as in the line, "*Nor* did he *not* perceive them," which com-

---

[15] *A Philosophical and Practical Grammar of the English Language* (New Haven, 1807), p. 37 note.
[16] *ibid.*, pp. 158–159.
[17] *ibid.*, p. 171.

pelled him to say that "Milton seems to have understood Latin better than English." [18] But in the main Webster found Milton so congenial to his purpose that in illustrating how easily the imagination substitutes an author's name for his works he wrote what appeared to him a self-evident truth: "Milton *resembles* Homer in sublimity and invention, as Pope *resembles* Virgil, in smoothness of versification." [19] If, in his chauvinistic *Grammatical Institutes,* Webster had suspected Milton of subverting American expression, he now shifted the base of his argument. In his *Philosophical and Practical Grammar* he presented Milton to American youth as a very model of effective use of the language.

Compilers of "readers" and "speakers" expanded the aims of grammarians to include moral as well as linguistic instruction. In his Preface to *The English Reader,* Lindley Murray declared that his purpose was "to improve youth in the art of reading; to meliorate their language and sentiments; and to inculcate some of the most important principles of piety and virtue." [20] To fulfill such purposes Murray turned to numerous literary treasures of the Western World, excerpting, as occasion demanded, generous passages from *Paradise Lost.* As an example of emphasis, he cited the opening lines of that poem. As a lesson in piety, he quoted the famous passage in Book IV describing Adam and Eve's vespers before they walked hand in hand to their nuptial bliss. Moral delicacy forced Murray to leave out Milton's lines depicting Eve's nakedness, an omission justified by his policy "to avoid every expression and sentiment, that might gratify a corrupt mind, or, in the least degree, offend the eye or ear of innocence." [21] Perhaps he quite rightly assessed postlapsarian weakness in American youth. But he seldom found in Milton a cause for

[18] *ibid.,* pp. 191–192 and note.
[19] *ibid.,* pp. 74–75.
[20] *The English Reader* (New York, 1799), sig. A2.
[21] *ibid.,* pp. 272–275, sig. A3.

embarrassment. Under "Didactic Pieces" he placed Adam's advice to Eve on how to avoid temptation,[22] that moving but fruitless admonition in the first part of Book IX; and in his *Sequel to the English Reader* he reproduced the passage on the coming of night in Book IV and gave a short biographical sketch of its author, in which he claimed that *Paradise Lost,* "notwithstanding the severity of criticism," stood as the "glory and boast of English literature" and "ranked among the noblest efforts of human genius." [23] Yet apparently Murray believed that mature students alone could profit from a study of *Paradise Lost.* When he compiled his *Introduction to the English Reader* for a younger class of readers, he failed to find any use for that glorious poem.

During the first decade of the nineteenth century American pedagogues increasingly depended on Milton for examples to instruct American youth in the arts of reading as well as in the precepts of morality. One of the most effusive was Daniel Staniford, whose *Art of Reading* presented lessons in elocution in a manner reminiscent of Burgh's remarkable *Art of Speaking.* Staniford offered as exercises in class instruction selections from many authors Americans admired; but he recognized, by both affirmation and practice, that Milton was a special witness for teaching a wide variety of oral expression. A reading of Milton, he asserted, required "a method peculiar to itself": Milton's style possessed "a pomp of sound and energy of expression" that demanded "a kind of *grandeur* of *utterance, look* and *manner.*" Milton brought into play in the speaker a combination of talents and efforts that made his works particularly valuable for classroom performance. But Milton fascinated Staniford not only because he possessed an "uncommon elevation and sublimity of diction"; he could also soften

---

[22] *ibid.,* pp. 286–287.
[23] *Sequel to the English Reader* (New York, 1811), pp. 220, 343. The first edition appeared in 1800.

into "tenderness" and melt "into the most heart-rending pathetic." [24] Staniford thus found in Milton a diversity of sentiments especially suitable for teaching voice modulation and bodily movement, from which he proceeded to develop in a series of lessons precise instructions on how they could best be declaimed.

Only a glance at Staniford's instructions and the passages he reproduced will show how American students learned to read Milton. Satan's startled address to his son Death toward the end of Book II of *Paradise Lost*, he explained, should be expressed with a *"boldness"* in *"look* and *manner."* Death's answer, beginning "To whom the Goblin, full of wrath, replied" should be spoken in a "lower tone," though soon the boldness in look and manner should be reassumed, as first recommended. Staniford presented similar instructions for reading Satan's apostrophe to the sun and his soul-searching soliloquy in Book IX, as well as "Eve's Speech to Adam": the first should be rendered with a tone both solemn and full, the second "most *affectingly,* but with a kind of *manly pathetic."* As for Eve's speech—this should be "read with the same glow and tenderness of expression as before recommended." [25]

Such selections represented to Staniford the height of grandeur and sublimity and hence required "in the reading, a suitable grandeur of utterance." More simple modes of expression demanded *"easy, unaffected"* yet dignified delivery. For such exercises he chose Adam's declaration of wonder when he first saw the beauty of Eve, followed by Adam's account of his own growing self-consciousness as he viewed the created world. The first, explained Staniford, should be recited "with a *glow* and *softness* of delivery," the second "in a manner entirely *unrestrained."* Finally, Staniford declared

---

[24] *The Art of Reading* (11th edn., Boston, 1816), p. 227. The first edition, presumably, appeared in 1800.
[25] *ibid.,* pp. 227–229.

that "Eve's Address to Adam," that humble plea in Book X asking Adam's forgiveness and prefiguring their mutual reception of Grace, should be delivered in a manner *"exquisitely pathetic."* [26]

The visions such rubrics now bring to mind compel a smile, if not laughter. Even young Americans of the day must have felt some sense of the ridiculous as they postured and grimaced, as they raised and lowered their voices to express grandeur or pathos. Yet in the first decade of the century perhaps no other kind of class exercise aided more in making Milton's language and sentiments a national possession: the line from school recitation to tract or journal or sermon was clear and direct.

Miscellaneous texts of the time helped to perform the same task. John Hubbard's *The American Reader* presented five substantial passages from Milton, ranging from the popular "Adam and Eve's Morning Prayer" in *Paradise Lost* to the relatively little know "Sampson's Soliloquy When Imprisoned by the Philistines" in his Hebraic tragedy. [27] In *The Understanding Reader* Daniel Adams taught explication and spelling through Milton's description of the creation of the world. [28] And in his *Compendious System of Rhetoric* Samuel Knox, the principal of Baltimore College, illustrated personification, apostrophe, and exclamation from *Paradise Lost,* praised *L'Allegro* and *Il Penseroso,* and placed Milton among the most distinguished and widely approved epic poets that critics had judged. [29]

Few texts of the day failed to praise Milton, or to present him as a model of moral and of linguistic virtue. But in the first decade of the century the most eminent was John Quincy Adams' *Lectures on Rhetoric and Oratory.* Adams published

[26] *ibid.,* pp. 230–231.
[27] (2nd edn., Walpole, 1807), pp. 205–212.
[28] (3rd edn., Leominster, 1805), pp. [105]–107.
[29] (Baltimore, 1809), pp. 45, 48, 53, 66, 69.

his lectures in 1810, five years after his appointment to the Boylston Professorship of Rhetoric and Oratory at Harvard. He praised Milton so highly and presented him so often as a model of excellence that even the "Advertisement" to the printed text recognized the extent of his debt. A few examples of how Adams combined value judgments with exercises in structure will show at once his method of instructing American youth.

In Lecture XXIII, Adams illustrated effective means of transition by references to the "incomparable" *Paradise Lost,* saying that the second edition of that poem, which expanded Books VII and X into four separate divisions, displayed the "uses and propriety" of that "form of speech" more "effectually" than could be "found in volumes of oratory." In Lecture XXV, Adams recalled Milton's vision of Moloch and Satan to illustrate the power of language. The suggestiveness of Milton's description placed Moloch above the usual superlative degree to a fourth degree of comparison, Adams declared; the power of words could not be raised to a higher pitch. And as for Satan: what could be more effective than to present him not simply so huge as to carry a shield as large as the moon on his shoulders, but to make him even more huge by magnifying the moon itself through the lifting powers of Galileo's telescope? Such amplification by inference, Adams went on, or the enlargement of some object to make another seem even more large, had received Quintilian's sanction. Milton had employed the device so effectively that even Virgil's Polyphemus shrank to pigmy size in comparison with Satan.[30]

Adams never wearied of instructing his classes at Harvard through materials taken from Milton. If Webster had praised Milton's idiom because he believed that it derived from a primitive language, Adams recommended Milton's construc-

[30] *Lectures on Rhetoric and Oratory* (Cambridge, 1810), II, pp. 107–109, 127–129, 130–131.

tions because he saw in his syntax the elements of Latin. Ronsard, declared Adams, who incorporated Greek and Latin into his French, would now be scarcely remembered were it not for the ridicule of Boileau. But Milton, "who strained the English tongue to the same bent," continued to be the "delight and glory" of the English nation. For such a literary phenomenon Adams offered a linguistic answer. Milton had discovered the power of classical syntax and had constructed his sentences in accordance with classical principles. He had, as had "no other writer in the language," furnished numerous examples of "forceful expression" effected "by the appearance of the most emphatic word in the front."

Adams believed the principle important enough to offer further instruction. Through such syntax, he explained, Milton had been not only "enabled to invigorate his thoughts by exhibiting occasionally the strong word at the head of the sentence; but he multiplied the use of this artifice, by presenting it in the front of the line, where its effect is equally striking, and where he could more frequently and more easily sweep away from before his frontispiece the rubbish of articles, auxiliaries, pronouns, and prepositions." [31] Some critics had found Milton's inversions offensive, but Adams considered them devices conducive to strength and advised his students to employ them in their own compositions.

After Adams, American pedagogues simply repeated positions on Milton already well known or incorporated into their lessons familiar excerpts from his poetry or prose.[32] In such lessons many illustrious names—Shakespeare or Dryden or

---

[31] *ibid.*, pp. 202–203.

[32] See, for example, Asa Lyman, *The American Reader* (Portland, 1811), pp. 196–199; Amos Jones Cook, *The Student's Companion* (Portland, 1812), pp. 57–64; Increase Cooke, *The American Orator* (Hartford, 1814), pp. 367–370; and Abner Alden, *The Reader* (4th edn., Boston, 1814), pp. 151, 167, 168–169, 183–184. Alden's text first appeared in 1802 and enjoyed popularity through the early years of the century.

Pope, whom Americans also held in highest esteem—appeared by his side. But during the early years of the Republic American schoolmasters presented Milton again and again as a special model for moral and linguistic instruction. Such insistence made him a constant companion and mentor of American youths, furnishing them not only with patterns of language and modes of oral expression, but also with moral precepts, affective images, and rhetorical aids to Christian piety and belief.

## III

Americans found Milton instructive on manners and morals in a number of ways,[33] but what they responded to most, or what they repeatedly recalled, was the picture of marital bliss Milton had painted in Book IV of *Paradise Lost*. This vision had long been a favorite among poets, as well as among schoolmasters and preachers; now it began to appear in tractates and journals as a design for connubial love.[34]

Precedent for presenting this vision as an archetype of nuptial love could be found in English admirers of Milton. The Reverend John Bennett, in his didactic *Letters to a Young Lady*, spoke often of Eve and of marriage in Eden, saying that here was a pattern that merited emulation and praise. The *Letters* appeared under an American imprint in 1796, four

[33] For random examples of the wide variety of ways, see *The Poetical and Miscellaneous Works of James Elliot, Citizen of Guilford, Vermont* (Greenfield, 1798), p. 231; *The Hive: Or a Collection of thoughts on Civil, Moral, Sentimental and Religious Subjects* (Hartford, 1803), pp. 26–28; James Abercrombie, in a "charge" delivered to the senior class of the Philadelphia Academy, *The Port Folio*, v, no. 30 (August 2, 1805), 234; *The Immortal Mentor: Or Man's Unerring Guide to a Healthy, Wealthy, & Happy Life* (Philadelphia, 1810), pp. 322–323. See also selections from John Aikin's *The Calendar of Nature: Designed for the Instruction and Entertainment of Young Persons*, which appeared in *The Weekly Magazine*, I, no. 11 (April 14, 1798), 332–334; *ibid.*, II, no. 18 (June 2, 1798), pp. 147–150; and *The New-England Quarterly Magazine* (April, May, June 1802), pp. 153–162, "On the Comparative Value of Different Studies."

[34] For an interesting comment on the status of woman in America, see Russel Blaine Nye, *The Cultural Life of the New Nation*, pp. 142–143.

years after *The American Museum* had reprinted from the original collection excerpts recalling Milton's idyllic scene.[35] Bennett declared that "the immortal poem of Paradise Lost should not only be in the *hands*, but graven on the *heart*, of every woman," for "above all other authors" Milton had described the "distinguishing graces of the sex," presenting in Eve "an exquisite pattern of female perfection." [36] What blessings are derived from the society of woman! Bennett exclaimed. How cheerless the "face of nature" without their companionship! Because Milton knew this he labored to make Eve "everything that could charm," everything "that could alleviate the infelicities of life." Bennett was so taken with Eve and with the amenities she offered to Eden that he enjoined the "libertine" of his day to examine Milton's picture of marriage, hoping that such a study would allow him to adjudge the "prevailing rage for impurity and seduction!" Though he failed to record whether his advice had the effect he desired, Bennett left no doubt about his moral position. Milton had presented in Eden an ideal of marriage, capable of reforming even an inveterate rake.

Mrs. Elizabeth Griffith recalled the idyllic vision of Eden to inform young women how to become good home makers and wives. Girls should follow the example of Eve in being "Not obvious, not obtrusive—but retired," [37] she advised in her *Essays Addressed to Young Married Women*, selections from which appeared under American imprints in *The Massachusetts Magazine* and *The Apollo*. Mrs. Griffith maintained

---

[35] *Letters to A Young Lady* (1st New York edn., 2 vols. [1796]). See also *The American Museum Or Universal Magazine* (January 1792), pp. 9–11; *ibid.* (February 1792), pp. 70–72; *ibid.* (April 1792), pp. 139–142.
[36] *ibid.*, I, 101.
[37] *The Apollo Or Weekly Literary Magazine*, I, no. 23 (July 20, 1805), 178. For other letters, see *ibid.*, I, no. 7 (March 30, 1805), pp. [49]–50, and I, no. 16 (June 1, 1805), [121]–122. See also *The Massachusetts Magazine Or Monthly Museum of Knowledge and Rational Entertainment*, VI, no. 1 (January 1794), 37–40.

that in so acting Eve had found the secret of holding man's esteem and affection. Had not Adam himself said as much in his confession to Raphael, when he spoke of the reasons for his fondness for Eve? Here Adam had declared that what attracted him most was not physical beauty but daily acts of kindness and love, an admission so revealing that Mrs. Griffith thought it wise to repeat from *Paradise Lost* the gist of what Adam had said:

> Those thousand decencies, that daily flow
> From all her words and actions, mixed with love,
> And sweet compliance, which declare unfeigned
> Union of mind, or in us both one soul;
> Harmony to behold in wedded pair,
> More grateful than harmonious sound to the ear.[38]

Wives would do well to take to heart Adam's confession, Mrs. Griffith implied, for in this archetypal setting Milton had uncovered one of the secrets of a happy marital life.

Dr. John Gregory invoked the same image in *A Father's Legacy to His Daughters*, which Americans reprinted in *The American Lady's Preceptor* and in a pocket library series addressed "To the Ladies of the United States." Dr. Gregory had advised his daughters to be gracious, modest, and dignified —to "possess dignity without pride, affability with meanness, and simple elegance without affectation." For such characteristics Dr. Gregory had gone to Milton's description of Eve in *Paradise Lost*, a procedure he revealed before he completed his discourse. Milton indeed had expressed his "idea" precisely:

> Grace was in all her steps, heav'n in her eye;
> In every gesture dignity and love.[39]

---

[38] *The Massachusetts Magazine Or Monthly Museum of Knowledge and Rational Entertainment*, VI, no. 6 (June 1794), 343–345. See also *The Ladies Magazine* (September 1792), pp. 175–179.

[39] *The American Lady's Preceptor* (Baltimore, 1811), pp. 40–45. See also *The Lady's Pocket Library* (Philadelphia, 1794), p. 97, and *The Christian's, Scholar's, and Farmer's Magazine* (June and July 1789), pp. 188–191.

Not only Dr. Gregory's daughters, but daughters everywhere, could do no better than model themselves after the Mother of Mankind. That Dr. Gregory and Mrs. Griffith had referred to the picture of Eve which later led Raphael to issue a warning about the nature of love and the dangers of infatuation apparently disturbed no one. The image of marital harmony, and of Eve's grace and beauty, captured the sensibility of the time.

Milton's image of Eve was so vibrant and his picture of love so attractive that Americans could not remain long content reprinting English letters and essays. They wished to make their own reading of life in the Garden, stressing its relevance to American life; and, though English admirers of Milton undoubtedly gave them suggestions, they focused more precisely on the character of Eve and on the psychology of marital happiness in Eden.

Some journals simply recalled the image of Eve to imply that women should model their lives after the Mother of Mankind. *The Ladies Magazine* suggested that "A Female Character" should be very much like the Eve who in *Paradise Lost* had heaven in her eye and grace in her steps.[40] Invoking the same image, *The American Lady's Preceptor* moved into an argument on "The Art of Improving Beauty," saying that Milton's picture of Eve, which stressed "lustre" of mind more than a Venus-like form, should convince even the "proudest fair one" that without the "irradiating power" of virtue "the most perfect features are uninformed and dead."[41] *The Massachusetts Magazine* picked up the identical description to define at some length the trait for which woman should be most esteemed. Dignity in feminine manners, this journal declared, commands attention in men but is hard to delineate

---

[40] *The Ladies Magazine* (September 1792), p. 182. Milton's lines preface the story.
[41] *The American Lady's Preceptor,* pp. 79–81.

with any precision. Corregio, Guido, and Raphael, to be sure, had in their pictures distinguished two kinds, the *majestic* and the *familiar*, as respectively shown in their representations of Minerva and Venus; and of these two the *majestic* more became womankind. But to define precisely this trait *The Massachusetts Magazine* turned not to Renaissance delineations of the Goddess of Wisdom but to Milton's picture of Eve. Here was a vision to command "admiration and esteem." Here was an ancient "model" of dignity and grace, indeed an "original," which could like the sun "impart" some of its "rays" to the "amiable sisters" of America for the purpose of correcting "their modern manners." [42] Majestic carriage as seen in the picture of Eve should be the "most commanding trait" in feminine character.

Milton's vision of Eve led John Cosens Ogden to make much the same observation. As Rector of St. John's Church, Ogden delivered an address at the opening of Portsmouth Academy, stressing, as might be expected, the importance of educating the youth of the land. The Bible, he said, furnished "excellent patterns" by which to inform character: the good wife of *Proverbs*, whose worth was far above rubies, should stand as a model for daughters of American men. But Eve, too, commanded attention as a pattern of feminine excellence—the Eve whom Adam had seen, graceful of step, divine of eye, replete with dignity and love. So "lovely" a character, Ogden went on, particularly when juxtaposed against "the horrid picture of furies," should compel even "vicious men" to turn away from the one and follow the other. [43]

A model for women and a magnet for men—such was the Eve Americans created from the picture Adam had painted for the sociable Raphael, a picture so fascinating that *The Monthly*

[42] *The Massachusetts Magazine Or Monthly Museum of Knowledge and Rational Entertainment*, II, no. 4 (April 1790), pp. 234-235.
[43] *An Address Delivered at the Opening of Portsmouth Academy, On Easter Monday, A.D. 1791* (Portsmouth, 1791), pp. 7-8.

*Register* of Charleston made it central to "A Vision of Female Excellence," or a dream of what woman should be. The dream itself followed a query asking how feminine worth could be ascertained. The answer came quickly. A goddess of "female excellence" would descend from the sky, embodying the highest ideals of the sex. Soon the dream goddess appeared—tall and graceful, simply yet elegantly clothed, showing a proper blend of youth and maturity. Whom should this figure closely resemble but Eve when Adam first saw her. In words Eve might have spoken the vision addressed an attentive audience around her. Be generous, good tempered, and modest she exhorted her feminine listeners; follow religion and virtue. With this, the dreamer awoke, well pleased with what he had learned.[44] Apotheosis of Eve could hardly be pressed any further.

Yet the image of Eve as an ideal of beauty and grace was too abstract and etherial, too statuesque and remote. Heaven might be in her eye, but Americans longed for a little of earth also. Milton himself had been careful not to leave her unfleshed and unblooded, not to present her as merely lovely and gracious, lacking sexual charm. Americans soon seized upon Milton's full characterization. The sight of Eve as Satan first viewed her, slender of waist and wanton of hair, served an essayist in *The Bureau* to give Eve a further dimension by praising her as God's lavish creation.[45] Here Eve stood naked and unashamed before God and man—chaste, beautiful, serene, but not without knowledge that "coy submission" and "modest pride" could lead Adam on, that her "sweet reluctant amorous delay" would arouse fires of love. Ideally, then, woman should

---

[44] *The Monthly Register, Magazine, and Review of the United States,* I, no. 7 (July 1805), pp. 201–210. The same essay appeared also in *The Bureau Or Repository of Literature, Politics, and Intelligence,* I, no. 19 (August 1, 1812), pp. 146–147.

[45] *The Bureau Or Repository of Literature, Politics, and Intelligence,* I, No. 15 (July 4, 1812), p. 113, in "Essays After My Own Manner."

be both pure and seductive, conjoining heaven and earth.

An Eve at once pure and desiring, at once innocent yet aware of her magnetic flesh so appealed to *The American Museum* that that journal reprinted the Reverend Lathrop's "Remarks on Female Honour," which began with Adam's recognition of her complex attraction.[46] Eve possessed virgin modesty, Adam had said, expanding his initial comments on her beauty and grace. She would be sought and if properly wooed could be won. Her very modesty made her desirable, her very honor the more worth possessing. Such a beginning allowed Lathrop to lament the current prevalence of hurried marriages and illegitimate children, the result of unbridled passion, not of innocent love. The fact that Eve's concept of honor contrasted so sharply with views of the time proclaimed her a model of excellence. Eve knew the real meaning of honor, and because of her so also did Lathrop. *The American Museum* simply desired to make the ideal Eve had embodied more widely known.

But Americans could not rest with an ideal that embraced only spiritual beauty and seductive though innocent flesh. As heirs of Puritan New England and of Benjamin Franklin, they desired in their women practical skills. The Scriptural Martha had long served as an ideal of domestic accomplishment, even if Mary had received greater praise, but now Eve took her place as a model in household achievement. Adam himself had praised Eve for her domestic interests on the fateful day of the Fall. She had been a model housewife in all she had done. She had properly cared for their angelic guest, serving as hostess when needed but retiring graciously when Adam and Raphael fell to their discourse. Tactful, efficient, understanding, Eve merited every word of Adam's praise, even had

---

[46] *The American Museum Or Universal Magazine* (December 1790), pp. 280–282, in an essay, "Remarks on Female Honour," by the Reverend Joseph Lathrop of Springfield, Massachusetts.

she not shown anew on the morn of the Fall her interest in domestic affairs by suggesting a plan to tidy the Garden. Adam's sentiment expressed so precisely the Puritan ideal of domestic accomplishment that a young man picked it up to advise his sister at school. Turn your thoughts frequently to household duties, he wrote; on the authority of the great Milton himself he could tell her

> *That Nothing lovelier can be found*
> *In woman, than to study household good.*[47]

So authoritative a statement on so important a matter served to define the policy of instruction in Mrs. Williams' Boarding School in New England. This school offered lessons "Calculated to improve the Manners, and Form the Character of Young Ladies," an aim which limited instruction to domestic accomplishments. Mrs. Williams purposed to develop the minds of her students, yes, but she "particularly endeavoured to domesticate them" by turning "their thoughts to the beneficial and necessary qualifications of private life." She therefore often stressed that nothing lovelier could be found in woman than household good, laboring at the same time "to convince them of the utter insignificance and uselessness" of some of Eve's later daughters, who had been

> Bred only and completed to the taste
> Of lustful appetence; to sing, to dance,
> To dress, and troll the tongue, and roll the eye.[48]

The contrast between Eve as a model of domestic virtue and of her daughters as inhabitants in the tents of wickedness defined even more precisely Mrs. Williams' practice and policy. Such a difference between educational aims and activities for women led the Reverend John S. J. Gardiner, in a sermon

[47] *The Ladies Magazine* (October 1792), pp. 231–235, under "Letters from a Brother to a Sister at a Boarding-School," dated August 27, 1785.

[48] *The Boarding School: Or Lessons of a Preceptress to her Pupils* (Boston, 1798), p. 7.

delivered before members of the Boston Female Asylum, to praise solid feminine accomplishments and to deplore the frothy and vain. Excoriating "trifling attainments," which tended "only to nourish vanity and self-conceit," he hailed the "modest female" who possessed "affable manners, good principles, good humour, and good sense." Gardiner mentioned neither Eve nor her daughters to strengthen his contrast, but he declared that education for women was futile unless they brought to their reading a full mind. To support this position, he quoted Christ's answer to Satan on the reading of books in *Paradise Regained*.[49]

Presentation of Eve as a model of domestic accomplishment paradoxically focused attention on her intellectual achievements. Americans had not forgotten the better part Mary had played, despite Martha's down-to-earth qualities. A person writing under the name of Sophia in *The Evening Fire-Side* regretted that poets like Homer and Milton had stressed the domestic role of woman in their visions of life. Hector's injunction that Andromache hasten to her spindles and loom, and Eve's finding her whole law in Adam placed too much weight on household accomplishments, Sophia declared. She therefore advised that women develop more of their intellectual powers.[50] An answer to Sophia in the next issue of *The Evening Fire-Side* implied that Milton had indeed endowed Eve with precisely such virtues, that, far from relegating her to the kitchen, he had given her mental endowments. Had not Adam himself in *Paradise Lost* said that "Authority and Reason" waited upon her? [51]

A "Moral Disquisition" on the education of women in *The*

---

[49] *A Sermon, delivered at Trinity Church, September 22nd, 1809, Before the Members of the Boston Female Asylum, Being their Ninth Anniversary* (Boston, 1809), pp. 15–16.
[50] *The Evening Fire-Side Or Weekly Intelligence*, I, no. 17 (1805), pp. 133–134.
[51] *ibid.*, I, no. 18 (1805), pp. 139–140.

*Massachusetts Magazine* had earlier developed this facet of Eve's character in a vision of the American future, which depicted men and women walking hand in hand "brightening each other's virtues," even "to the close of life." But such a happy companionship, this vision revealed, could be achieved only if women would neglect the "toilet and looking glass" for the "acquirement of science," only if they would leave off "unsatisfying amusements for the improvement of the heart and the refinement of manners." Through education the dream could come true: American women could become second Eves, could be like the intellectual companion Adam had delineated to Raphael, shortly before Raphael's instruction on man and the universe closed:

> Yet when I approach
> Her loveliness, so absolute she seems,
> And in herself complete, so well to know
> Her own, that what she wills, to do, or say,
> Seems wisest, virtuousest, discreetest, best.
> All higher knowledge in her presence falls
> Degraded. Wisdom in discourse with her,
> Loses discountenanced, and like folly shews.[52]

Adam's hyperboles, which made Raphael uneasy, failed to disturb prophetic Americans enmeshed in the optimism of the Enlightenment. Eve as a model of intellectual companionship so impressed Daniel Bryan that he sought in *Paradise Lost* a physiological reason for such a psychological phenomenon. In his *Oration on Female Education,* he asserted that Eve was a proper help "meet" for Adam because she had been made from his rib. Adam himself was his authority for this position. To have Eve by his side, Adam had said, was simply to regain a part of himself.[53]

[52] *The Massachusetts Magazine Or Monthly Museum of Knowledge and Rational Entertainment*, v, no. 2 (February 1793), 92–93.
[53] *Oration on Female Education; delivered before the Visitors and Students of the Female Academy in Harrisonburg, August 4th, 1815* (Harrisonburg, 1816), pp. 7–8.

Graced with physical and spiritual beauty, chastely seductive, gifted in household affairs and accomplished in mind, Eve appeared to Americans, as the Reverend John Bennett had said, "an exquisite pattern of female perfection." As a model of womanly excellence she called out even more praise in that she had flawlessly played one of her primary roles: she had ameliorated the human condition. A Gentleman of Connecticut saw her fulfilling precisely this role, saying, as Adam had informed Eve, that the sweet intercourse of looks and smiles had brought to man a rational happiness denied to beasts of the field. Without the kind of companionship Eve had given to Adam the world would be little more than a "wide waste." [54] So deep and satisfying was this companionship that *The Boston Spectator* pointed, though perhaps with some irony, to Adam's choice to disobey God and to risk his fortunes with Eve after her Fall as one of the highest examples of human love and affection.[55] But Americans apparently realized the dangers of pressing so Satanic an argument too far. More often they pictured Eve making life in the Garden engaging and sweet, showing how from the very beginning she had softened the human condition. Such was the view *The Boston Spectator* had presented in an earlier issue. Eve's life in the Garden, that journal declared, though drawn by the "imagination of a poet," showed along with "innummerable instances" from history that "woman *always* possesses a benign and commanding influence" in social affairs.[56] In *Paradise Lost* Eve had simply prefigured a long line of women that followed.

The Honorable James Wilson dignified this argument in a lecture on the origin and development of laws. A professor

<hr>

[54] *The American Lady's Preceptor*, in an essay, "Ledyard's Character of Women," 56–58. This had appeared earlier in *The Literary Magazine and American Register*, VI, no. 34 (July 1806), 55, and in *The Port Folio*, II, no. 39, New Series (October 4, 1806), 195.

[55] *The Boston Spectator*, I, no. 26 (June 25, 1814), 103.

[56] *ibid.*, I, no. 5 (January 29, 1814), 19.

in the College of Philadelphia, and long an Associate Justice of the Supreme Court, Wilson delivered a series of Lectures on Law, in which he stressed the relation between government and manners. In his introductory lecture on the "Study of Law in the United States" Wilson declared that the ladies of his audience might be secretly asking what they had to do with the formation of governments. He would answer succinctly: women affect manners, and manners affect laws. To illustrate this relationship Wilson pictured Adam and Eve in the Garden. In that "pure and perfect commencement of society," he explained, Adam's large fair front and eye sublime declared that he was formed for contemplation and valor. Eve, on the other hand, showed sweet attractive grace; and from her flowed all the amenities that made life in Paradise perfect. Thus nature evinced from the beginning that women "were destined to embellish, to refine, and to exalt the pleasures and virtues of social life." Now, since to "protect and to improve social life" is "the end of government and law," women have a "most intimate connexion with the effects" of a good legal system, even if they fail to share in its actual formation.[57]

With this bit of Philadelphian legerdemain, performed with the image of Eve to dazzle the eyes of his audience, Wilson argued the position that women indirectly affect laws enacted by governments. Perhaps neither Zenobia nor Queen Elizabeth I nor Semiramis of Nineveh, whom Wilson had mentioned earlier as examples of great women, would have been convinced by this argument, but some Americans apparently succumbed. At any rate, *The Monthly Register* categorically stated that American women had begun "to learn" that their lives should not be given over to "lustful appetence" and song, after the manner of the daughters of evil Michael had pic-

---

[57] *The Works of the Honourable James Wilson,* L.L.D. (3 vols., Philadelphia, 1804), I, 33–37. *The American Museum Or Universal Magazine,* IX (January 1791), 21–24, reprinted extracts from Wilson's lecture.

tured to Adam. In actuality, American women had begun "to discover" that God had given them "high capabilities of excellence," "acute perception," "tender feeling," "lofty imagination," and "ardent and honourable affection" not to serve "man's brutal appetite," but rather to become "his companion and his guide," the "soother of his sorrows" and the "heightener of his joys," the "object of his proud submission, his dignified obedience, his chivalrous adoration," the being whose "smile" formed the "joy of his life, and the sunshine of his existence." [58] If Eve's name was not attached to this newly discovered intelligence, it should have been. For she clearly informed the vision which *The Monthly Register* asserted had begun to serve as a model for American wives.

The image of Eve as a prototype of perfection comprised only a part of the idyllic picture of Eden American journals spread through the early Republic. A companion like Eve meant marriage, and marriage meant the relationship Milton had spelled out in his hymn in Book IV of *Paradise Lost*. This great apostrophe, as previously shown, sang of wedded love as unique, as the mystical tie joining woman with man. Such love engendered mutual respect and attraction, drove adulterous lust out of life, and raised sense experience to a spiritual plane. Nuptial love was founded in reason, was just, loyal, and pure; from it sprang close family relationships, some of the dearest possessions in human society. Above all, wedded love contrasted sharply with casual amours or the bought smiles of harlots, so often condoned in wanton song and courtly romance. So exalted a view of marriage and love (which Milton himself had gleaned from Puritan thought of his day) [59] so captured the imagination of journalists that they even an-

[58] *The Monthly Register, Magazine, and Review of the United States,* IV (December 1807), 5–6.
[59] See William and Malleville Haller, "The Puritan Art of Love," *The Huntington Library Quarterly,* V (1942), 235–272.

nounced prominent weddings with words of the hymn;[60] but more significantly they made its lines serve as texts for meditations on marital bliss, or allowed its values to permeate their feeling and thought.[61] As a letter in *The New York Magazine* declared, Milton's hymn had presented an "admirable" concept of connubial love.[62]

Sometimes a journal simply quoted a few lines from the hymn, finding its cue in a striking image or sentiment to be developed later in the form of a discourse. An essay "On Matrimonial Happiness" in *The Weekly Magazine*, for example, opened with Milton's romantic image:

> Here love his golden shafts employs, here lights
> His constant lamp, and waves his purple wings,
> Reigns here and revels.

The argument of the essay itself moved from and beyond this romantic conception, stating, with Milton, that wedded love is unique, that its joys derive from mutual respect, that dissimulation and uncontrolled passion have no place in such a relationship.[63] A discourse on "Marriage" in *The Weekly Museum* followed a similar procedure. Prefaced by two lines of the hymn, this essay extolled conjugal life, contrasted libertine and true love, and described the satisfying delights of familial ties.[64]

[60] See, for example, *The Weekly Museum*, x, no. 469 (June 24, 1797), under "Court of Hyman." See also *idem.*, xii, no. 619 (September 6, 1800); xiii, no. 654 (May 9, 1801); and *The Weekly Visitor Or Ladies' Miscellany*, iv, no. 16 (February 15, 1806), 126.

[61] *The Massachusetts Magazine Or Monthly Museum of Knowledge and Rational Entertainment*, ii, no. 7 (July 1790), essay on "Conjugal and Domestick Happiness," p. 393, and *The American Museum Or Universal Magazine*, x (July 1791), essay on "Important Considerations on Matrimony," p. 54. The latter essay was taken from *The Universal Magazine*.

[62] *The New York Magazine Or Literary Repository* (June 1795), pp. 358–361.

[63] *The Weekly Magazine*, i, no. 5 (March 3, 1798), 153–154. The same essay appeared later in *The Weekly Visitor Or Ladies' Miscellany*, ii, no. 53 (December 17, 1803), 4.

[64] *The Weekly Museum*, ix, no. 441 (December 10, 1796).

So close a parroting of Milton's sentiments reached fullest expression in a consideration of "Conjugal Love" published in *The Massachusetts Magazine*, where nearly the entire hymn appeared, surrounded by commentary explaining Milton's position and fitting it into the thought of the day. "Of all the pleasures that endear human life there are none more worthy of the attention of a rational creature than those that flow from the mutual return of *conjugal love*," the essay began. Such an exordium called to mind the great Milton himself, who, after describing "the nuptial bower of *Adam* and *Eve* in *Paradise*," had praised their "blissful state," making their lives serve as a pattern of marriage and love. Milton's vision indeed had embraced the "full completion of the blessings of humanity." For "if reason and society" distinguish man from the "other animals," the argument continued, then "an excellence in these two great privileges," which center in wedlock, "must raise" him in "happiness" above all living things. In short, in marriage "the noblest passions of which the human soul is susceptible join together, virtuous love and friendship." One supplies it "with a constant rapture," the other regulates it "by the rules of reason." [65] Such emphasis on society and reason in marriage echoed ideals of the Enlightenment, but the image of marital bliss and the values it embodied derived from *Paradise Lost*. *The Massachusetts Magazine* had come close to absorbing Milton's entire concept.

*The Vermont Baptist Missionary Magazine* reprinted Isaac Watts's sentimental story "The Rake Reformed in the House of Mourning" to show how Milton's hymn could effect a changed attitude toward marriage and love. Florino, an apparent gay blade about town, had tried to comfort his friend Lucius at the death of Serena, his wife, by suggesting that they go to a play or a concert. But Lucius would have none of

---

[65] *The Massachusetts Magazine Or Monthly Museum of Knowledge and Rational Entertainment*, IV, no. 2 (February 1792), 102.

this, lamenting that nothing could take the place of Serena and asking that his steps be directed to heaven, where he should see her again. Such a show of affection astounded Florino. As he mused on what he had heard, he suddenly realized that "some vast and unknown pleasure" must exist "in a virtuous love," a feeling that reached "beyond all the madness of wild and transient amours."

Milton's hymn, which he had always read before "as mere poesy and fable," now began to impress him as true; and after repeating it to himself he exclaimed: O "Blessed poet! that could so happily unite love and virtue, and draw so beautiful a scene of real felicity," which prior to his present experience he had always considered "merely romantic and visionary." Lucius' love for Serena had taught Florino to understand Milton's sentiments, had aroused in him "a strange new sensation." He now was convinced that "the blind poet" had seen "deeper into nature and truth" than he himself could have ever imagined. Such a conviction allowed him to declare that "a union of virtuous souls, where happiness is only found," could become a reality; and, perceiving "some glimmerings of sacred light" rising within him, he panted for "such a partner and such a life" as Lucius had experienced, and as Milton had envisioned in Paradise. His new understanding even turned his wandering steps back to God.[66]

Perhaps few Americans experienced such a dramatic conversion upon reading Milton's hymn to nuptial love, but the ideals it encompassed, the image of perfect understanding and bliss it presented, haunted their minds. They longed for the vision Milton had painted, hoping somehow to find such a life. As *The Ladies Magazine* implied, the happiness of our first parents as portrayed in the nuptial hymn showed by

[66] *The Vermont Baptist Missionary Magazine*, I, no. 5 (January 1812), 143–150. See Isaac Watts, *The Improvement of the Mind* (New Edition, London, 1810), pp. 408–417.

contrast the low state of love in degenerate modern times.[67]

Americans so longed for such a life that they searched the psychology of Eden to discover the secrets of Adam and Eve's bliss. That a wife should be as perfect as Eve has already been noted. She should be chastely seductive, the soul of honor and virtue, accomplished in household affairs and intellectually active. No one would question the desirability of such qualities, or their contribution to an ideal companionship. But what of the subtle relationships between husband and wife, the attitudes of mind and day-to-day acts that produce bitter fruit or unparalleled joy?

In a reply to "An Old Bachelor's Reflections on Matrimony" *The Weekly Museum* turned to Adam's assessment of Eve for an answer. Adam had told Raphael how much he respected Eve's intuitive knowledge, beside which his own reason seemed sometimes inferior; he had praised her so highly that the angel later demurred. But the picture of marital bliss Adam had drawn served to answer the Old Bachelor's reflections. Adam bowed to Eve's intuition, and she responded with love—a companionship so understanding and sweet that every day spent in solitude seemed lost.[68] Surely, here was one secret of connubial bliss.

*The Weekly Museum* returned to the topic in a subsequent issue and revealed an additional secret. Adam had also told Raphael of his joy in Eve's understanding and of his delight in her daily ministrations of kindness and love. All her actions and words, mixed as they were with love and compliance, declared unfeigned union of mind, Adam had said. Such sentiments now buttressed an essay on "Marriage," pointing to the reasons for successful companionship in Eden.[69] Eve had graciously acted, and Adam had responded with affection and

---

[67] *The Ladies Magazine* (June 1792), pp. 34–37, in an essay "On Love."

[68] *The Weekly Museum*, IX, no. 468 (June 17, 1797), "Happiness of the Married State—A Reply to the Above."

[69] *ibid.*, XI, no. 553 (April 6, 1799), "Marriage."

praise. Married couples could thus learn from our First Parents how to live together in joy.

The "sweet and enchanting picture" of "connubial felicity" in Eden allowed Dr. Robert Cecil to advise a young friend on a delicate marital problem. Should a wife be informed of financial difficulties? By all means, replied Dr. Cecil; nothing should be hidden in marriage. For the "most pure and exquisite happiness of that state" consists "in the free and unreserved communion of spirits," in "that perfect correspondence and unity of knowledge and feeling," which identifies "their two persons" and makes them "one person and one soul." Such a relationship had held the key to Adam and Eve's happiness until the Tempter arrived, and "such would always be the case" where the "bosom" is "free from the consciousness of guilt and the understanding unclouded by error and folly." [70] The exemplum was clear. Dr. Cecil's young friend should no longer doubt the path he should follow.

Gracious act and response, freedom from hidden guilt or festering conscience—on such indeed could a successful marriage be founded. Yet Americans searched even further into the relationship between Adam and Eve to discover the subtle foundations of happiness. Neither man nor woman could be happy alone—that was clear. For as Adam had said, and as *The Weekly Visitor* repeated,

> In solitude,
> What happiness? Who can enjoy alone,
> Or, all enjoying, what contentment find?

God had implanted in man the desire for companionship and had instituted marriage to fulfill that desire. [71] But such a

[70] *The Old Bachelor* (Richmond, 1814), no. XX, pp. 129–131. The letter of inquiry, addressed to Dr. Robert Cecil, was signed "Romeo."

[71] *The Weekly Visitor Or Ladies' Miscellany*, I, no. 12 (December 27, 1802), 92, in an essay, "The Necessity of Esteem in the Marriage State." See also *The American Museum Or Repository*, VI (November 1789), 377.

companionship had to be carefully nurtured, had to be fed with expressions of liking and joy; if a wife attended to her husband's wishes and interests, he in turn should speak of the happiness such attention had brought.

An epistle "On the Happiness of a Domestic Matrimonial Life" in *The Columbian Letter-Writer* plumbed this secret more deeply. One of a number of articles "Calculated for the Amusement and Instruction of the Youth of America," this epistle presented a husband writing a letter to a much beloved wife. He might, the writer conceded with masculine vanity, have made another woman a good husband; but only his wife could have brought *him* the happiness he had enjoyed. Her "amiable disposition and virtues" had so made her the bliss of his life that he could only exclaim, as Eve had to Adam, that their companionship had sweetened all the varieties of human experience. Conversing with her he had forgotten all time. Neither the silence of evening nor the breath of morn, neither the charm of earliest birds nor the fragrance of earth, was sweet away from her presence. Eve's exclamation of joy had expressed so precisely what he felt in his heart that he put the whole passage down in his letter so that his wife would know the depth of his love. Such a husband might be considered old-fashioned, as a friend looking over his shoulder observed. But his expression of joy in companionship reflected more than two decades of marital happiness, and in turn ensured future bliss.[72]

Yet neither pleasing actions nor union of mind nor expressions of joy in companionship told the whole story of wedded happiness in Eden. From the very beginning God had created man and woman with different, complementary natures. A knowledge of their separate natures was therefore essential to

[72] *The Columbian Letter-Writer, or, Young Lady and Gentleman's Guide to Epistolary Correspondence* (Alexandria, 1811), pp. 83–84. *"We'll learn sound morals whilst we learn to write"* was the motto appearing on the title page of this book.

the achievement of harmony, argued John E. Hall in "The American Lounger" column of *The Port Folio*. Hall opened his discourse by quoting Milton's familiar sentiments on woman and household good, after which he digressed on the specious notion of equality, an argument currently pressed, he said, by young republicans and Jacobins in a manner reminiscent of Milton's devils.

But Hall had digressed for a purpose: he was leading up to his position that the proper relationship between men and women was not that of equality, which had been "so zealously maintained" in current disputes, but that *"excellent form and happy state"* of inequality, which Milton had presented through the eyes of Satan when he first glimpsed Adam and Eve in the Garden. The "entire passage" could not "be too often quoted," Hall exclaimed. For here Milton had not only stressed Adam and Eve's different natures—his inherent authority and her sweet submission; he had prized Eve's mind more than her body. What interested Hall was not so much the Renaissance great scale of nature, which allowed Milton to place Adam above Eve, as the psychological differences between male and female, a knowledge of which would promote matrimonial happiness. He became so enamored of Eve's distinct characteristics that he called them to the attention of his "fair countrywomen," for whom, he hoped, they would serve as an inspiration and stimulant. To troll the tongue and roll the eye might "ensnare the passions," as had been the aim of Eve's latter day daughters in Michael's vision of wickedness; but such feminine accomplishments could "not gratify the mind" or "bind the heart" and therefore should not be highly commended. Let women consult the picture Milton had painted, Hall implied; let them recall Eve, or Shakespeare's Imogene, or Spenser's Belphoebe. Let women "hold the *mirror up to nature*" and criticism of them would be retorted, for they would then, as upon the touch of Ithurial's spear, "not display a single stain on the white robe of their purity." [73] God had created man and woman with separate and pure natures; to fulfill the intent of creation would alone produce harmony.

If recognition of Adam and Eve's different natures brought happiness to Eden, failure to do so condemned that joyous state to one of mutual accusation and mistrust. So suggested *The Port Folio* in a report on "Law Intelligence" from England, which recalled how Thomas Erskine had cited in a case of adultery Eve's recrimination and Adam's admission of guilt after the Fall. Eve rightly accused Adam of "leaving her unprotected from the wiles of the seducer," the report seemed to say. Had Adam acted according to nature and asserted his proper authority Paradise might have never been lost. Eve now knew this truth and Adam came to it belatedly. Bitter experience alone had disclosed that a husband should never "desert the guardianship of his wife's purity and honour," the true "source" of his "comfort" and "happiness." [74] A word to wise Americans should be sufficient.

Yet Americans rarely referred to Adam and Eve after the Fall, however salutary the exemplum might be. They repeatedly recalled the picture of prelapsarian bliss in the Garden, to which they felt obliged to add a final stroke of detail. The wedding hymn had sung of happy family relations, and Eve herself on the morning of the Fall had hinted to Adam that soon young hands would join them to keep the Garden in trim. Who bids abstain? Only "our destroyer, foe to God and man," Milton had said, just before he opened his song to nuptial love. This sentiment had earlier encouraged a young lady in "The Maid's Soliloquy" [75] to give up her freedom for

[73] *The Port Folio*, II, no. 39, New Series (October 4, 1806), [193]–195. John E. Hall wrote under the pseudonym of "Sedley."

[74] *ibid.*, III, no. 26 (June 25, 1803), 204–205.

[75] The same soliloquy appeared again in *The Weekly Visitor Or Ladies' Miscellany*, IV, no. 26 (April 26, 1806), 203.

marriage; now it crowned an essay "On Matrimony," which listed the joys of family life. Marriage not only brought comfort and ensured solace against loneliness; it entailed the pleasures of parenthood. The relations dear of the hymn—the education of children, "their progress in learning, the unfolding of their minds, the prognostics whence to form an opinion of their dispositions"—now became by projection a part of the image of pristine happiness in Eden.[76] The ideal vision of marriage Americans found in *Paradise Lost* at last was complete.

Presentation of Eve as a pattern of wifely perfection and of marriage in Eden as an archetype of nuptial love held steady during the early years of the Republic. Americans still recalled the Biblical story of Ruth and referred to the good wife of *Proverbs* as guides to a happy connubial life. But Milton's picture of Eden now supplanted the older images of marriage, at least in the popular mind. If few journalists grasped the whole picture at once, they responded to parts that appealed to their individual temperaments and instinctively perceived that Milton's delineation of paradisial love corresponded to a deep-seated yearning in human experience. They discovered, as had Milton, that the soul longs for natural simplicity, for a happy state based on mutual understanding and love, where the senses may deploy in complete innocence, unencumbered by guilt and shame.[77] Such a fulfillment of nature made casual amours appear tawdry and cheap, and even the happiest marriages seem by comparison incomplete and self-conscious. Such perfection, and the reasons for it, fascinated Americans during the early Republic; and if, as Milton himself became less widely known, the picture gradually faded from the national

[76] *The Literary Miscellany Or Monthly Review*, I, no. 2 (June 1811), 105–107.
[77] Wylie Sypher (*Four Stages of Renaissance Style*, New York, 1956, pp. 192–194) sees Milton's baroque presentation of Adam and Eve in the Garden as an example of "unified sensibility."

scene, it has never ceased to enamour readers of *Paradise Lost*. Even the most sophisticated critics of Milton in the twentieth century respond to the idyllic vision of Eden, finding in it an authentic expression of the hopes of mankind.[78]

## IV

Ministers and lay preachers of the early Republic found Milton no less authentic as a witness for piety and Christian belief. Edward Williams stated in England that *Paradise Lost* and *Paradise Regained* should be on the shelves of "The Preacher's Library," a recommendation Americans endorsed by publishing his view under a Philadelphia imprint soon after the turn of the century.[79] But Americans needed no reminder that Milton had spoken to eternal spiritual values, or that he should be within easy reach of the clergy. Samuel Cooper Thacher possessed copies of Milton's two great poems,[80] and Joseph Lathrop and Leonard Woods advertised him on a list of "valuable" theological works in the back pages of their sermons and tracts.[81]

Evidence everywhere suggests that religious Americans made Milton a close companion. Samuel Worcester even argued for the appropriateness of sacred music on earth by reference to Milton's vision of angelic harmony in heaven;[82] and Joseph Goffe enlivened his sermon on *The Flaming*

---

[78] See, for example, John Peter, *A Critique of Paradise Lost* (New York, 1960), Chapter 5, "Adam and Eve in Paradise"; and *The Living Milton*, ed. Frank Kermode (New York, 1961), Chapter 6, "Adam Unparadised."

[79] *The Christian Preacher* (Philadelphia, 1810), p. 333.

[80] *Catalogue of the Entire and Select Library of the Late Rev. Samuel Cooper Thacher* (Boston, 1818), p. 19.

[81] *Discourses, on the Mode and Subjects of Christian Baptism* (Boston, 1811), at the conclusion; and *A Sermon Delivered Before the Massachusetts Missionary Society, on their Thirteenth Anniversary, May 26, 1812*, at the conclusion.

[82] *An Address, on Sacred Music, Delivered before the Middlesex Musical Society and the Handel Society of Dartmouth College* (Boston, 1811), p. 15.

*Sword* with Milton's popular portrait of Adam and Eve's expulsion from Eden.[83] Eulogies on persons of national importance, like General Washington [84] or the Honorable James Bowdoin,[85] the character of a worthy servant [86] or of an unworthy divine [87]—all could be articulated by reference to Milton.

But ministers found him more helpful in mounting attacks on skeptical thought of the Enlightenment and in furnishing imagery and rubrics of worship to reaffirm ancient beliefs. He became a witness for Christianity *par excellence:* tendencies to interpret religious experience in terms of *Paradise Lost* evident as early as Benjamin Colman and John Adams now became common practice.

A glance at the religious scene will readily show how Milton could serve to answer skeptics of the Enlightenment. The eighteenth century had witnessed a softening in Calvinistic theology and a rise in benevolism, a change stemming largely from Deistic thought and its attendant ideals of perfectibility and progress.[88] Charles Chauncy had already preached universal salvation, which questioned the doctrines of original sin and of the Atonement of Christ; and now in a series of sermons and tracts Hosea Ballou, a New England clergyman of some fame, advocated universalism. To make matters worse

---

[83] *The Flaming Sword* (Worcester, 1816), title page.

[84] Joseph Dana, *A Discourse on the Character and Death of General George Washington, Late President of the United States of America, Delivered at Ipswich, on the 22nd. February, A.D. 1800* (Newburyport, 1800), p. 26.

[85] Thaddeus Mason Harris, *A Tribute of Respect, to the Memory of the Hon. James Bowdoin, Esq.* (Boston, 1811), p. 32, the "Obituary Notice."

[86] William Collier, *The Gospel Treasury* (Charlestown, 1810), p. 453.

[87] *The Christian's, Scholar's, and Farmer's Magazine* (February and March 1790), p. 687.

[88] For the best discussion of this change, see Joseph Haroutunian, *Piety Versus Moralism: The Passing of the New England Theology* (New York, 1932). See also Russel Blaine Nye, *The Cultural Life of the New Nation,* Chapter 9, "The Building of an American Church," and Chapter 10, "The Great Revival of American Faith."

Thomas Paine had presented to an uneasy world *The Age of Reason,* a tractate so secular in tone and so skeptical of mystery that it seemed to undermine all that pious Christians held dear.

In *An Oration on the Influence of Social Institution upon Human Morals and Happiness* Tunis Wortman accurately summarized the skeptical element in American thought. Here he asserted that the doctrine of original sin, or of the debasement of human character, had in the past only served tyrants, but the "philosophy of modern times" had now "exploded the prejudices and delusions" that had so long "shackled" literature of earlier ages. He further maintained that as man probed more deeply into the "theory of mind" the more he understood that evil springs from "human and secondary causes," a source amenable to social change; and this, far from arousing doubts about Providence, should confirm the "wisdom or the benevolence of Heaven." [89] This best of all possible worlds Wortman had found mainly in Locke and Montesquieu, though his American experience no doubt contributed to it. An amiable God, an ethical Christ, and man possessed of infinite possibilities for advancement seemed more acceptable than an angry God, a sacrificial Christ, and man beset with original sin. The old piety had given way to the new moralism.

But defenders of the old piety soon arose in their wrath to smite down such skeptics, and to do so they called upon Milton. Lemuel Haynes attacked Hosea Ballou in *Universal Salvation A Very Ancient Doctrine,* a sermon so popular that it ran through six editions within two years. Taking the text for his attack from Genesis 3:4, Haynes first spoke of Satan's temptation of Eve; but if the text came from the Bible, the picture Haynes presented came from *Paradise Lost,* with

<hr />

[89] *An Oration on the Influence of Social Institution upon Human Morals and Happiness, Delivered before the Tammany Society, at their Anniversary, on the Twelfth of May, 1796* (New York, 1796), pp. 6–7.

Ballou himself appearing in the role of the Tempter. Happy indeed was the primitive state of man, Haynes declared. Adam and Eve could regale themselves with "all the delicious fruits" of the Garden with the exception of that which grew on one tree. "Happy were the human pair, amidst this delightful paradise," Hayes continued, "until a certain preacher, in his journey, came that way, and disturbed their peace and tranquillity, by endeavouring to reverse the prohibition of the Almighty, as in our text—'Ye shall not surely die.'" Like Satan, Ballou had stopped at this point, Haynes implied, thereby hoping to establish the doctrine of universal salvation; and to clarify Ballou's omission and to establish orthodox Christianity Haynes supplemented Genesis with Milton's version of Eve's temptation and fall:

> She pluck'd, she ate;
> Earth felt the wound: nature from her seat,
> Sighing through all her works, gave signs of wo,
> That all was lost.

The completed image from *Paradise Lost* thus allowed Haynes to turn back on Ballou the sense of Scripture itself. Ballou had presented only part of the story. The whole picture, clarified by reference to Milton, showed Satan himself to be the author of Universal Salvation.[90]

Pious Americans found Thomas Paine's *Age of Reason* an even greater cause for concern. Perhaps they felt Paine had betrayed them in this late popular tract. Andrew Broaddus observed that he had admired Paine's earlier political views, but now opposed his present positions. What Milton had said of Lucifer after his fall could be "accommodated" to Paine by substituting *genius* for *archangel*, Broaddus declared. To him Paine now appeared no less than a genius impaired, the excess

---

[90] *Universal Salvation A Very Ancient Doctrine . . . A Sermon, Delivered at Rutland, West-Parish, Vermont, in the Year 1805* (7th edn., New York, 1810), sig. A2.

of his glory obscured.[91] For, during the Revolution, he had called men to heroic action; but now he shone the dry light of reason on the main Christian story, questioning its mysteries and doctrines. Such apostasy, Broaddus implied, demanded an answer; and the Reverend Uzal Ogden supplied it in *The Deist Unmasked*

In this long and pedantic answer Ogden found the testimony of Milton pertinent on two crucial points: (1) the justice of God and (2) the Atonement of Christ. Paine had felt no need for expressing duty to God, Ogden declared; he had shown concern for man only, for loving mercy and doing justice so as to make the human race happy. The *awful* attributes of the Deity had indeed seemed to Paine less important than His *amiable* qualities. In short, a God of benevolence had superseded a God of stern justice; and such theology, Ogden continued, was not that of Christians but of infidels. To present the true picture of man's relation to Deity Ogden cited God's pronouncement on man as Milton had phrased it in Book III of *Paradise Lost*. "Dye hee or Justice must," God had said,

> unless for him
> Some other able, and as willing, pay
> The rigid satisfaction, death for death.[92]

Such a God was the God of true Christianity, Ogden believed, and Milton's image had allowed him to bring Paine's views into proper perspective.

To set Paine right on the Atonement, Ogden followed an identical procedure. Paine had argued that moral justice could not punish the innocent for the guilty, even if the innocent agreed to such punishment—a position Ogden answered in the

---

[91] *The Age of Reason & Revelation; or Animadversions on Mr. Thomas Paine's Late Piece, Intitled The Age of Reason, &c.* (Richmond, 1795), pp. 5–6.

[92] *Antidote to Deism. The Deist Unmasked: Or An Ample Refutation of all the Objections of Thomas Paine, Against the Christian Religion* (Newark, 1795), I, 85–87, in a series of notes.

words of a "justly esteemed poet" that the Messiah had made precisely the plea Paine had rejected. For God's only Son *had* offered Himself for man's sins; and as Ogden quoted additional lines from Book III, the whole picture Milton had painted came to mind: the hushed choir, the stern edict, and the gift of a life for a life so that fallen man might live again.[93] Ogden knew that the doctrine of the Atonement lived in that scene; he knew also that he could answer Paine best by recalling its drama.

Scenes from *Paradise Lost* indeed served as a standard answer to the skepticism of Paine's *Age of Reason*. At the trial of Thomas Williams, Thomas Erskine summarized the argument of Milton's poem to refute Paine's contention that the Christian story was merely one of the "more ancient superstitions of the world"—a refutation Americans considered important enough to print at least twice before the century closed.[94] As the Calvinist preacher Thomas Williams declared, better "err in company with the immortal *Milton*, the philosophic *Baxter*, and other writers of equal celebrity" than be skeptical with Paine.[95] But of course no Christian could believe Milton had erred.

Yet Americans turned to Milton not so much to refute notorious Deists as to articulate meditations on God. In *Paradise Lost* Milton had pictured the Christian story as had no other poet: his genius had presented a panorama of doc-

---

[93] *ibid.*, II, 138–139.

[94] *The Speeches of the Hon. Thomas Erskine, in the Court of King's Bench, June 28, 1797* (Philadelphia, 1797); and *Poor Richard Revived: Or Barber and Southwick's Almanack, For the Year of Our Lord, 1798* (Albany).

[95] *The Age of Infidelity: In Answer to Thomas Paine's Age of Reason* (Philadelphia reprinted, 1794), p. 42. See also David Simpson, *A Plea for Religion and the Sacred Writings: Addressed to the Disciples of Thomas Paine, and to Wavering Christians of Every Denomination* (Baltimore, 1807), pp. 70, 91, 143, 199, 218, 239, 265, 275, 282, 284. Simpson, an English divine, found Milton's testimony most helpful. See also *The Weekly Monitor: A Series of Essays on Moral and Religious Subjects* (Philadelphia and Charleston, 1810), nos. 12, 13, and 14.

trine in action, a narration of images dramatically structured, but each possessing a special force of its own. Americans responded less to the great argument in its entirety than to individual scenes, of which the most often invoked was Adam and Eve's morning worship in Book V, following Eve's premonitory dream of the temptation. This hymn of worship had already appeared in earlier poetry and almanacs,[96] and remained a staple in texts of the day. Now it furnished Americans with something very much like a rubric of praise, rivaled in popularity by the great hymn to nuptial love alone.

Paradoxically Adam and Eve's morning hymn served old pietists and new moralists alike. Both paraphrased its thought or framed their own worship after its sentiments; they differed in their concept of God and in what man should praise. New moralists stressed God's benevolence, His bounty and goodness in creating the world for man's delectation. He merited praise not because of His awful power and might but because He had wrought so minutely for His creatures' comfort and joy. As Milton had said, He was "Parent of Good." Such a sentiment allowed Azel Washburn to "adopt" with "the greatest propriety" the "language of the poet" in a discourse on the power and wisdom of God, delivered in the college chapel at Dartmouth. "How exactly" are all the "heavenly bodies balanced to keep their motions harmonious and regular," Washburn observed; how precisely the whole universe works "so that all creatures may be furnished with comfortable subsistence." Even the "formation of the smallest animal" showed infinite wisdom, even the operation of his lungs and the circulation of his blood. Such a reflection on God and his creatures led Washburn directly to Adam and Eve's morning hymn, which informed his own feeling and structured his praise.[97]

[96] Almanacs still reprinted it. See, for example, *The Almanack of Poor Richard the Second: Or An Astronomical Museum, For the Year of Our Lord, 1802* (Boston), title page.

[97] *Two Discourses Delivered in the College Chapel, At Hanover, New Hampshire* (Hanover, 1795), p. 8.

In a similar manner William Woodbridge guided his meditation on nature in his *Sermon on the Care of the Soul*, delivered in North Killingworth. Orthodox at his opening, Woodbridge expounded the first great commandment, but soon he began to reflect tendencies of the Enlightenment. Contemplation of the heavens, he declared—contemplation of the "established laws of nature" would lead man's soul directly to God; and with this he expressed the benevolism of the day, supported by the language and structure of Milton's hymn. God became an "all-bountious Parent supplying the wants of every living thing"; and if He inspired in Woodbridge a feeling of awe, He also because of His benevolence appeared friendly. God's thunderous voice and the laws of nature combined to teach "the awful and amiable attributes of deity." [98]

The "amiable attributes of deity." Such a concept of God moved from the pulpit into popular journals of the day, still bearing the impress of Adam and Eve's song. *The American Museum* presented a discourse on the water pine and the water withe of Jamaica, taking its cue from Milton's statement that even the lowest works of creation declare the goodness and power of God.[99] Could it be possible, "that amidst such evident proofs of design" in such plants, anyone could doubt or deny the existence of a Supreme Being? Such a query answered itself. Rather than ask such questions, the meditation continued, man should rejoice that the Creator stood ready to supply all his wants, and to observe all his necessities, comforting him in

[98] *A Sermon on the Care of the Soul, Delivered to the Society in North-Killingworth* (Middletown, 1798), pp. 27–28.

[99] William Derham had expressed such a view earlier in his *Physico-Theology: Or, A Demonstration of the Being and Attributes of God, From His Works of Creation* (10th edn., London, 1742), p. 423n. Here Derham reported that his friend, Dr. Sloane, had furnished him with an account of the *"Water-with of Jamaica,"* which the inhabitants of that place *"celebrated"* as *"an immediate Gift of Providence."* Since Derham's book was widely read during the eighteenth century, it no doubt furnished new moralists with many of their fundamental positions.

his life on earth and inviting him to prepare for life to come.[100] Scientific observation had shown God to be man's great and good Friend, but Milton had furnished both a language and form to celebrate the discovery.

Benjamin Waterhouse pursued a similar reflection on plants in *The Monthly Anthology*, finding his conclusion in the last part of Adam and Eve's hymn. Here Milton had described plants and trees, waving their tops in obeisance to God: through motion or sound, life on earth praised the Creator of all. Such a description of worship in nature declared the benevolence of creation for man. The "traits of wisdom" Waterhouse uncovered, the discoveries he made in the flora of nature simply instructed him "how kindly P R O V I D E N C E restrains, impels, and directs all things to a beneficient end." [101] What Milton had expressed in song, Waterhouse had discovered through his researches.

Meditations based on Adam and Eve's hymn sometimes reached out to include larger operations of nature, such as the rhythm of seasonal change. Could anyone observe vales enameled with flowers, or see frowning hills rising sublimely about him, without lifting his voice in praise to the Creator? Each season afforded its particular pleasure, and only an insensible mind would not feel impelled by sensations of gratitude and joy to join in the "general chorus, and say with Milton, 'These are thy glorious works, Parent of Good!'" [102] The *Philadelphia Repository* joined the chorus in some "Reflec-

---

[100] *The American Museum Or Universal Magazine*, IX (May 1791), 279–280, in a reflection called "Physico-Theology." Like Derham, the author of this mediation also called on the testimony of Dr. Sloane.

[101] *The Monthly Anthology and Boston Review*, IV (August 1807), in a lead article entitled "The Leaf," under a series called the "Botanist," by Benjamin Waterhouse. See Lewis P. Simpson, *The Federalist Literary Mind* (Baton Rouge, La., 1962), p. 13.

[102] *The Massachusetts Magazine Or Monthly Museum of Knowledge and Rational Entertainment*, IV, no. 6 (June 1792), 376–379, in a reflection on the "Rashness of Censuring the Laws of Creation," by Edmund Rack, Esq., an English Quaker.

tions on Spring," a season whose bounties asked for uninhibited praise. Who could contemplate a prospect in spring and "not feel his heart overflow with gratitude to that all-bountiful and omnipotent B E I N G ," Who had poured down his "blessings" and delighted in the "happiness" of his creatures? The succession of day and night, of seed time and harvest, of cold and heat revealed the "glorious truth" that God is a *"kind and universal* P A R E N T ,*"* and mankind *"brothers* and *sisters* of one great F A M I L Y .*"* [103] Such words strained the purpose of Adam and Eve's morning hymn, however closely they followed part of its thought. The benevolism of the Enlightenment had forced a meaning beyond Milton's intent.

Old pietists worshipped God through the frame of the hymn much more traditionally. Milton had presented Adam and Eve praising the Creator Himself, not His works, which simply manifested His infinite bounty. In his discourse on astronomy the Angel Raphael made this position clear when he disclosed that the book of creatures should inspire not curiosity but admiration and wonder, should impress upon man the mystery and power of God.[104] God had created the world for *His* pleasure, not *man's:* His should therefore be the power and glory, not His laws, which gladdened the heart and worked for the benefit of mankind.

Such was the spirit that animated Timothy Dwight as he incorporated the first part of Milton's hymn into some concluding remarks in a sermon entitled "The Earth." He had already imitated the hymn in *The Conquest of Canäan,* where he made it speak against the infidelity of sun worshippers; now he turned it against the infidelity of his age. First he an-

[103] *Philadelphia Repository and Weekly Register,* III, no. 21 (May 21, 1803), 163–164, "Reflections on Spring," signed by A. W. of Gray's Ferry.

[104] *The Monthly Anthology and Boston Review,* IV (September 1807), 489–492, in an essay on the "Superiority of Practical Philosophy to Scientifick Researches," comments on this point.

swered the infidels' objection to miracles by saying that the creation itself was a miraculous act; the laws of nature followed, not preceded, the appearance of earth's goodly frame. All that was "beautiful, useful, majestic, or exalted" only displayed the "beauty, excellence, greatness, and sublimity" of the Divine Perfection. How naturally, then, the "language of the great English Poet" expressed Adam and Eve's praise, Dwight observed. "What a Mind must that be, which could contain an exact, as well as comprehensive, scheme of all the parts, characteristical qualities, and operations, of such a work; which, without confusion, or mistake, could see through the whole, and discern every consequence, even in the remotest ages of being." Had Dwight dwelt at "the side of our first Parents," how instinctively *he* would have exclaimed: "*Worthy art thou, O Lord, to receive blessing, and glory, and honour, and power, for thou hast made all things, and for thy pleasure they are, and were created.*" [105] Such a cry of exultation and praise arose from ancient Christian tradition: Milton and Dwight had followed a rubric of worship viable in the Church since primitive times. But Milton's hymn helped Dwight articulate his conclusion, which sharpened the distinction between the old piety and the new moralism.

The same spirit animated a "Lady of Connecticut" as she compiled *A Real Treasure for the Pious Mind.* One selection in this compilation, most of which came from English writers of pious repute, meditated on "The Glory of God in his Works of Creation, Providence and Redemption." This particular reflection referred to only two lines of Milton's hymn, but it paraphrased a number of its sentiments. God so moves through nature than man should adore and confess His power, the meditation ran. Thunder and lightning, "summer and winter, the shady night, and the bright revolutions of the day"

---

[105] *Theology; Explained and Defended, in a Series of Sermons* (5 vols., Middletown, 1818), I, 360–362, in the sermon "The Earth."

all manifest the presence of a great Creator. If He shows Himself "thus illustrious" in His works, what then must be His "essential majesty and beauty"; and if "discoveries" of His "power and wisdom are thus delightful," how "transporting" must be the "manifestations" of His manifold "goodness"! [106]

Thomas Branagan presented a similar attitude in a meditation on "The Order and Beauty of the Visible Creation," which he included in his *Flowers of Literature*. Opening his discourse with the first lines of Adam and Eve's song, he moved quickly to exclamations of devotional joy, after commenting on the "sublime dignity" of the created universe. "What proportion do the most sumptuous and finished monuments of human power and skill bear to the magnificence of the creation! How low and contemptible are all the proudest works of men compared to those of God!" Such expostulations led Branagan to state that the effect of the visible world upon man could best be explained through an imaginative incident. Suppose, he said, a man ignorant of nature and light suddenly saw "an ample prospect of the sublime canopy of heaven, the blazing sun, the illumined atmosphere, and the florid earth diversified with its various landscapes." How would this "appearance astonish and transport him, and stamp at once on his mind the new ideas of grandeur and beauty, and excite his veneration of the wisdom and power of God!" [107]

Even the study of natural history could command traditional piety when channeled through Adam and Eve's morning hymn. *The Port Folio* declared that the book of nature—"the plainest, the most easily comprehended, striking, and impressive" record of creation—perpetually inspired "the highest

[106] *A Real Treasure for the Pious Mind. Compiled by a Lady of Connecticut. From the Collections and Writings of the Countess of Huntingdon, Mrs. Rowe, Miss Harvey, Dr. Watts, Mr. Perin, Mr. Smith, and Others* (Hudson, 1806), pp. 43–47.

[107] *The Flowers of Literature* (Trenton, 1806), pp. 281–285.

conceptions of the Creator." Such a book animated man with "the purest spirit of devotion," increasing his "amazement" on "every fresh survey." A study of nature forced man to exclaim "in the rapturous language of the poet" the wonders of creation. No better rubric could be found than Adam and Eve's morning hymn to declare the power and wisdom of an eternal, Supreme Being.[108]

So habitual a use of the language, sentiments, and form of Milton's song to the Creator testifies to its efficacy. If Americans saw any heresy here or elsewhere in *Paradise Lost* they remained silent, at least until the discovery and publication of *De Doctrina Christiana*, which William Ellery Channing believed argued the Unitarian cause. But Americans found little in Milton during this period to support denominational conflicts. The Reverend John Bowden might regret *"Milton's sneering* observations" about Episcopal church government,[109] and the Reverend John S. J. Gardiner might happily place Milton within the Trinitarian fold.[110] Yet Americans rarely called on Milton for testimony in disputes over church organization or dogma, apparently believing, as Daniel Roberts declared, such controversies to be as futile as the arguments of the fallen angels in Hell.[111]

What Americans sought and found in Milton in addition to a language and form of devotion was reassurance of the spiritual world. The Newtonian world view had subverted the old scale of nature, by which men had earlier argued the existence of angels. Sir Thomas Browne had rightly foreseen

---

[108] *The Port Folio*, I, no. 6, New Series (June 1809), 511.

[109] *The Apostolic Origin of Episcopacy Asserted* (2 vols., New York, 1808), I, 57.

[110] *A Preservative Against Unitarianism: A Sermon, Preached on Trinity Sunday, At Trinity Church, June 9, 1811* (Boston, 1811), p. 15.

[111] *Some Remarks on Modern Arianism* (New York, 1802), p. 5. See also John Bowden, *A Full-Length Portrait of Calvinism* (2nd edn., New York, 1809), pp. 15–16 and note.

that a break in the great chain of being would cast doubt not simply on witches but on the entire realm of spirit. But if under the pressures of science the great chain no longer seemed valid, *Paradise Lost* still lived to assert the reality of the whole range of being from lowest forms to the essence of God. A reviewer of Joseph Lathrop's discourse on the soul thought Milton "no despicable theologian" mainly because he had pictured "malignant as well as benevolent spirits" acting "through invisible agents in this lower world." [112] The "great and justly admired" Milton had in truth written that man is continually "surrounded with invisible beings," watching his actions and serving as guardian angels.[113] Such testimony was enough to solace a grieving father at the death of his son. In one of the most reprinted essays at the turn of the century he saw his child as an angel, hovering over him and perhaps even guiding his hand. Had not the "great Milton" said,

> Millions of spiritual creatures walk the earth,
> Unseen, both when we sleep and when we wake.[114]

Besides comforting early Americans, Milton's spiritual creatures confirmed the actuality of transcendent existence. Seth Payson informed the Governor, Senate, and House of New Hampshire that the "celebrated Milton did not exhibit the creature of a poetical fancy, but a solemn truth, when he represented sin bringing forth death." [115] Even the militant Deist

[112] *The Monthly Anthology and Boston Review*, III (April 1806), 313.

[113] *A Sequel to an Antidote to the Miseries of Human Life, Containing a Further Account of Mrs. Placid and her Daughter Rachel* (New York, 1810), p. 56.

[114] *The Massachusetts Magazine Or Monthly Museum of Knowledge and Rational Entertainment*, III, no. 12 (December 1791), 746–748; *The American Museum Or Universal Magazine* (May 1792), pp. 222–223; *The Massachusetts Magazine Or Monthly Museum of Knowledge and Rational Entertainment*, VII, no. 5 (August 1795), 281–282; and *The Rural Magazine Or Vermont Repository* (September 1795), pp. 447–449.

[115] *A Sermon Preached at Concord, June 6th, 1799* (Portsmouth, 1799), p. 6. For the image of death taken from *Paradise Lost*, see also *The American Museum Or Universal Magazine*, VIII (November 1790), 227–228.

Elihu Palmer, in an extended attack upon revealed Christianity, admitted that Milton had "given to the most enthusiastic fictions" the appearance of "real existence," an artistic feat which forced him to add that *Paradise Lost* had "done more to immortalize the marvellous character" of Satan "than even the bible itself." As a tractate observed, the "*orthodox doctrine* of the devil," as Milton had presented it, was considered "by thousands, as solemn truth," however "chimerical" the story of Satanic activities might appear to reasonable minds.[116] If rational thought could no longer support the great hierarchy of creation, Milton's epic of God's ways to man could.

Pious Americans indeed believed that *Paradise Lost* validated the whole Christian story. In a commencement address at Yale College Timothy Dwight remarked that Milton had turned to Scripture for some of his scenes. The incomparable apostrophe from Isaiah, he said, "How are thou fallen from heaven, O *Lucifer*, Son of the Morning!" had undoubtedly given "*Milton* the first thought of Satan's rebellion, and war." [117] But if Milton drank from the fountain of truth, he added to its stream by dramatizing the providence of God and by furnishing details of the narrative where the Bible had been silent. As Andrew Fuller explained, the "christian, borne on the wings of faith, may adopt the language of Milton, and in a much more real and interesting sense." Even as Urania had led Milton into the heaven of heavens to breathe "empyr-

---

[116] Elihu Palmer, *Principles of Nature, Or A Development of the Moral Causes of Happiness and Misery Among the Human Species* (3rd edn. [New York], 1806), p. 158; and *Light Shining in Darkness, and the Darkness Comprehending it Not* ([Charlestown], 1811), p. 6. See also the *American Review and Literary Journal*, 1, no. 4 (October, November, and December 1801), 454.

[117] *The Sublime and Beautiful of Scripture: Being Essays on Select Passages of Sacred Composition. To Which is Added, Dr. Dwight's Dissertation on the Poetry, History, and Eloquence of the Bible* (New York, 1795), pp. 242–243. Delivered and published first in 1772, Dwight's address now supported the thesis of Samuel Jackson Pratt's collection. Pratt himself quoted from Milton many times.

eal air," so faith could lead the Christian into an understanding of Christ's love.[118] Yet Milton's vast panoramas of Heaven and earth not only allowed Americans to breathe rarefied air; they testified with all the strength of Milton's pictorial power to the truth of Christian faith and belief. The living drama of *Paradise Lost* verified what long had been known but had never before been so picturesquely expressed.

To present the divine nature of man to the graduating class at Union College Eliphalet Nott recalled the picture of Adam and Eve in the Garden. This vision had informed Benjamin Colman nearly a century earlier, and Americans had seen it again in a sermon of John Wesley, which Thomas Coke and Francis Asbury reprinted to promote faith in a new land.[119] Journalists had by now made the whole sweep of Eden familiar in their presentation of Milton's concept of marriage and love. But as President of the College Nott wished to impress the graduating class not so much with the idyllic state of our First Parents as with man's Christian nature and destiny. To stress the superiority of man over the animals, to advise his charges of man's "port, his attitude, the texture of his frame," Nott conjured up the vision of Adam and Eve when Satan first glimpsed them. Here they stood tall and erect, Nott declared: "Godlike erect, with native honor clad," seeming lords over all. "No wonder the primeval state of man, excited in the Poet such ideas"; no wonder the picture Milton had painted inspired confidence not simply in man's physical greatness but in the grandeur of his mind.[120] Com-

[118] *Dialogues, Letters, and Essays, on Various Subjects* (Hartford, 1810), pp. 204–205. English theologian and Baptist missionary, Fuller received the degree of D.D. from Yale and Princeton, and published a few of his works under American imprints. Two American editions of the *Dialogues* within two years indicate the relevance of Fuller's arguments to the American religious scene.

[119] *The Arminian Magazine* (December 1790), pp. 589–592.

[120] *The Addresses, Delivered to the Candidates for the Baccalaureate, At the Anniversary Commencements in Union College* (Schenectady, 1814), p. 165.

mencement tradition demanded that Nott stress the nobility of man: to emphasize the clouding of man's reason on such an occasion would speak ill of his charges, to say nothing of the deficiencies of the President and faculty. But Abiel Holmes seized on the picture to verify the depth of man's fallen condition. In a *Sermon* preached at the ordination of the Reverend Jonathan Whitaker he explained that man, when "in the paradise of God," communed freely with his Maker; but when he fell and "Brought death into the world, and all our woe," his "understanding became darkened, and the will depraved." [121] Milton's lines served to recall the tragic contrast between Adam and Eve before and after they tasted the fruit, which in turn allowed Holmes, as Christian doctrine demanded, to present the full implications of man's first disobedience and Fall. Azel Backus said much the same thing in *An Inaugural Discourse*, though he dramatized his position with imagery from another part of *Paradise Lost*. "Had not man apostasized," he said, "reason had been a competent support and an unerring guide"; but since the Fall had darkened man's mind even the "wisest heathen" and the "most acute infidel philosophers," when speaking of moral subjects, "resemble M I L T O N 's description of Satan floundering in chaos." Once revolted from God, man, without Revelation, became simply an "Arabian desert, without chart or compass." [122]

Nott and Backus and Holmes invoked Milton's images for rhetorical as well as for doctrinal reasons. They knew that scenes from *Paradise Lost* could sharpen their visions, dramatize their arguments, and hence make their discourse more

[121] *A Sermon, Preached at the Ordination of the Rev. Jonathan Whitaker to the Pastoral Care of the Church and Society in Sharon, Massachusetts, February 27, 1799* (Dedham, 1799), p. 7.
[122] *An Inaugural Discourse, Delivered in the Village of Clinton, Dec. 3, 1812, on the Day of his Induction into the Office of President of Hamilton College* (Utica, 1812), pp. 12–13.

efficacious. They aimed not so much to define a doctrinal stance as to give abstract concepts color and life. But occasionally Americans found that Milton could verify Christian positions through imagery informed with a precise theological language. In *The Ruin and Recovery of Man* Alexander Proudfit called on Milton to define the nature of free will and original sin. Adam was completely qualified for the important trust God vouchsafed him, Proudfit began. He was upright, created in the image of his Maker, and had been given sufficient light to apprehend God's perfection. "Such was the character of Adam when the Lord God appointed him our representative in the covenant of works, and as the station was dignified and responsible he was amply qualified for filling it." To clarify his position Proudfit turned, as he revealed in a note, to the image of the heavenly throne in Book III of *Paradise Lost,* where God pronounced on man and his Fall. Here, Proudfit declared, the *"prince of poets"* had expressed his sentiment precisely *"in language both scriptural and sublime."* God had made man just and right, Milton had said—*"Sufficient to have stood, though free to fall"*; and so it was with the etherial powers, too: *"Freely they stood who stood, and fell who fell."* [123]

The sharpness of God's words, the pedantic tone which so grated on Alexander Pope and subsequent critics, Proudfit assessed as a linguistic virtue. He apparently believed, as had Henry Alline several years earlier, that Milton was one of the "clearest writers" ever to pronounce on the "disputed point" of original sin, that he had in truth spoken "for God in this matter." [124] Neither Scripture nor commentary had been more precise or as graphic.

---

[123] *The Ruin and Recovery of Man. A Series of Discourses on the Distinguishing Doctrines of Christianity* (Salem, 1806), pp. 77–78 and note.
[124] *Two Mites, Cast into the Offering of God, For the Benefit of Mankind* (Dover, 1804), pp. 3–4, 11.

Proudfit returned to Milton in "The Righteousness of Jesus Infinitely Sufficient for the Justification of All Who Embrace It" in order to define the doctrine of the Atonement. Since the Messiah "both obeyed and suffered in the nature which had sinned," he explained, it "was indispensably requisite, in order to our reconciliation, that the law of Jehovah should be honored, both in its precept and penalty, by our nature which had offered the insult." To support such an orthodox position he offered Milton's picture of God on his throne, pronouncing man's eternal doom unless someone could be found to pay the debt incurred by the Fall.[125]

This great image from Book III served Andrew Fuller with even greater precision in a dialogue on "Substitution." Here Fuller spoke at length on the meaning of the Atonement. This doctrine should not be construed as simply a payment of debt, where "satisfaction being once accepted justice *requires*" the debtor's "complete discharge," Fuller began. It could be likened more accurately to a payment for crime, where the criminal makes satisfaction "to the wounded honour of the law, and the authority of the lawgiver"—where "justice, though it *admits* of his discharge, yet no otherwise *requires* it than as it may have been matter of promise to the substitute." Yet this analogy failed to reveal fully the nature of the Atonement, Fuller continued. Nor could Christ's sacrifice be said to conform to the "law of innocence," which simply stated to the transgressor, "Thou shalt die." Were this true, "Every child of man must have perished," and God's pronouncement on man in *Paradise Lost* "would be inaccurate." But Milton had made no mistake: God had said in the poem that justice must die unless someone would willingly pay for man's disobedience with his own life. "The sufferings of Christ in our stead, therefore, are not a punishment inflicted in the ordinary course of distributive justice,"

[125] *The Ruin and Recovery of Man*, pp. 153-154.

Fuller went on; "but an extraordinary interposition of infinite wisdom and love: not contrary to, but rather above the law, deviating from the letter, but more than preserving the spirit of it." [126]

The pronouncement which allowed Fuller to define the Atonement also served to preface a letter "The Death of Christ a Propitiatory Sacrifice," one of a series Thomas Cleland wrote to Barton W. Stone on "Some Important Subjects of Theological Discussion," in reply to his address to Christian Churches in Kentucky, Tennessee, and Ohio.[127] Milton's image of God on his throne pronouncing man's doom sharpened exegesis of doctrine to the very edge of the frontier.

Yet Americans turned to Milton not so much to define as to clarify and enliven Christian belief. In order to quicken the doctrine of Repentance, the Reverend Henry Holcombe recalled in a letter to his brother the picture of Adam and Eve standing in prayer at the beginning of Book XI, Prevenient Grace having descended to prepare their regeneration. The sight of our First Parents—or painting, as Holcombe noted the scene—receiving the ministrations of the Holy Spirit infused the doctrine of Repentance with drama and meaning.[128] Here was doctrine in action, here was a moving picture of the conditions mankind must meet before God would vouchsafe His Grace.

But woe to Americans who hardened their hearts and shut themselves off from God's generous gift. To impress such sinners with the reality of eternal punishment ministers conjured up Milton's vision of Hell. In a sermon preached at the

---

[126] *Dialogues, Letters, and Essays, on Various Subjects*, pp. 165–166.

[127] *The Socini-Arian Detected: A Series of Letters to Barton W. Stone, on Some Important Subjects of Theological Discussion, Referred to in his 'Address' to the Christian Churches in Kentucky, Tennessee, and Ohio* (Lexington, Kentucky, 1815), Letter V, p. 51.

[128] *The First Fruits, in a Series of Letters* (Philadelphia, 1812), Letter XXII, pp. 186–187.

ordination of Edward Richmond, David Gurney pictured the state of the damned as conjectured by Belial in Book II of *Paradise Lost,* where he had told the Infernal Council that the condemned might be placed

> Under that boiling ocean wrapt in chains;
> There to converse with everlasting groans,
> Unrespited, unpitied, unreprieved,
> Ages of hopeless end.[129]

The scene Belial had imagined and Gurney had pictured presented only a part of the grand panorama ministers recalled to stress the tortures of Hell. In a sermon on immortality Samuel Whelpley turned to the horrible sights Milton had earlier shown, where he had dramatized the regions of eternal darkness and pain. Whelpley began by saying, "Let us pursue the soul and trace, if we can, her destiny beyond the grave." The idea so exhilarated him that he soared to rhetorical heights. "But, ah!" he exclaimed, "who has drawn aside the curtain which hides eternal things? Who can describe that undiscovered country, from whence no traveller returns?" Inspiration could, with God's help—divine inspiration could disclose the "habitations of angels" or the "awful prisons" of "wrath and justice."

Since Shakespeare had offered no glimpse of the country from whose bourn no one returns, Whelpley focused on the divine inspiration of Milton. He asserted first that the doomed soul would sink into Hell—"a gloomy region, inhabited only by devils and the spirits of the damned." As he directed his eyes to that place, he saw "souls of the wicked" banished from good, "eternally given up a prey to their own vileness, the unceasing sport of tormenting passions." They had rebelled against God and now reaped the fruit of their doing. Souls so damned would find "no cessation" of "discord,

---

[129] *A Sermon Preached December 5, 1792* (Boston, [1793]), p. 14.

blasphemies or woes! The sweet and chearing beams of peace
. . . [would] never dawn on the blackness of darkness where
they dwell." Such familiar details made the incorporation of
Milton's picture almost superfluous: Whelpley's paraphrase
presented enough of Milton's grim scene to give his parting
injunction an understandable urgency. "O sinner, remember
the day of retribution, and fly from that dire destruction that
awaits thee, and make the Judge thy friend." [130] Jonathan
Edwards himself could hardly have been more dramatic.

To ministers of the early Republic Milton was an articulate
and a helpful companion. For some, he sharpened and answered vexing theological queries; for others, he stood as a
rock against skeptical forces of the Enlightenment; for still
others, he dramatized doctrine and enlivened the invisible
world with colorful figures and scenes. As he moved from
ministerial studies into the world of journalism and of lay
speculation, he gave a language and form to spiritual longing
and a sense of reality to an eternal, transcendent realm. The
great argument of *Paradise Lost* no longer commanded very
much interest: the paradox of the happy fall, central to Milton's justification of God's ways to man, now moved to the
periphery of religious contentions. But Milton's imagery by
this time had become an inextricable part of the tale of sin and
redemption, supplementing the Bible with pictorial details
and giving a further dimension to the Christian story itself.
Such an enrichment of the Christian tradition heartened many
an American during the early Republic, lending him, for a
moment at least, a fresh sense of piety and a renewal of faith.
*Paradise Lost* had become inseparably bound to American
religious experience.

---

[130] *A Sermon on the Immortality of the Soul. Delivered at Newark, April
11, 1804* (Newark, 1804), pp. 12–13.

## IV

Imagery from *Paradise Lost* spread beyond the moral and religious life of the nation into the heart of political conflict. Washington had hoped that with the establishment of the Republic men would rise above faction; but he had scarcely finished swearing his inaugural oath before human nature asserted itself and sharp disputes on foreign and domestic policy divided the country, splitting it into the Federalist and Republican parties. To sway public opinion to their positions Federalist and Republican alike resorted to libel and Billingsgate, to parody and satire, to sketches of both men and affairs —ancient weapons of party dispute already in evidence on the American scene. Milton was no stranger to Americans who had employed such tactics. Jonathan Odell had earlier made *Paradise Lost* an instrument to assassinate character; Freneau and Trumbull had turned scenes from the same poem into rollicking, satiric verse. Politicians of both parties now followed their lead. From the arrival of Citizen Genêt through the Alien and Sedition Acts to the War of 1812, propagandists used Milton's imagery and symbols as weapons of choice, operating on the rhetorical principle that one familiar picture would be more effective than a thousand logical words.

Party disputes occasionally reminded Americans that Milton had argued directly for freedom, or that he had contributed to the Revolutionary cause. From 1795 to 1802 three separate reprints of *The Spirit of Despotism* by the Englishman Vicesimus Knox recalled that Milton had "discovered a noble spirit of independence," that "his writings contain[ed] some of the finest passages" on freedom ever composed, and that he and John Locke stood as "great names on the side of liberty." [131] Levi Lincoln remembered that no less a figure than

---

[131] *The Spirit of Despotism* (reprinted Philadelphia, 1795), pp. 228–229. Other reprints appeared in Morristown, 1799, and in Trenton, 1802.

John Adams had confessed his dependence on Harrington, Milton, and Locke, to mention a few of his political mentors; [132] and John Taylor of Virginia, hoping that the difference between Adams the Revolutionary and Adams the President would focus attention again on the great issues of freedom, observed what now was well known—that Milton was among the inspirers of that great man's early political activity.[133]

James Cheetham expanded such recollections to include the whole tradition of freedom Americans had inherited from England. Some of the principles Jefferson had stated in the Declaration of Independence, he said, sprang from Locke; a phrase or two on "reason and free inquiry" in his *Notes on Virginia* came from *Areopagitica*. But Cheetham not only desired to point out Jefferson's debt to great Englishmen; he wished to establish, particularly in view of French influences present in American life, that the success of the Revolution owed much to English activity and to ancient traditions of liberty nurtured on British soil. Englishmen, Irishmen, and Scotsmen had joined together to help win the Revolution, Cheetham maintained—particularly men like General Gates, whose contribution to the happy conclusion of the War had been singular. Cheetham wished to remind Americans further that Gates had been born on an Island that had given birth to "Shakespeare and to Milton, to Newton and to Locke, to Sydney and to Russel; to many sages or martyrs of freedom," from whom all "correct notions of civil liberty" had been drawn.[134] Such reminders should keep fresh the English sources of American political liberty.

In a Fourth of July oration published at the request of

---

[132] *Letters to the People. By a Farmer* (Salem, 1802), p. 93.

[133] *An Inquiry into the Principles and Policy of the Government of the United States* (Fredericksburg, 1814), pp. 520–521. For a recent study of Taylor's importance as a political thinker, see Eugene Tenbroeck Mudge, *The Social Philosophy of John Taylor of Caroline* (New York, 1939).

[134] *The Life of Thomas Paine* (New York, 1809), pp. 53–54 and note, 131 and note.

The '76 Association Benjamin Elliot presented a variation on the same theme. "Is monarchy inspiring?" he asked. If so, why had so many men of genius and learning spoken so contemptuously of kings? In France, Voltaire and Montesquieu had cried out against monarchy; in England, Milton and Sidney and Locke. In America—here Elliot could express his patriotism and his love of freedom through hyperbole only. He hoped that no American was "so vile" as to love monarchy, and that a single republican sentiment united Americans everywhere. For should an American give up his heritage of freedom he would become only a thing fit "to crawl on earth; and Earth herself would shrink at her own debasement, when knowing this was her true offspring." [135] Elliot reminded Americans that men of the past had formulated ideas of liberty Americans now held, that they had indeed contributed to the American triumph, the fruits of which all now enjoyed.

But if memory of Milton as a spokesman for freedom and as one of the spiritual fathers of the Revolution animated patriots still, few felt compelled to parade the old arguments. The battle against monarchy had been won. Rather, Fourth of July orators now sought to exalt American achievements and destiny, for which purpose they found Milton's symbols and imagery particularly helpful. Timothy Fuller reminded his fellow countrymen at the historic battle site of Lexington that the Revolutionary War could be likened to the dispute between Satan and God in *Paradise Lost,* a conflict so profound

> That never could true reconcilement grow
> Where wounds of deadly hate had pierc'd so deep.[136]

In so likening the American struggle to the archteypal conflict in Heaven, Fuller invested the War with more than his-

---

[135] *An Oration, Delivered in St. Philip's Church, Before the Inhabitants of Charleston, South-Carolina; On Friday, the Fourth of July, 1817* (Charleston, 1817), pp. 17–18.

[136] *An Oration Pronounced at Lexington, Massachusetts, on the Fourth of July, A.D. 1814* (Boston, 1814), p. 10.

toric significance: it was simply a repetition on earth of the eternal clash between Evil and Good. In like manner William Richardson implied that the landing of the Puritans in New England was a working out of God's Providence. Even as Adam and Eve had left Paradise and faced the wilderness before them, Richardson proclaimed in a Fourth of July discourse, so the Puritans had left home to find freedom "amid wilds and wolves" of a new land. The founding of America was an enterprise so grand, the winning of independence from England a culmination so happy, that only reference to the closing scene of *Paradise Lost* could suggest the importance of these events in the providential scheme of God's ways to man.[137]

Recollection of the War and of independence from England so exhilarated J. S. Richardson that he called on Milton's picture of the portals of Heaven to describe the fruits of the struggle. If during the War the sword had been sanctioned, Richardson said, if the doors of Hell, as depicted in *Paradise Lost*, had been opened to release havoc upon men, after the defeat of the British "Heaven opened wide/ Her ever-during gates" to pour her riches over the land.[138] Such symbols of war and of peace, such images of mortal conflict or of errands into the wilderness served no particular party or man; but they enhanced Fourth of July oratory and allowed Americans to read their achievements in terms of transcendent truth. Politicians now picked up such symbols and images, recognized their power, and turned them into propagandist devices to fight party disputes of the day.

[137] *An Oration, Pronounced at Groton, July 4, 1801* (Amherst, 1801), pp. 6–7.
[138] *An Oration, Delivered in St. Michael's Church, Before the Inhabitants of Charleston, South-Carolina, on Monday the Fifth of July, 1813. (The Fourth Being Sunday)* (Charleston, 1813), pp. 4–5. In his *Lectures on Rhetoric and Belles Lettres*, Blair had illustrated the affinity of sound and meaning in Milton's poetry with these two images. See p. 116.

Imagery from *Paradise Lost* indeed argued fundamental issues in conflict from Washington's inauguration to the Era of Good Feeling. The Revolution had secured independence from England, but had failed to weld factions or to define a united national policy. Republicans rejoiced at the French Revolution, dulling their eyes to its bloodshed and excesses. Federalists viewed it as a great menace to mankind, a threat to sound morals and established religion. From the overthrow of the French monarchy to the defeat of Napoleon events on the Continent shaped disputes on American soil. The course of the French Revolution, as Colonel Higginson said, drew a sharp line through early American history: it divided parties and molded them, giving them "their demarcations, their watchwords and their bitterness." [139]

To party conflicts thus guided by events on the Continent, Americans now brought *Paradise Lost*, finding in its symbols and imagery weapons of singular strength.

The image of Pandemonium as a weapon of choice appeared shortly after Citizen Genêt arrived in America in 1793. Greeted enthusiastically by Americans over the country, Genêt created among Republicans a state of mind that can be described only as phenomenal. Some Republicans sang French songs, some addressed each other as *citizen*, and the more radical founded Jacobin Clubs, modeled after the Société des Jacobins in France. Even the Olympian Washington, who normally stood above party disputes, spoke sharply in his message to Congress in 1793 about these societies, whose business, *The Massachusetts Mercury* declared, was "to denounce citizens, pack juries, abuse Government, instruct Congress," and, for all that was known, to "erect guillotines." [140]

---

[139] As cited in Charles Downer Hazen, *Contemporary American Opinion of the French Revolution* (Baltimore, 1897), [ix]–x.

[140] Charles Warren, *Jacobin and Junto* (Cambridge, 1931), p. 54. Warren quoted directly from *The Massachusetts Mercury* for November 29, 1793; he cited other journals expressing similar sentiments.

Gallicization of America soon reached such proportions that Federalists felt compelled to strike back. Unless they rooted out the growing menace of Jacobinism, they firmly believed, government would soon be subverted, trade exalted and learning degraded, and, who knew, their wives raped and their daughters deflowered. To expose what they thought was the true nature of the Jacobin threat to the American people and hence to bring the nation to its senses Federalists mounted a program of exposure and vilification, drawing part of their ammunition from Milton's picture of the conclave of devils.

Here was a scene all Americans could immediately grasp— evil incarnate plotting against God and the right, devils joined together in a desperate attempt to overthrow hierarchical values through the subterfuge of democratic debate. Satan on his throne in Pandemonium had long been a familiar image, and now John S. J. Gardiner invoked it in his *Remarks on the Jacobiniad,* one of the first significant attacks on the Republican radical wing.

To carry out his attack Gardiner created an imaginary mock-epic poem, to which he addressed running commentary in notes to the text. He could have taken the cue for his poem from de Villenave's mock-heroic *La Jacobiniade,* which had appeared in France perhaps as early as 1794. But of importance now is neither its source nor its commentary but the relevance of Milton's image to the Jacobin movement in America. To point out the nature of Jacobins Gardiner described a supposed meeting of the Boston Jacobin Club in the Green Dragon Tavern, which he called Pandemonium, a place where fools, artisans, and knaves met for the purpose of undermining the nation. A more motley crew would be hard to find:

> At *Pandemonium,* meets the *scoundrel* throng,
> Hell in their heart, and faction on their tongue.

．　　．　　．　　．　　．　　．　　．　　．

Who are the men, these caitiff chiefs command?
A strange, unlettered, multifarious band.
Some with weak heads, but well intentioned hearts,
Are simple dupes to antifederal arts;
Who, viewing tyrant acts in useful laws,
Mistake foul *Faction's*, for fair *Freedom's* cause.
The rest are genuine progeny of *dirt*,
Who, for a pint of rum, would sell their *shirt!*
With heads of adament, and hearts of steel,
The *worst* of passions are the *best* they feel:
An envious, restless, swearing, drinking crew;
Whom sense ne'er guided, virtue never knew;
Some foreign ruffians, hireling tools no doubt,
*French, Irish, Scotch,* complete the '*rabble rout*.' [141]

Here Gardiner is at some of his best. The image of Pandemonium showed Jacobin leaders as false as Satan's cohorts in
Hell, their witless followers as gullible as the numerous
fallen angels crowding below Satan's magnificent throne. The
whole scene made the Jacobin movement appear monstrously
evil, yet at the same time ridiculous, a movement evil enough
to be thoroughly crushed yet so futile as to arouse in the
Federalist Heaven ironic laughter, even as God had never
relented against his rebellious angels yet smiled at their
foolish activities.

As propaganda, the image was no doubt highly effective, as
the immediate success of the *Jacobiniad* would imply. Gardiner had called attention to what he considered a very real
menace and had branded it with a stamp of recognized evil.
Such a procedure showed him to be more perceptive than
Timothy Dwight, who, in investing good men with Milton's

---

[141] *Remarks on the Jacobiniad: Revised and Corrected by the Author.*
Part Second (Boston, 1798), pp. [9], 12. See also *Remarks on the Jaco-
biniad. Part First* (Boston, 1795), pp. 26–27, for some lines modeled on
Satan's speech to his fallen angels. For Gardiner's estimate of Milton's moral
and political conduct, see *The Monthly Anthology and Boston Review*, VI
(February 1809), 87–88. Lewis P. Simpson reproduced this estimate in *The
Federalist Literary Mind*, pp. 87–88.

symbols of evil in *The Conquest of Canäan,* confused his primary intentions. Gardiner knew precisely what he wanted to do and within the frame of temporal politics succeeded. Only in the perspective of literary history could his achievement be questioned.

Successful use of the image of the Infernal Council in attacks against radical Republicans had not come unheralded. In *Democracy: An Epic Poem,* Brockholst Livingston had already fastened the picture on a meeting of demagogues in New York, gathered there for the purpose of prescribing to Congress the adoption of measures hostile to Britain. Calling on Chaos to inspire his song, Livingston presented Republican demagogues in a scene reminiscent of the great Council in Book II of *Paradise Lost,* including several speeches by Satan's cohorts and thunderous applause from the audience. To the evil attached to Republican activities by the image itself, Livingston added the symbol of Milton's Chaos and Old Night, terms Federalists often used to describe the result of Republican policy.[142]

So choice a weapon could even be effective in intraparty maneuvers, or at least so thought Richard Alsop, who apparently chided Livingston in particular and Gardiner in general in *Aristocracy: An Epic Poem.* The poem itself is often playful and charmingly ironic; and as it presented aristocracy as a form of government unfriendly to the American dream, it invoked Pandemonium to make clear that some Federalists had gone much too far in their advocacy of Britain and her kind of rule. To press his point Alsop turned the Infernal Council into something of an extreme Federalist conclave, in which Satan harangued his fallen angels on the happy state of America, after the epic hero Aristus had retired to a grove to meditate his devilish role:

[142] *Democracy: An Epic Poem* (New York, [1794]), *passim.*

'Mid Pandemonium's walls, in awful state,
High on a throne exalted, S A T A N sate.
Around, in order meet, on either hand.
Powers and Dominions, Thrones and Princes stand:

Satan soon spoke to the social revolution in America, informing the devils assembled before him that in that country men worked for the good of mankind. Such a society was disquieting, Satan explained, and for this reason he rejoiced that Aristus roamed about in America and there labored to extend Satan's sway.[143] In short, Alsop apparently wished to remind the extreme wing in his own party of the dangers aristocracy held, and he seized upon the image of the Infernal Council to argue his point.

But the weapon of the Infernal Council must have been ineffective employed against Federalist positions. After all, Federalists stood for established religion and law, and any attempt to accommodate the symbols of revolt to either their activities or thought wrenched the image almost beyond recognition. Once, to be sure, and that much later, Republicans ridiculed the Hartford Convention by presenting its activities in the light of the Satanic conclave. That gathering of New England Federalists, spurred by the machinations of the Essex Junto, had moved close to treason in its presumed intention of declaring a Northern Confederacy.[144]

To compare that meeting with the risible activities of the fallen angels in their rebellion against God, as "Hector Benevolus" did so aptly in *The Hartford Convention*, showed a considerable amount of political acuity. Dissension among advocates—described in the Argument of this poem as "*Satan's speech—he is angry—Mr. O's attempt to appease him—*

---

[143] *Aristocracy: An Epic Poem* (Philadelphia, 1795), p. 14, Book I. This poem has been attributed to Alsop, but whether it is his is questionable.

[144] See Charles Raymond Brown, *The Northern Confederacy* (Princeton, 1915), Chapter 6.

*Satan's indignant reply—The little Rebel in a rage—attempts to strike his infernal majesty, and is transformed into a monkey"*—put the abortive meeting into a proper historical perspective and helped laugh the Essex Junto out of existence.[145]

But John S. J. Gardiner possessed a surer political instinct when he discovered a certain similarity between the rebellious, restless activity of Jacobin clubs and the false democratic jockeying in the great consultation in Hell. So successful had he been in damning the Jacobin movement through Milton's image of evil that Pandemonium became almost a monopoly of Federalist authors.

The image proved particularly effective in conflicts arising over the passage of the Alien and Sedition Acts, the Government's answer to the increasing flow of vilification and libel issued by the Jacobin wing of the Republican party. In a sense, the Government passed such laws to stem the stream of radical ideas emanating from the French Revolution itself; but in spite of Government action Republican journals pressed attacks on conservative institutions and men. As "Master Read" said in an oration delivered at the Latin School Boston, Jacobins called Washington an assassin and John Adams an old dotard; in haranguing the "gaping mechanic" and "admiring truckman" they would say anything to achieve their nefarious ends. They reminded Master Read of Satan himself, who had broken the order of God and then had declared it better to reign in Hell than serve in Heaven.[146]

---

[145] *The Hartford Convention in an Uproar! And the Wise Men of the East Confounded! Together With a Short History of the Peter Washingtonians; Being the First Book of the Chronicles of the Children of Disobedience: Otherwise Falsely Called 'Washington Benevolents'* (Windsor, 1815), p. 9.

[146] Read's oration appeared in the *Columbian Centinel* (July 25, 1798), p. 2. It was delivered on July 14, Bastille Day.

But the Alien and Sedition Acts had been a Federalist triumph. The law itself proclaimed the evils of Jacobin journalism, and as Federalists now looked at the political scene they saw that their best tactic would be to make Jacobins appear ineffectually ridiculous. To do so they again invoked the image of the Infernal Council, developing the risible possibilities of the scene that John S. J. Gardiner had touched only lightly.

In *The Political Green-House* Richard Alsop pictured happy Federalists and disconsolate Jacobins sitting together, the latter so discomforted by the turn of affairs that they seemed to have "burrs in their seats," or, more appropriately, appeared like a drove of "Satan's Deacons,"

> When from the burning lake, in ire,
> They sat their feet on solid fire,
> To find if war, or sly pollution,
> Could raise in Heaven a revolution.[147]

Alsop felt so secure in the Federalist triumph that through the image of the Infernal Council he could laugh at the way Jacobins squirmed. Federalists laughed even harder in *The Demos in Council*, a poem ridiculing through the picture of Pandemonium the imprisonment and release of Abijah Adams, bookkeeper for the *Independent Chronicle*, a Jacobin journal indicted for libeling members of the Massachusetts General Court.

Francis Dana, Justice of the Massachusetts Supreme Court, presided over the trial. A conservative Federalist, he concluded his charge to the jury with a homily against Jacobinism, even going so far as to describe several liberal members of the Massachusetts legislature as "worse than infidels," as abettors of "a traitorous enterprise to the government" of the coun-

[147] *The Political Green-House, For the Year 1798* (Hartford, [1799]), p. 6. Alsop may have had collaborators in this poem.

try.[148] Such strong feeling from the bench predicted the verdict: Abijah Adams was fined and sentenced to thirty days in the Suffock County jail, a victim, Republicans trumpeted, of legal oppression. Whether a victim or not Federalists saw in his imprisonment a chance to ridicule the plight of Republicans caught up in the new laws. To picture a Jacobin come to justice would be great good fun in itself; to show him plotting against the law of the land, as Satan had plotted against God, would reveal the futility of evil and help laugh Republican claims out of court.

*The Demos in Council: Or 'Bijah in Pandemonium* indeed parodied Republican tactics and principles through Milton's popular scene. The poem began with a picture of Adams incarcerated, high in a room in the county jail, by merit of his imprisonment raised to bad eminence and now ready to rally his Jacobin friends:

> H I G H , in a room of legal state, which far
> Outvied the strength of *Dedham*, or of *York*,
> Or e'en the *Concord*, which with heavy hand
> Clanks on her slaves her barb'rous chains, and bars,
> 'B I J A H exalted sat, by merit rais'd
> To that bad eminence; and from despair,
> Insatiate to pursue vain war with laws,
> His proud imagination thus displayed:
> "Cits, lawyers, doctors, brother Jacos all
> For since this gaol, within its walls, can hold
> Me but a month, tho' sad, oppress'd and fall'n,
> I give not all for lost.[149]

The opening scene set the tone of the whole poem. Being jailed by the Federalists would only glorify "gallic virtues"

[148] See John C. Miller, *Crisis in Freedom* (Boston, 1951), pp. 121–122, for an account of Adams' trial. Miller cited *Springer's Weekly Oracle* for May 18, 1799, and the *Independent Chronicle* for March 7, 1799 for reports of this charge.

[149] *The Demos in Council; Or 'Bijah in Pandemonium. Being a Sweep of the Lyre, In Close Imitation of Milton* (Boston, 1799), p. 3.

of the Republicans, 'Bijah announced. Such oppression would actually strengthen their forces, since they now had been freed from envy and rank, the curse of their Federalist foes. So 'Bijah continued his parody of Satan's false discourse before the conclave of devils, even to the assertion that a concord of misery gave further advantage of union, a firmer faith and accord than could be found among Federalists. For this reason 'Bijah now pressed a reopening of conflict, a renewal of their customary opposition against government, the means for so doing they now would decide, whether by "open war" or "covert guile."

The great consultation which followed at once parodied and revealed Republican aims and maneuvers. Speaking like Moloch, Honee [150] called for an alliance with France, for a joining of strength so that Jacobins could force their "resistless way" over the "fair land" of America. Junius, like Belial, argued for ease, and Tummas spoke in the manner of Mammon. But all plans gave way before the scheme of Democritus, "than whom, 'Bijah except, none higher sat." Since another attack on the government seemed fruitless, Democritus proposed a great Jacobin gathering to celebrate 'Bijah's release from incarceration: songs could be sung, music played, and 'Bijah himself could be borne shoulder high through the streets of the town. Such a suggestion, which described Jacobin activities on memorial occasions, elicited swine-like sounds of delight and approval. And on the appointed day Jacobins carried 'Bijah triumphantly, hailing him as a martyr and "pris'ner elect."

But Federalists turned even this triumph into a ridiculous rout. At the height of the celebration the sheriff arrived, bringing law to the town and fright and dismay to the Ja-

---

[150] Perhaps Benjamin Curtis, Jr. a Boston Jacobin known as "Honestus." See Charles Evans, *American Bibliography*, for a number of conjectural identifications.

cobins: 'Bijah "skipt" from his throne and the assembly fled far from sight, to renew their feasting and singing in realms no verse recounted, no muse inspired.[151] So ended the liveliest attack of the time on Jacobin political activity, based on the image of the Infernal Council.

The allegiance of Republicans to France, and, in Federalist eyes, their martyr complex, their specious arguments for freedom, their subversion of established laws, and their love of demonstration to forward political aims all were there—characteristics and maneuvers Federalists made appear unquestionably evil, even as the archetype of such activities in Satan had been evil, but ridiculous too, since both Adams and Satan had rebelled against an order established by God. Seldom had Federalists laughed so heartily at their Republican foes.

As the country moved into the bitter disputes of the new century, Milton's symbols and imagery served to affix labels on political figures, living and dead. John S. J. Gardiner had already employed such a tactic to smear the character of Jefferson. The Vice President, he had said, displayed the same cowardice and fear that Satan's "Infernal Majesty" had shown in *Paradise Lost*.[152] Now John Thomson arose to attack John Marshall's positions on the Alien and Sedition Acts. Marshall had risen to power, Thomson implied, in ways that could only be described as Satanic. His "boldness and ability" in defending "the most reprehensible measures of the federal government," his energetic, zealous, and violent efforts to create a monarchy or an aristocracy from the ruins of the Republic had brought him to his present "bad eminence." [153]

---

[151] *The Demos in Council; Or 'Bijah in Pandemonium, passim.*

[152] *Remarks on the Jacobiniad: Revised and Corrected by the Author,* Part Second, "Dedication." Reminiscences of Milton appear through a good part of this work.

[153] *The Letters of Curtius, Written by the Late John Thomson of Petersburg* (Richmond, 1804), Letter I, p. 1.

But if symbols of evil could condemn, symbols of good could exalt. Because he had refused a political bribe in New York, thereby showing himself to be a man of "integrity" and "honour," *The Examiner* called Ruggles Hubbard a faithful Abdiel.[154] Because he possessed a "variety and versatility" of talents, allowing him to exercise extraordinary powers of management, the *Boston Repertory* likened Alexander Hamilton to Milton's God.[155]

To present George Washington as the most commanding figure the country had known Americans likened him to both Abdiel and God. Richard H. Dana saw him possessed of intelligence and of indomitable courage, standing, like Abdiel among powerful enemies,

> Unshaken, unseduced, unterrified.
> Nor number, nor example with him wrought
> To swerve from truth, or change his constant mind.[156]

Such a granite-like figure reminded Elijah H. Mills of Milton's description of God as He created the world. Washington's imperviousness to popular clamor, Mills proclaimed in a famous Fourth of July oration—his power to halt the "progress of faction" and to save the "country from the horrors of war" during his tenure as President merited a comparison with what God had wrought. Washington also had ruled the "wild uproar"; he also had stamped confusion and chaos with order.[157] Washington was a man of such stature declared Isaac Bates that, when Edmund Randolph tried to incriminate him, he could only look away from so exalted a figure and stand

---

[154] *The Examiner*, III, no. 20 (March 18, 1815), 421.

[155] William Coleman, *A Collection of the Facts and Documents, Relative to the Death of Major-General Alexander Hamilton* (New York, 1804), pp. 231–232, in a sketch taken from the *Boston Repertory*, presumably written by Fisher Ames.

[156] *An Oration, Delivered Before the Washington Benevolent Society at Cambridge* (Cambridge, 1814), p. 16.

[157] *An Oration Pronounced at Northampton* (Northampton, 1813), pp. 7–8.

abashed, seeing how "awful goodness is" and "Virtue in her shape how lovely." [158] Through Miltonic symbols the Father of his Country had already begun to assume the image of greatness that history has so firmly secured.

But politicians turned more often to Milton for symbols to blacken political foes. In 1804 *The Corrector* presented through two consecutive issues a "PANDAEMONIAN GALLERY" of "ORIGINAL PICTURES" by "*American artists*," a collection of political portraits designed to sway public opinion following Jefferson's election as President. The idea for such a collection probably sprang from the opening of a Milton gallery in London in 1799 to show Henry Fuseli's illustrations of *Paradise Lost*.[159] But however inspired, the gallery appearing in *The Corrector* served a political purpose. DeWitt Clinton was on the political rise, after a series of appointments that earned him the reputation of fathering the spoils system in New York; [160] and the English-born journalist James Cheetham not only supported Clinton's positions but had attacked Aaron Burr, whose duel with Hamilton was only a few months away. The central position of New York in national politics shortly after Jefferson took office focused attention on such politicians, whose party affiliations, though chiefly Republican, remained as flexible as expedience demanded.

[158] *An Oration, Pronounced Before the Washington Benevolent Society of the County of Hampshire, on their First Anniversary, 1812* (Northampton, [1812]), pp. 18–19.

[159] See *The Repository and Ladies' Weekly Museum*, VI, no. 15 (March 29, 1806), 113–114, for a comment on the 1799 showing and on the 1805 revival. See also Peter Bayley, *Poems* (Philadelphia, 1804), p. 27. Here, in "An Apology for Writing," Bayley said:

> Lo! where soars Fuseli, through realms of light
> Darting with ardent glance his piercing sight;
> On high he rides: terror around him flings,
> And visits scenes that Milton only sings.

[160] See Howard Lee McBain, *DeWitt Clinton and the Origin of the Spoils System in New York* (Columbia University, 1907), for a partial vindication of Clinton.

But if conspiracy and shifts in allegiance characterized the political scene in New York, one fact was clear: Clinton's skill as a politician secured him in office and made him a prime target of personal abuse, particularly among Federalists, who became more frantic as their plans to regain power repeatedly failed. To give a new twist to an old tactic *The Corrector* hit on the device of having each enemy sketch his own portrait from *Paradise Lost*. Number I of the series, for example, was a "superb painting of the Arch Fiend, seated upon his royal throne at the opening of the Council," drawn by the "youthful hand and promising pencil" of DeWitt Clinton. The picture itself simply reproduced lines from *Paradise Lost*, so presented as to be interpreted in the context of Clinton's own political career.

In this context Satan's words spoke unequivocally. Clinton himself had secured office not by merit but by fraud and deceit; his portrait revealed him not as a promoter of public good, as was argued, but as a politician of the worst sort, feeding his own pride and power. But even Milton's portrait of Satan failed to reveal the fullness of Clinton's wickedness or the depth of his guile. Clinton might be "deficient in *spirit* and in majesty" to Satan, but opinion agreed that in his expression, he "excelled, if possible, the malignancy of the devil himself." [161] Even the image of the Father of Lies could not describe all that Clinton had done.

James Cheetham fared even worse. As a "foreign artist of great notoriety," *The Corrector* explained, Cheetham painted a portrait of the "serpent biting the heel of woman's seed," that is, the picture of Sin at the end of Book II of *Paradise Lost*. *The Corrector* thus presented Cheetham as the serpent armed with "mortal sting," the grisly offspring of Satan, around whose middle hell hounds unceasingly barked—in short the journalist creature of Clinton who vexed the land

---

[161] *The Corrector* (April 14, 1804), no. 6, p. 22, picture 1.

with the hideous noise of his brood.[162] Such an image should have been sufficient to stigmatize the alleged activities of both Cheetham and Clinton, but *The Corrector* had not yet completed its task.

Far down the corridor appeared the portrait of Nisroch, the defiant "prime" Principality who in the midst of angelic warfare Milton presented as calling for new weapons to vanquish the foe. This, *The Corrector* declared, James Cheetham had claimed as his own; but "connoisseurs" had pretended to find in it "many strokes of the sublimely horrid pencil" of DeWitt Clinton himself, implying that the picture was a joint venture.[163] In this manner the Pandaemonian Gallery blackened the characters of New York politicians: some appeared as Moloch and Belial, or as Mammon and Beelzebub; others as Satan in his many disguises and forms. Whether such portraits accurately described the accused mattered little: they hung on public figures all the crimes their archetypes had displayed, precisely as *The Corrector* intended. By 1804 symbols from *Paradise Lost* had become weapons *par excellence* in disputes of the day.

Such weapons remained handy as events moved toward the War of 1812. As President, Jefferson aroused such bitterness in the Federalist camp that only Satan seemed sufficiently evil to describe his character and his activities in office. John Pierpont accused Jefferson of being a dupe of Satan's devious ways, even as conservatives in America now tar liberals with the Communist stick by calling them unwitting tools of the Kremlin. During his tenure as President Jefferson allowed Jacobinism to cover America like a cloud, Pierpont explained —a covering comparable to the mist that concealed Satan as he slipped by Urial's guard into Eden. "No wonder *jacobinism* should elude the utmost efforts of human sagacity." Not "even

---

[162] *ibid.*, picture 5.
[163] *ibid.* (April 21, 1804), no. 8, p. 31, picture 11.

the keenness of angelic vision could detect, till too late, the movements of its great archetype." How could Americans, then, have been expected to uncover the evil designs of the Republican Party? For as Satan through subterfuge had entered Eden and seduced Adam and Eve, so Jefferson under the cover of Jacobin guile had brought his country's honor to an early grave.[164]

Charles Prentiss attacked Jefferson much more directly. Jefferson was, he said, a very Satan himself, a figure like Milton's Fallen Angel filled with "obdurate pride" and "steadfast hate," a President casting about his "baleful eyes" as he dismissed Washington's wise councillors and chose his own devilish advisors.[165] Even the Louisiana Purchase allowed Elijah H. Mills to blacken Jefferson's name. He likened that vast territory to Milton's picture of the outskirts of Hell, a waste of dark and dreary vales, of "Rocks, caves, lakes, fens, bogs, dens, and shades of death"—by extension the property of Satan himself, purchased at the expense of a friend.[166] Most of Jefferson's accomplishments, to Federalists at least, matched the evil of the Enemy of Mankind, an image that history has failed to sustain.

From the vantage point of the end of the period Mathew Carey looked back and saw that politicians had pressed such tactics too far. As a leading publisher in the early Republic, he observed that exaggeration, without laughter, could defeat its own purpose.[167] With hardly an exception, he said, Federalists and Republicans had made their own partisans "all angels of light" and their opponents "demons incarnate." The

[164] *The Portrait. A Poem Delivered Before the Washington Benevolent Society* (Boston, 1812), pp. 24–25 and note.

[165] *New England Freedom: A Poem Delivered Before the Washington Benevolent Society* (Brookfield, 1813), pp. 9–10; 23 and note.

[166] *An Oration Pronounced at Northampton*, pp. 10–11.

[167] See James Playsted Wood, *Magazines in the United States* (New York, 1949), pp. 19–27, for the importance of Carey in early American journalism.

one became "all beauty, with little resemblance to the pretended original"; the "other a hideous caricature, equally foreign from honour, truth, and justice." [168] Carey failed to record whether Milton should bear some of the blame for such tactics, but he well could have done so. For some of the portraits of key figures owed much of their evil or good to the imagery of *Paradise Lost*.

But if politicians erred in presenting their friends and foes as good or evil incarnate, they made no mistake in their efforts to paint the French Revolution as a drunken orgy of blood, followed by the blight of Napoleon. Even American Jacobins, though still loyal to the ideals of French freedom, felt uneasy as Napoleon locked the Continent in the iron grip of his might; and New England Federalists became so alarmed at the Government's neutrality that a few conspired to secede from the Union. An America still divided over policies toward France called for a rigorous campaign to reveal the Revolution in its bloody reality; and to do so politicians turned to the imagery and symbols of *Paradise Lost*.

As already noted, Federalists had long attached to Jacobin Clubs the image of the Infernal Council. Edmund Burke had employed a similar tactic in his parliamentary address against the French Constitution of 1788 when he damned that document with a quotation from Milton's picture of Death—a maneuver, *The Port Folio* implied, particularly appropriate to the occasion.[169] Such a maneuver seemed so appropriate that Federalists ransacked *Paradise Lost* for imagery to paint the French Revolution in its actual colors, a procedure that often

---

[168] *The Olive Branch: Or Faults on Both Sides, Federal and Democratic* (2nd edn., Philadelphia, 1815), p. 21. *The Columbian Phenix and Boston Review* (January 1800), pp. 36–37, had presented the same view, with a further comment on the power of a free press.

[169] *The Port Folio*, VI, no. 6, New Series (December 1811), 616. In *The Monthly Anthology and Boston Review*, IX (July 1810), 19 an essay entitled "Burke-Milton" had recalled how Burke had recited the speeches of Moloch and Belial at a meeting of a Dublin literary society.

called for a contrasting view of their own revolutionary struggle, which they wished to dissociate from events on the Continent.

John Lowell of Boston had drawn such a distinction, declared a reviewer of Lowell's Fourth of July oration for 1799:
the French Revolution had invited him to contrast the two
recent struggles for freedom, particularly since some circles
confused them. But the reviewer thought Lowell had pictured
the evils of the French Revolution too loosely; and to sharpen
the image he turned to the "sublime and forcible language"
of Milton for an appropriate comparison, which he found in
the vision of the outskirts of Hell. There, Milton had said,
dwelt

> Perverse, all monstrous, all prodigious things,
> Abominable, inutterable, and worse
> Than fables yet have feigned, or fear conceived,
> Gorgons, and hydras, and chimeras dire.[170]

Such a vision alone could contrast the hell of France to
heavenly America. To reveal the evils of France by reference
to Milton's description of Hell became commonplace among
politicians of the early republic. As Zechariah Lewis declared,
with the Revolution Satan erected his empire in France; her
"atheists" wrote on their standard the cry of Old Anarch:
"HAVOC, AND SPOIL, AND RUIN ARE OUR
GAIN."[171] But no one maneuvered Milton's symbols more
skillfully than Tristam Burges, who invoked the image of
Sin to explain to the good people of Providence the seductive
evil of France. When the Revolution first presented its al-
lurement of freedom, he said, she seemed like a "woman to

---

[170] *The Monthy Magazine and American Review*, I, no. 5 (August
1799), 373–375.
[171] *An Oration, on the Apparent, and the Real Political Situation of the
United States, Pronounced before the Connecticut Society of Cincinnati,
Assembled, At New-Haven, For the Celebration of American Independence,
July the 4th, 1799* (New Haven, 1799), p. 23.

the waist, and fair." But such was an illusion. In reality French freedom was like "Milton's Portress of Hell Gate,"

> foul in many a scaly fold,
> Voluminous and vast; a serpent arm'd
> With mortal sting,—

a serpent that "would have coiled" America within its "contaminating embrace," had not Washington declared neutrality.[172]

No wonder James Burnet cried out in the meeting house in Weston that French freedom was poisonous. "If you set a value upon your liberty, if you have any regard for your families, if you wish for the promotion of Christianity, if you have any reverence for your Saviour and your God," he exclaimed, "resolve to oppose the intrigues and encroachments of the French nation and flash your vengeance like the forked lightning, on those enemies of man, for in Frenchmen is concentrated every enormity." Burnet failed to enliven this particular cry with Miltonic imagery, but he envisioned the pollution of American women "by the deadly contagion" of France as comparable to Eve's Fall from innocence.[173] William Hunter's assertion that not even Milton's imagination was "bold and wild enough to realize any analogy of a French revolution" proved to be completely erroneous.[174] Federalists found *Paradise Lost* a mine of apt phrase and sentiment: no other one source furnished more appropriate scenes or more powerful symbols in their campaign to turn Americans against France.

As Napoleon's ambition inexorably moved the armies of

---

[172] *Liberty, Glory and Union, or American Independence* (Providence, [1810]), p. 16.

[173] *An Oration, Delivered on the Fourth of July, 1799* (Newfield, [1799]), pp. 17–18.

[174] *An Oration; Delivered in Trinity-Church, in Newport, on the Fourth of July, 1801* (Newport, 1801), p. 13. Hunter had found unsatisfactory Milton's image of the comet, shaking from its hair pestilence and war.

Europe toward Waterloo, Federalists stepped up their campaign of denigration. If the Revolution had turned France into the Devil's domain, they reasoned, Napoleon himself could be pictured as Satan. Such propaganda was the logical climax of a campaign Federalists had presented to the American people for more than two decades. William Cobbett, for example, had described the first National Assembly of the Revolution as a collection of demagogues, who by definition made their motto Satan's defiant pronouncement "rather reign in hell than serve in heaven"; [175] and Ezra Sampson had presented Marat as Napoleon was to appear later, as Milton's horribly grinning, ghastly Death.[176] As Napoleon tightened his grip on the countries of Europe, Federalists culminated their attack on revolutionary France by picturing the Continent as a vast scene of horror and death, a territory of flame and desolation, ruled by the Prince of Darkness himself.

Such was the tactic of Andrew Bigelow in an address before the Washington Benevolent Society. "Amidst the universal dismay" of Europe, he said, "a gigantic form, mantled in every terrour, arose on the bewildered view; and, like Milton's Satan, strode resistless along the flaming waste. Of boundless ambition, he grasped at universal empire; of daring impiety, proudly 'shook his hand against the mount of the Daughter of Zion.' " [177]

Out of his pride and ambition Napoleon, like Satan, soon met defeat. To celebrate the triumph of good, Josiah Dunham not only recalled reasons for the holocaust in Europe but presented Napoleon as Satan, soliloquizing over his fall.

---

[175] *The Bloody Buoy, Thrown out as a Warning to the Political Pilots of America* (2nd edn., Philadelphia, 1796), pp. 215–216.

[176] *The Sham-Patriot Unmasked: or, An exposition of the Fatally Successful Arts of Demagogues, To Exalt Themselves, By Flattering and Swindling the People* (Concord, 1805), p. 8; and Thomas G. Fessenden, *Pills, Poetical, Political, and Philosophical* (Philadelphia, 1809), pp. 91–93.

[177] *An Oration, Delivered Before the Washington Benevolent Society at Cambridge, July 4, 1815* (Cambridge, 1815), p. 8.

Jacobinism—"the fiend of society" and "the foulest enemy of the human race"—had brought on the reign of terror, he declared. Jacobinism—"Fierce as ten furies" and "terrible as Hell"—had pronounced government a tyranny and religion a mummery, had turned the temples of Jehovah into temples of Venus and houses of prayer into dens of revolutionary thieves. What then, Dunham asked, must be the thoughts of Napoleon, could he be viewed as his conscience waked him to despair? You could behold a wretch stung even to agony, he declared; you might even hear him lament in Satan's own words:

> Me miserable! which way shall I fly
> Infinite wrath, and infinite despair?
> Which way I fly is Hell: myself am Hell!
>
> .    .    .    .    .    .    .
>
> With diadem and sceptre high advanced,
> The lower still I fall, only supreme
> In misery! *Such joy ambition finds!* [178]

As a parting shot, Dunham wondered whether Madison, who Napoleon had said was his friend, would partake of the same feeling should he be given the same leisure time to reflect; but such a thought only passed through his mind. Dunham's main aim was to show through the Satanic figure of Napoleon the evils of the French Revolution, to reveal to the American people through images they all understood the inherent peril of friendship with France.

At the close of the period James H. Price revealed in a

---

[178] *An Oration Delivered at Hanover, in the Vicinity of Dartmouth College, Before the Several Washington Benevolent Societies of Hanover, Lebanon, Lime, Norwich, and Hartford, on the Thirty Eighth Anniversary of American Independence; And in Commemoration of the Great Events in Europe, Which Have Terminated so Honorably to the Allied Arms, and So Triumphantly Glorious to the Cause of Humanity* (Hanover, 1814), pp. 14, 22–23. See also *The Port Folio*, III, no. 3, New Series (March 1810), 195, for a comment on Napoleon with reference to Milton.

satirical poem depicting a Fourth of July celebration how habitually Americans had made *Paradise Lost* speak to disputes of the day. In a foreword, he explained that a number of patriots had "ransacked" Milton's poem "from its centre to its circumference" to embellish some sixty or seventy toasts drunk in honor of American independence. Now and then these patriots had "culled" a *"rose"* from "that great parterre of flowers, to be offered up as incense to the nostrils of Federalism." Here and there they had "carefully selected" a *"thorn"* from its "ample shrubbery to wound the bare and bleeding toes of stubborn and incorrigible democracy." The appearance of these toasts in the *Troy Gazette,* as well as the sentiments they expressed, inspired him to write a rollicking poem upon the occasion.

The poem itself related the main events which had made that patriotic day memorable. What struck him at once was that *Paradise Lost* had furnished so many people with such appropriate sentiments that he wished Milton himself could have been in attendance to hear lisping maids and youths, matrons and graybearded men, reciting wise sayings from this his greatest of poems. Of particular interest would have been the sight of an elderly Federalist peeping into its pages, only to find such a "striking resemblance" between "Milton's Devils" and "some leading Republicans" that he fell to the floor senseless, unable to utter more than "Da a-a-mn Je-e-efferson." [179]

Here was a double irony indeed. An architect of the Revolution, who had called on Milton to support religious freedom, was now being damned through the imagery of *Paradise Lost.* And Milton himself, a publicized witness of the revolutionary tradition, was now being invoked to testify in conservative causes. Such ironies, however, rather than arguing that Milton possessed two political faces—a radical one in his

[179] *Miscellany, in Verse and Prose* (Albany, 1813), pp. 71–75.

youth, a conservative one in old age—simply suggest that the fable of *Paradise Lost* had become well enough known in the early Republic to serve as an archetype of human affairs. Its transcendent personages and scenes could now evaluate any historical event, from attempts at political bribery in New York through the presidential activities of Washington, Jefferson, and Madison to the great sweep of the French Revolution and the Napoleonic Wars. Americans had turned Milton's epic into a measuring rod to read and assess political life of the times.

## V

One measure of the print Milton left on poetry of the early Republic lies in the abundance of political verse just examined. The imagery of *Paradise Lost* moved through a large body of satire and parody, sometimes illuminating a single stanza or line, sometimes governing the structure of a whole poem. But beyond such occasional verse lay an even larger body of belles lettres directed more to the poetic than to the political community. Much of it appeared in weekly or monthly journals; some, in slender volumes signed by names now unknown or forgotten. Such poetry reveals that the Revolutionary enthusiasm to create a great national literature had somewhat subsided, though Timothy Dwight still labored up Parnassus in *Greenfield Hill* and Joel Barlow painstakingly reshaped his earlier epic into *The Columbiad*.[180] But if the urge to write a national poem comparable in aim to the *Aeneid* had waned, such a diminution failed to lessen the flow of American verse. As John T. Cooper observed, "insaniæ severiores" covered the land as "Thick as Autumnal leaves that strow the brooks/ In Vallombrosa," most of which

---

[180] Leon Howard (*The Connecticut Wits*, p. 229) heard a few echoes of Milton in the fifth part of *Greenfield Hill*.

were of the "most barren fertility." [181] For the low state of poetry at this time many reasons could be offered, the most obvious being the absence of talent and genius, but some of the blame rests on admirers of Milton.[182] Dangers of Miltonic imitation evident as early as Mather Byles and William Livingston now appeared everywhere.

One danger lay in incorporating Milton's phrases and lines into the context of a serious poem. John Trumbull had successfully used imagery from *Paradise Lost* to satirize political activities of Tories and Whigs: the grandeur of Milton's pictures had rendered by contrast some of the action of *M'Fingal* ridiculous. But in a serious work, or in one not meant to be risible, Milton's lines had to be worked in with considerable care, or the weight of the original would overpower the poem or blur its intention. No one would object to John Pitman's including "With loss of Eden" in a poem on the progress of society,[183] or to Paul Allen's assessing Shakespeare as "Fancy's darling child" who "warbled forth his wood-notes wild" in a verse upon taste.[184] Such lines merely indicate, along with John Shaw's *"light fantastic toe,"* [185] Richard Snowden's "Say, heav'nly muse," [186] and John Woodworth's *"horribly he grinn'd a ghastly smile"* [187] how indelibly Milton's phrases had printed themselves on the minds of American poets.

---

[181] *An Oration, and Poem, Delivered before the Government and Students of Harvard University, at the Departure of the Senior Class, July 31, 1811* (Cambridge, 1811), pp. 10–11.

[182] See Tunis Wortman, *A Treatise, Concerning Political Enquiry, and the Liberty of the Press* (New York, 1800), pp. 61–65, for a comment upon the extraordinary requirements of genius in imitating epic poetry.

[183] *A Poem on the Social State and its Future Progress* (Providence, [1811]), p. 7.

[184] *Original Poems, Serious and Entertaining* (Salem, 1801), p. 133.

[185] *Poems by the Late Doctor John Shaw* (Baltimore, 1810), p. 130.

[186] *The Columbiad: Or A Poem on the American War* (Philadelphia, 1795), opening lines.

[187] *The Spunkiad: Or Heroism Improved* (Newburgh, 1798), p. 21.

But Catharine Weller's incorporation of Milton's "Sweet is the breath of morn" into the first line of her poem on *The Sabbath* presents a problem in poetic decorum. Catharine Weller sought to picture the triumph of Christ on the morn of His resurrection, "that morn most sweet/ Which saw its conquering Lord rise." In an attempt to make her image impressive she opened her scene with Eve's answer to Adam in Book IV of *Paradise Lost*, where Eve had confessed to her consort her enjoyment in his daily companionship.[188] Milton's line recalls and in itself expresses a perceptive enjoyment of nature, the sort so charmingly portrayed at even greater length in *L'Allegro*. But in the context of a religious poem on the central event in the Christian story it elicits the wrong sentiment, making the whole stanza seem discordant and strained.

Nathaniel L. Frothingham encountered a similar difficulty in his song celebrating the departure of the senior class from Harvard University. Frothingham hoped to dignify the occasion by likening departing students to Adam and Eve's expulsion from Eden, a scene in *Paradise Lost* heavy with tragedy yet cheered with the hope of mankind's future redemption. Memories of Adam and Eve's solemn departure from Paradise failed to enhance the song Frothingham had composed for his classmates, as a glance at its concluding stanza will show:

> We'll onward then undaunted,
> And every toil deride;
> For 'the world is all before us' spread,
> 'And providence our guide.'
> With virtue's purest pleasures blest,
> With love and friendship's glow;
> We'll disdain to complain,

---

[188] *The Medley* (New York, 1810), p. 90. In another poem, "Address to Peace," Catharine Weller works the vision of Death, "grinning horribly," into her argument.

Though the storms of life may flow,
Though the clouds of grief may veil our joys,
And the storms of life may blow.[189]

As the strains of this song died away a perceptive few in the audience must have smiled. The lilt of the lines, combined with a recollection of Milton's solemn occasion, presents an incongruity that must have overwhelmed the risibilities of even tolerant relatives and friends. Who would wish to think of a commencement in terms of an expulsion, however bright the future might be?

Incorporation of Milton's lines into verse of the day reached a height of absurdity in the ubiquitous American almanac. Occasionally these annuals printed original poems—dismal compositions of doggerel interlaced with well-known lines or images excerpted from Milton, or from Thomson or Young or Gray. *The Wilmington Almanac*, for example, began *Lines Written by A Young Man, After He was Seized With a Consumption* with a phrase from Milton's famous lament on his blindness in the introduction to Book III of *Paradise Lost*. This moving lament, so expressive of bitter loss and of resignation to Providence, became worse than incongruous in its new context of physical illness:

> Now spring returns: but not to me returns
> The vernal joy my better years have known:
> Dim in my breast life's dying taper burns,
> And all the joys of life with health are flown.[190]

But no one committed a greater offense against poetry than Archable Gibson, who combined in a number of verses most of the Miltonic infelicities of the age. Desirous of exalting his

---

[189] Frothingham's song was printed at the conclusion of *An Oration, and Poem, Delivered before the Government and Students of Harvard University, at the Departure of the Senior Class, July 31, 1811.* It was sung to the tune of "Ye Mariners of England."

[190] *The Wilmington Almanac, or Ephemeris, For the Year of Our Lord 1794,* Sig. [D3].

lucubrations on the seasons and weather, he changed the blank verse of *Paradise Lost* into heroic couplets, sometimes paraphrasing a whole section of that poem into lines of incredible stupidity. Altogether, he incorporated Milton's language into four of his efforts, drawing from Adam and Eve's morning hymn, the famous night scene in Book IV, and Raphael's answer to Adam on forbidden knowledge in Book VIII. The first two couplets from his effusions for July 1–10, 1794, will illustrate the puerile nature of his accomplishment:

> To give both life and breath to all that live,
> First day and then the night alternative,
> Solicit not thy thoughts with matters hid,
> Leave them to God alone, him serve and fear.[191]

A worse quatrain than this would be difficult to find in the whole range of literature. At the very least Frothingham worked Milton's lines into an intelligible syntactical structure, however incongruous its elements. Gibson could not even mesh Milton's words with his own.

Yet American poets persisted in embellishing their lines with well-known phrases from Milton, or in announcing the source of their imagery in notes to their texts. They apparently believed they could enhance their poetry not simply by making his language their own, but also by revealing the name of the man from whom they had drawn. Such a practice allowed them to establish a connection with the great Milton himself, a relation that proclaimed their fitness as poets, as well as their discrimination in taste. Thus in his commencement poem on *The Present State of Literature* Warren Dutton explained that his phrase "Awake, arise!" had originated in Milton.[192]

---

[191] *An Almanack, For the Year of our Lord 1812.* April 15–23, June 16–30, July 1–10, and November 8–30.

[192] *The Present State of Literature; A Poem, Delivered in New-Haven, at the Public Commencement of Yale-College, September 10, 1800* (Hartford, 1800), p. 10 and note.

In like manner, R. H. Rose glossed his use of "light mantle" in a description of night with a reference to a phrase in Milton's picture of evening in Book IV of *Paradise Lost*.[193] The practice of glossing phrases and lines became so commonplace among poets of the early Republic [194] that Charles Prentiss filled his edition of Robert Treat Paine with notes calling attention to earlier authors, among whom Milton was one of the most prominent. Paine himself never achieved lasting greatness. A satirist of some skill, eccentric in manner and facile in versification, he became famous for a while through his popular *Adams and Liberty* and was considered by his contemporaries a genius. Affiliation with Milton, Charles Prentiss must have thought, would consolidate Paine's position, heighten his fame, and place him squarely in a great poetic tradition. If reference to Milton failed to secure Paine among the immortals, the fault lies in Paine's verse, not in Prentiss' editorial activity.

For Prentiss commented at length on Paine's debt to Milton in notes to his text. On an untitled poem reminiscent of Milton's descriptions of nature, for example, he observed: "The whole paragraph is not inelegantly imitated from several passages of the Paradise Lost. It shews that Milton was among the authors, with whom Mr. Paine was early conversant." Sometimes Prentiss limited himself to reminiscence alone, as in the suggestion that Paine's stanza describing zephers laden with rich perfumes came from Milton's depiction of "gentle gales/ Fanning their odoriferous wings." Sometimes he was sharply critical, as in his comment that Paine's ear "was but little enamoured of the full and stately harmony of Milton's rhythm." A casual reading of Paine's redaction

---

[193] *Sketches in Verse* (Philadelphia, 1810), pp. 11–13 and note. His editor, Joseph Dennie, could have made the gloss.

[194] See, for example, *The Untaught Bard: An Original Work* (New York, 1804), p. 24n. and *The Port Folio*, VI, no. 1, New Series (July 1811), 18.

of Adam and Eve's morning hymn to the Creator, one of his obvious borrowings from *Paradise Lost*, confirms such a judgment:

> These are thy wonders, great Jehovah; these,
> As all their various orbits they perform,
> Speak forth thy majesty and endless praise.
> The mighty pillars of the universe,
> The etherial arch, with starry curtains hung,
> Thy hands have made; through the stupendous frame
> Loud hallelujahs and hosannas sound,
> Wafting thy glory to unnumbered worlds,
> In Nature's language, understood by all.[195]

Of importance here is neither Paine's poor imitation nor Prentiss' judgment but the practice of glossing Miltonic echoes. Milton had become by this time such a power in the poetic community that authors and editors alike felt compelled to defer to his greatness in notes to the text. Such a practice verified their literacy, confirming in the public mind their own great good taste, as well as their right to be heard. Attempts to reach Milton's heights was now no more important than affiliation with the great man himself.

Yet several poets still tried to improve their effusions by direct imitation of his language and subjects. Few paid much attention to John Blair Linn's caveat that to follow Homer or Milton could stifle original genius.[196] Most cherished Thomas Dermody's observation that Milton was "nearly a pattern of perfection." [197] To say that many writers of the time wished to "sweep the string" in the manner of Milton, as a poet in *The Port Folio* implied, would not be far from the truth.[198]

Such a desire led Richard B. Davis to "versify" Eve's love

---

[195] *The Works, in Verse and Prose, of the Late Robert Treat Paine, Jun. Esq. With Notes* (Boston, 1812), pp. 7–14, 425–427.

[196] See *supra*, Chapter I, Section III.

[197] See *supra*, Chapter I, Section III.

[198] *The Port Folio*, VI, no. 13, New Series (September 24, 1808), p. 208, under "Original Poetry."

song to Adam and nature in Book IV of *Paradise Lost;* [199] and
periodicals and fugitive volumes published poems with titles
such as "Eve Upon Leaving Paradise," "Heaven's Last Best
Gift," and "The Test," the last being a verse on Eve's Fall.[200]
Yet as popular as Milton's Eve was, both as a model of wifely
perfection and as a subject for verse, she inspired fewer poetic
efforts than *L'Allegro* and *Il Penseroso.* Esteemed by Blair
in his *Rhetoric* and by Knox in his catechetical lessons,[201]
these poems now fixed the expression of mood into inflexible
patterns of language and structure. As James Fennell exclaimed in his *apologia:* "I am the slave of feeling—sometimes
*l'Allegro*—sometimes *Il Penseroso.*" [202] To describe the joys
of mirth or the satisfactions of melancholy through any other
form would insult the literary taste of the time.

Slaves either to feeling or to patterns of verse would not
be likely to produce poetry of a very high order. Hopkinson
had earlier shown considerably more skill in his adaptations of
Milton's twin poems, and Philip Freneau, in *The Power of
Fancy,* excelled every effort at imitation either before or after
his time. Imitations of *L'Allegro* and *Il Penseroso* in the early
Republic are important not because they are intrinsically good,
but because they show, by their numbers and forms, the dangers of freezing a mood into patterns unsuited to divergent
motivations and aims. Consider, for example, Richard H.
Townsend's untitled imitation of *L'Allegro,* one of the best
to appear during the period. Following typical imitative prac-

---

[199] *Poems by Richard B. Davis* (New York, 1807), pp. 94–95. This
poem had appeared earlier in *The New York Magazine Or Literary
Repository* (June 1795), pp. 377–378.

[200] See, for example, *The Weekly Monitor,* I, no. 13 (September 8,
1804), 52; *The Weekly Museum,* VIII, no. 373 (July 4, 1795); and Henry
C. Knight, *The Cypriad in Two Cantos: With Other Poems and Translations* (Boston, 1809), pp. [31]–34.

[201] *A Compendious System of Rhetoric,* p. 66.

[202] *An Apology for the Life of James Fennell* (Philadelphia, 1814),
p. 34.

tice of the day, Townsend avoided Milton's intricate introductory rhyme scheme, casting his whole poem into tetrameter
couplets; but from the opening line to the concluding sentiment the presence of *L'Allegro* is everywhere evident. Milton's allusive and heavily imaged injunction, Townsend
turned into a simple plea that melancholy depart so that he
could be gay:

> Now I'm much in love with Folly,
> Leave me, leave me Melancholy!
> Hie thee to some dismal cell,
> And with blackest midnight dwell;
> There, to bitterest notes of woe,
> Let thine eyes forever flow—
> Hence! and leave me to be gay,
> For thou shalt no longer stay.

Here, all vigor and drama of the original have vanished—all
the horrid dreams and shapes engendered by melancholy,
which by contrast in Milton's poem rendered the appearance
of Mirth so light and attractive. Only the language remains,
and the thought—husks so dry that words no longer function
responsibly. For Townsend had not fallen in love with Folly,
as he said; or at least not with the Folly mentioned in the
introductory lines of *Il Penseroso:* he had asked for the companionship of *gaiety*, a quite different thing.

As Townsend developed his thought his dependence and
barrenness become even more evident. Milton's invitation to
Mirth, and all his images of a happy day in the country,
Townsend condensed into a few banal lines:

> Come, sweet laughter-loving power!
> Lead a votary to thy bower,
> Lead, O! lead me on the way,
> Happy, merry, blithe and gay!
>
> Over beds of fragrant roses,
> Where young joy with love reposes;

> Whilst with dance and sprightly song,
> Paphia leads the hours along!—

Skipping Milton's haunting vision of night, with its lantern light and tapers clear, Townsend hurried his journey to an abrupt conclusion, reminiscently saying that Mirth had brought him such charms that he would choose to follow her.

> Now I taste, I feel thy charms!
> O! what bliss my bosom warms!
> Lead, and I will follow thee,
> Wild as thou art, and as free.[203]

Such was typical of Milton's impress on mood poetry at the turn of the century, though some of it presented more sprightly individual lines.[204] No genuine feeling moved through Townsend's adventure with Mirth, no serious attempt to assess a significant mode of experience motivated his poem. All was hackneyed; all was patterned. The iron mold of *L'Allegro* had shaped all Townsend could say.

The mold of *Il Penseroso* shaped the poetry of melancholy with the same definitive power. Scarcely a poem on that topic could forego a contrast with Mirth, or omit scenes reminiscent of Milton's bowers and halls, brightly tapered or religiously dim. *The Port Folio*, for example, boasted that one such poem —*Address to Melancholy*—presented the "best" description of that "goddess, sage and holy" that had appeared since the time of Burton. The allusion to Milton was accurate, however untrue the boast; for the poem simply unfolded a variation of scenes within Milton's general frame. The poet asked that

---

[203] *Original Poems, by A Citizen of Baltimore* (Baltimore, 1809), pp. 124–125.

[204] See, for instance, Samuel Blauvelt, *Fashion's Analysis: Or, The Winter in Town* (New York, 1807), pp. 19–20; Richard Beresford, *Nugæ Canoræ; Consisting of a Few Minor Poems* (Charleston, 1797), pp. 22–23; *The Connecticut Magazine, and Gentleman's and Lady's Monthly Museum*, I, no. 3 (March, 1801), 173; and *Keatinge's Washington Almanac, For the Year of Our Lord 1806* (Baltimore).

Mirth be removed from his sight, that her "gaudy form" stay away from his path; then he invoked "meek-ey'd Melancholy" to lead him far from the "resort" of "folly." The course of his journey with Melancholy took him past lofty castles and halls, ringing loud with merriment and song; some scenes echoed *L'Allegro,* some *Il Penseroso:*

> Lo! the gilded ceilings shine
> With many a taper blazing bright,
> While the gorgeous train advance,
> Mingling in the measur'd dance,
> And mirth, and laughter, and delight
> Bid the festal bliss abound,
> And the joyous song resound.[205]

Soon the path led to a forest, choired with birds and studded with oaks, and from here his steps moved to the graveyard itself. The journey ended, the poet paused to reflect, invoking Melancholy for guidance and help: he would learn from her, as Milton had learned,

> how to prize aright
> The fleeting objects of delight.

Milton's image of a journey through life with the guidance of Melancholy governed a similar poem in a later issue of *The Port Folio.* Here, the poet hailed the "lonely goddess of the midnight gloom"; here, he "fled each thought of noisy Folly." And as he viewed the tribulations of life—its sorrows, its blasted hopes, its anguish keen—he could only ask that Melancholy come live with him, that they dwell together in darkness and solitude until life's tapers burned out. The poet here twisted Milton's original sentiment, but some of his exact words appear, now fixed in set formulations:

[205] *The Port Folio,* I, no. 40 (October 3, 1801), 320, under the section "Selected Poetry."

> Come, and with me love to dwell
> In some dreary dismal cell,
> Where the sun-beams never shine
> There in solitude we'll pine,
> There to sigh and weep we'll learn,
> Till life's dim tapers cease to burn.[206]

Such lines illustrate clearly how far Milton had ritualized the poetry of melancholy and of mirth: the injunctions "hence" and "come" had become almost indispensable to the expression of mood, however trivial or serious the occasion.

John E. Hall's poem *The Adieu* shows with even greater precision how far such a ritualization had gone. Announced in advance of its appearance in *The Port Folio* that it was an imitation of *L'Allegro* and that it was "beyond all compare the most ingenious, correct, and harmonious" Hall had produced, *The Adieu* turned out to be upon publication a close rendering of *Il Penseroso*, adapted to articulate a personal emotional crisis. Hall had decided to give up poetry for the practice of law, a decision apparently accompanied with some anguish of mind. To present his mood properly, he began with an injunction to poetry:

> Hence, now, the poets' life forlorn,
> Of Vanity, and Fancy born—
> 'Tis but a wild delusive joy,
> And shall no more my peace annoy.

Poetry had been sweet and Hall regretted to leave her; but the call of the law was strong, and he chose its demands over the delights of the muse:

> But come! thou judge, sedate and sage,
> Come and unfold thy learned page.
> Oh how shall I thy name invoke?
> Chief Justice, or my master Coke!

[206] *ibid.*, v, no. 7 (February 23, 1805), 56, "To Melancholy."

The conclusion followed the popular if by now worn-out pattern, even to the incorporation of some of Milton's own phrases:

> And may, at last, my weary age
> Find out the Judge's 'hermitage',
> 'Where I may sit, and rightly spell',
> Which cause is bad, and which is well.
> And where, without the Lawyer's strife,
> My income settled is, for life.
> These things, Judge Coke, oh! deign to give,
> 'And I, with thee, will choose to live.' [207]

Hall here could have intended to laugh at his predicament through a parody of *Il Penseroso;* but if so, his humor failed in its aim. More likely he followed the practice of other poetasters of the day, imposing Milton's language and form upon the expression of personal mood. Posturing such as this could scarcely become more empty of meaning.

But imitations of *Paradise Lost* in the early Republic presented even greater affronts to the name and nature of poetry. Earlier attempts to reach sublimity through Milton's language and syntax had been unhappy enough, as witness Joel Barlow and Timothy Dwight; but *The Vision of Columbus* and *The Conquest of Canäan* had possessed some freshness and vigor and had at least captured a spirit then moving the nation. Their subject matter had been of sufficient scope to ask for epic expression. Now, however, the machinery of *Paradise Lost* overpowered lesser intentions, or reduced to mere ceremony attempts to articulate religious experience.

Charles Love's *Poem on the Death of General George Washington* exemplifies how fully *Paradise Lost* overpowered serious verse of the day. One of a host of eulogists on the oc-

---

[207] *ibid.*, v, no. 11, New Series (March 12, 1808), 175–176, under "Original Poetry." *The Adieu* was signed by Sedley, that is, John E. Hall. *ibid.*, v, no. 10, New Series (March 5, 1808), 159 had announced the acceptance of Hall's poem.

casion of Washington's death, Love began his blank-verse poem of two books with an invocation to Liberty, reminiscent of Milton's invocation to the Holy Spirit. Like Milton, he asked aid to soar on adventurous wings; like Milton, he sought to assert eternal Providence and justify the ways of God to man. Love did not say this precisely, for he was apparently incapable of crystallizing his thought in verse form; but if his lines are often opaque Milton's imprint is nonetheless clear:

> We mean to soar,
> On untry'd wing, if thou thy aid vouchsafe,
> Up to Eternity's advent'rous height;
> From thence to earth we come, thence mount to Heav'n,
> Exploring regions mid, in devious space,
> Yet unexplor'd: Come! and thy genial glow,
> Dear Goddess lend—or best impart fit warmth;
> Whilst buoyant we, upborne amid the spheres,
> In sympathising mind, together roam;
> Or o'er th' Empyrean tract, research pursue
> Of *Providence, unusual fraught with grief;*
> The *cause* inexplicable, full conceive,
> And amplify to mourning Man below,
> In just epitome of reas'ning sound,
> And Fancy apt, things Moral and Divine.

With the aid of Liberty, Love soared to the highest Empyrean, to the very throne of God Himself, surrounded by adoring angels. Here in Miltonlike terms he described the "Light ineffable" of heaven; here in a scene recalling the great vision in Book III of *Paradise Lost,* he presented God speaking of Washington's role in America, telling of his life and his destiny. On the reception of such information the angelic host shouted "Glory to GOD," and cried "prepare ye—prepare ye—for WASHINGTON / A Place—a Wreath—a Crown." "Nor feigned their notes," Love continued in imitation of Milton: for God had explained Washington's death and had bid their sorrows surcease. With this a heavenly glow of confidence moved through the angelic host, revealing their submission to God's "sole righteous will." [208]

After so exalted a scene the mundane details of Washington's death on a cold, snowy day appear anti-climactic, though more honest and genuinely sorrowful. Perhaps the acid comment of *The Monthly Magazine* on Samuel Low's eulogy on Washington could apply with equal justice to Love's poem: "The introduction of the spirit of Washington into heaven, and its coming up to its Maker and making a bow, is neither awfully grand, nor *elegantly* little." [209] In comparison, even Mather Byles's imitations of Milton appear fresh and exciting.

Yet such obvious failures, far from discouraging serious authors, inspired in a number of lengthy religious poems an even closer rendering of Milton's language and imagery. After all, Milton still stood as a prime witness for Christianity: he had dramatized Christian doctrine and had articulated a wide variety of religious experience. That religious poets of the early Republic should turn to him to renew the old verities would therefore be only natural. But unfortunately such versifiers possessed little talent or vision and hence could only repeat what Milton had already said. A poem entitled *True and Infernal Friendship* could present Adam and Eve *only* in Milton's Garden of Eden, could speak of Hell *only* in terms of the Infernal Council, could present Adam's instruction by Raphael and the temptation of Eve *only* as these events had been told in *Paradise Lost*. The completeness with which the imagery of *Paradise Lost* dominated the poem pro-

---

[208] *A Poem on the Death of General George Washington, Late President of the United States* (Alexandria, Virginia, 1800), pp. 8, 21, 38–39 of Book I; and Book II. George Washington also inspired Thomas Northmore, an Englishman, to write *Washington, or Liberty Restored*, an epic based largely on *Paradise Lost*. An edition of this work appeared in Baltimore, in 1809.

[209] *The Monthly Magazine and American Review*, III, no. 1 (July 1800), 56–58.

claimed the power of Milton in the same measure it detracted from the power of the poem.[210]

Even more imitative was *The Propitiation*, a long poem on the life and passion of Christ appearing in successive issues of the *Philadelphia Repertory* from May 25, 1811, to February 1, 1812. Here the machinery of the Infernal Council moves through the whole narration—from the appointment of Chemos for the purpose of discovering the nature of Christ's mission, through the announcement of Calvary, to the descent of Judas Iscariot into Hell. Frequent gatherings of the Council of Devils, as well as numerous Satanic soliloquies, serve as props to give this loose and tedious effusion a semblance of structure.[211] But perhaps the most ambitious and most artificial imitation of *Paradise Lost* to appear at this time was Thomas Brockway's *The Gospel Tragedy: An Epic Poem: In Four Books*.

As a minister, Brockway aimed to tell the story of Christ from the recognition of His incarnation by Satan through the moving events of the Passion. Scarcely a page in the epic fails to record the weight of Milton's language, imagery, and thought, though Book I was most clearly Miltonic, as its "Argument" shows:

INTRODUCTION. *The powers of darkness alarmed at the incarnation of the Saviour.—Satan calls his Council.—They meet in the upper part of the atmosphere.—Satan's address, and narration.—The broken Peer.—His crime.—The resentment of the Council applauded by Satan.—Reasonings of a succeeding Peer.—No fear of conquest argued from the necessity of contrast.—An assault upon Christ urged. —His human body and spirit, fit objects of attack.—His arguments*

[210] *True and Infernal Friendship, Or the Wisdom of Eve. And the Character of the Serpent, with the Situation, Joys, and Loss of Paradise* (Providence, 1813).

[211] *Philadelphia Repertory*, from May 25, 1811, through February 1, 1812, or thirty-seven issues. In a prefatory comment to this poem, the author acknowledged his debt to Milton.

*refuted by a succeeding speaker.—His philosophick abilities.—His enmity to the Divine character.—Private temptation recommended and carried.—Satan nominated and chosen.—His acceptance.—The Council Dismissed.*

Such dependence on Milton in the argument of Book I was a mere token of the print of *Paradise Lost* and of *Paradise Regained* on the text of the poem. Brockway invoked Holy Light for instruction, presented Satan in heroic rebellion, and envisioned the disbanding of the Infernal Council, allowing each spirit to wander at will. He even pictured Satan *"left to his own reflections,"* desperate over his diminishing lustre, and presented the temptation of Christ in the wilderness as this event had appeared in *Paradise Regained*. Only in Books III and IV, "The Ministry of Christ" and "The Crucifixion" respectively, was Miltonic influence to lessen, and even here lines and phrases from Milton's two poems echo often enough to sound like a refrain.[212] Milton had stamped the stories of Satan and Christ with such memorable images that Brockway could only repeat them. The appearance of *Smoking a Segar in the Manner of Milton,* a poem burlesquing the heroic manner, penetrated the stale atmosphere of the time with a tang most refreshing.[213]

So dismal a record of Miltonic poetry in the early Republic lends at first glance some credence to T. S. Eliot's twentieth century injunction that young authors should eschew a study of Milton lest he infect their own style. For if *L'Allegro* and *Il Penseroso* had earlier sinewed American verse, giving it a toughness of texture seldom seen at that time, by the end of the century these twin pieces had frozen mood poems into artificial and meaningless postures, even as *Paradise Lost* had

---

[212] *The Gospel Tragedy: An Epic Poem: In Four Books* (Worcester, 1795), The Argument of Book I; pp. [7], 14, 17, 30, and 48 particularly in Books I and II; *passim* in Books III and IV.

[213] *The Port Folio,* II, no. 5 (February 6, 1802), 40, under "Original Poetry."

forced serious poetry into dull and predictable patterns of language, imagery, syntax, and form. Ironically, the more forcefully Milton spoke to the moral, religious, and political life of the day, the more he overpowered poetry, to its distinct disadvantage. Yet T. S. Eliot's position, upon which so many critical empires have been founded, hardly explains the desert of verse at this time. The same warning could be uttered for Dryden or Pope, or for Thomson or Young or Gray, whose poems early Americans copied with the same dessicating effect. Milton's more distinctive language and syntax simply revealed with a special clarity and force the derivative nature of early American literature. Milton *could* stir the imagination, *could* furnish an imagery and thought to create a very high form of art, as later seen in Herman Melville's *Moby Dick*, for example.[214] But before such could happen Americans had to break the mold of neoclassic imitation and fashion a fresh idiom to accommodate their heritage of spiritual greatness. A Romantic movement had to sweep aside husks that had been gathering for decades.

[214] See Henry F. Pommer, *Milton and Melville* (Pittsburgh, 1950).

FIVE

# Diminishing Stature

The very years that saw Milton reach a pinnacle of influence and fame ironically called out views that began to diminish his stature. His sayings and sentiments so prominently featured in textbooks and sermons, in almanacs and journals and fugitive tracts focused attention on his poems as a whole, and this in turn elicited a spate of critical essays, some of which sharply queried his art. With the appearance of such essays the process of flawing his image slowly began.

For years to come many critics would still see Milton as a man of titanic stature, overshadowing even Homer and Virgil; among a few he would never lose height. But in the early Republic, as the literary community moved from the dominance of neoclassical theory to the acceptance of Romantic principles, comment no longer maintained an almost unanimous front about Milton's supremacy. A schism born of that transitional period and still evident in Miltonic criticism began to appear, followed by a distrust in his style and by an uneasiness about what he said. Such views had not yet gone very far, but soon they would spread, probing his art, undermining his sentiments, and even questioning his right to be heard. In time, he would be known and admired less in the nation at large than in coteries and schools: as a popular symbol of authority he would gradually fade from the American scene.

## II

Yet schism among critics of the early Republic appeared to have had little immediate effect on popular opinion. The old clichés about Milton's inspiration and grandeur, or about his sublimity and prophetic visions still fell from American lips, often with little comment or thought. His popular image of authority and greatness allowed him to remain exemplary and doctrinal to the American nation. As *The Monthly Anthology* had observed, his mind was so great and his learning so sound, his taste so perceptive and his fancy so exuberant, that to doubt what he said could prove perilous.[1] Such *obiter dicta*, however, could not long satisfy a literary community searching for poetic principles and standards of judgment. In consequence, Americans created a small body of Miltonic criticism, most of it fragmentary and chiefly derivative, but significant in that it grappled with basic problems of language, subject, and style relevant then and of recurring interest to poets and critics. Some of this criticism supported the popular image of Milton's greatness; some of it attempted to diminish his stature.

Critical support of Milton's greatness centered attention for the most part in his language and imagery. Other considerations, to be sure, often aroused comment, such as his classical learning, his Biblical topics, or his musical ear; but the heart of his greatness, as *The Literary Magazine* declared, lay in his unique poetic language. The most difficult task of the poet, this journal explained, was the formulation of style, that is, the creation of a diction truly distinctive. The most stubborn step to scale on Parnassus was to discover an idiom distinguished from prose, as well as a poetic expression markedly different from the utterance of others. Most poets

---

[1] *The Monthly Anthology and Boston Review*, IV (September 1807), 489–492.

unfortunately lacked such distinction, *The Literary Magazine* went on, simply because the general cast of their language showed "little variation." They embellished their verse by interweaving expressions "nicely picked out of the performances" of others, with the result that, though they combined new ideas and found happy subjects, they made few contributions to "the poetical treasury of diction."

Now Milton's distinction lay precisely in his additions to the treasury of poetic language. His "notions of poetry were of the most exalted nature," *The Literary Magazine* continued. Milton indeed constructed a new diction, or, as he himself said of Edward King in *Lycidas*, he built the lofty rhyme. If in his minor verse he was content to employ the words of his contemporaries, "without pursuing any particular system," in *Paradise Lost* he created a new language suited to the grandeur of his theme. Out of the rich linguistic treasures of the past—out of Hebrew and Greek, Italian and Latin—he coined an original idiom, capable of expressing not only nice variations of feeling and thought but also bold images and vast scenes. The language of the moment, *The Literary Magazine* concluded with a warning from Gray, could never be the language of poetry. For thinking it could, Wordsworth and Southey had descended into common, colloquial talk. But Milton—ah! Milton had surmounted the highest obstacle a poet encounters: he had created a language that made poetry poetry, and this was the chief reason for his towering greatness.[2]

Such a position bespoke disapproval of Romantic doctrine and tacit assent to neoclassic principles of typicality and generalized diction. Yet admiring Americans found especially annoying Samuel Johnson's stricture that Milton's language was perverse and pedantic. *The Universal Asylum* reprinted

[2] *The Literary Magazine and American Register*, v, no. 30 (March 1806), 172–176, in an essay "On Poetical Expression."

an essay from *The Transactions of the Royal Irish Academy* which turned back on Johnson identical charges; [3] and *The Ladies Magazine* arose to defend Milton's blank verse as well as his style from Johnson's pronounced views. Johnson had been too severe, *The Ladies Magazine* declared, in saying that blank verse had put the measures of English poetry into the periods of a declaimer. This was simply not true. Milton particularly had so "admirably disposed" the "variety" and "judicious changes of the pause" that the ear scarcely tired: in his poetry no "perpetual sameness" appeared, no "recurrence of sound which in common blank verse is so insufferably disgusting." Nor was Milton's poetry for the eye only, as Johnson had said; nor could it be claimed that the power of his verse sprang from the sublimity of his sentiments or from his arrangement of words. Milton's sentiments *were* noble and lofty, yes; but his meter was "inexpressibly rich, mellow, and harmonious." Whatever "hypothesis" about poetry might be adopted Milton would "have every praise,—of sentiment,— of imagery,—of modulation." [4]

Whatever hypothesis about poetry might be adopted. Nothing could state more precisely the practice of most American critics, who paused in various contexts to drop words of praise.[5] In *The Monthly Anthology* "Silva" chided Joseph Addison for not "bestowing more encomium on one of the most magnificent conceptions ever formed in the mind of uninspired man," that is, Milton's picture of the world as seen through Satan's eyes,

> In the bigness of a star,
> Of smallest magnitude, close by the moon.

[3] *The Universal Asylum and Columbian Magazine* (April 1791), pp. 237–240, in an essay "On the Style of Dr. Samuel Johnson."

[4] *The Ladies Magazine* (September 1792), pp. 151–159, in an essay "On the Nature and Essential Qualities of Poetry, as Distinguished from Prose."

[5] See Clarence Arthur Brown, *The Achievement of American Criticism* pp. 14–28 for a good discussion of critical cross-currents in the age of transition.

So vast a picture could not be paralleled for sublimity "in the whole body of poetry, ancient or modern," Silva declared.[6] Nor could Milton be matched for the precision of his words or the flow of his lines. *The Port Folio* praised the harmony of his monosyllables in Adam and Eve's morning hymn;[7] and *The Literary Magazine* found his alliteration in "so talk'd the spirited sly snake" particularly artful in that he had here attained "the perfect hiss of the serpent."[8] Such fugitive comments in journals reiterated what Lindley Murray had proclaimed in his *Grammar:* that Milton had so mastered his medium that he could make the sound of his words speak their sense. But critics of the early Republic praised Milton most for his imagery, which they thought was superlatively affective and bold.

*Paradise Lost* furnished most of the grist for such comment. *The Port Folio* observed that Milton's simile, "As one who long in populous city pent," enhanced the joys of a walk in the country,[9] and later declared that *"Milton's well-known pictures of Sin and Death"* stood among the "finest passages of descriptive poetry in the English language."[10] John Blair Linn became so entranced by the imagery of the first books of *Paradise Lost* that he struck off a few encomiastic lines, which he recorded on a blank page of a copy of that poem. The picture of Satan defying almighty God, the glimmer of infernal light, the great panorama of Hell—these and other scenes so crowded his mind that, as Milton's imagination carried him

[6] *The Monthly Anthology and Boston Review,* IX (October 1810), 239–241, in an essay, "Milton and Addison."
[7] *The Port Folio,* V, no. 1, Third Series (January 1815), 66–71, in an essay "The English Language."
[8] *The Literary Magazine and American Register,* II, no. 10 (July 1804), 291–292, in an essay "On Alliteration in Verse," by Miss Seward.
[9] *The Port Folio,* I, no. 16, New Series (April 26, 1806), 252, in a sketch extracted "from a paper."
[10] *ibid.,* VI, no. 6, Third Series (December 1815), 614–615. See also *ibid.,* no. 5, New Series (November 1811), 493–495, for a discussion of Milton's pictures of the Devil and Death.

through Chaos to the edge of the world, he could only exclaim:

> Great God! what wonders meet my searching eyes!
> Worlds circling worlds, on systems systems rise! [11]

Linn had praised Milton earlier in a formal critical notice published in *The Literary Magazine*, where he had shown himself to be a critic of cultivation and taste. He knew and loved the classics, as well as such epics of the Italian Renaissance as Tasso's *Jerusalem Delivered*. But of all the great poems of the world, Linn declared, none could match *Paradise Lost* for vast and sublime imagery. What could be more exalted than the vision of Satan being cast out of Heaven in Book VI, a scene which for words and conception could not be exceeded in "strength?" Or what of Milton's description of how the waters abated after the Flood? "None but the most mighty imagination could have given birth to such a picture, and none but a giant in intellect could have begotten such gigantic personifications."

Linn recalled other affective scenes in *Paradise Lost*, such as the vision of Eve leaving her beloved flowers and shrubs; but clearly the grand panoramas moved him most.[12] If in his earlier career Linn had praised simplicity of expression, warning young Americans against invoking either Homer or Milton, he now saw true poetry speaking not of common particulars but in superlative generals. Poetry neither described immediate scenes nor related ordinary events; it "was sublime divination, through which earth-bound man caught quick and breath-taking glimpses of God's will." [13] *Paradise Lost* vouch-

---

[11] *The Literary Magazine and American Register*, III, no. 17 (February 1805), 134, under "Poetry . . . Original." Linn's poem was entitled: "Lines, Written by the Late Dr. J. B. Linn, in a Blank Leaf of Paradise Lost."

[12] *ibid.*, I, no. 1 (October 1803), 15–21, under "Critical Notices," signed "I.O.," that is, John Blair Linn.

[13] Lewis Leary, "John Blair Linn, 1775–1805," *The William and Mary Quarterly*, IV, Third Series (1947), 171.

safed man such visions of spiritual truth, and for this reason, Linn thought, was the greatest of all poems.

Praise for the minor poems followed much the same pattern, accompanied with occasional excursions into neoclassic doctrines of verse. Journals still delivered *obiter dicta*, as when, for example, *The Port Folio* announced that *Lycidas*, *L'Allegro*, and *Il Penseroso* contained the "very essence of poetry"; [14] but critics now attempted to plumb the secret of Milton's great popularity by a close examination of his minor works. *The New Haven Gazette* undertook such a task by centering attention in *L'Allegro* and *Il Penseroso*, twin poems so often admired that they had frozen mood verse into inflexible patterns of language and form. To arouse interest in its project, as well as to facilitate reading, the *Gazette* first printed both poems, announcing at the same time that a subsequent issue would publish an appraisal.

Associational and pictorial principles of verse guided a good part of the analysis that followed. The *Gazette* prefaced its appraisal with a sentiment from Horace: *Non satis est pulchra esse poemata; dulcia sunto*, hoping that such a pronouncement would strengthen its case. *L'Allegro* and *Il Penseroso* could indeed be described as beautiful and sweet; but what interested the *Gazette* most was the way they affected the reader. Images in both poems, the argument began, pleased more than individual objects in nature because they gave a unity of impression not possible in nature. Their power to excite kindred and united emotions sprang precisely from the "unity and consistency" of their sentiment, however many inconsistencies of language and versification might mar individual parts. Painter and poet alike should seek such effects, the *Gazette* further declared; the person of "true taste" should be affected not so much by the "mere perception" of external objects as by "the general influences of their union and correspondence." To be

---

[14] *The Port Folio*, VIII, no. 1, New Series (July 1812), 84–85.

specific, not the perception of a particular cavern or tree but only a picture of unity could arouse "uncommon sensations" to elevate heart and soul, and this was the power that bespoke "genuine excellence" in a poem. For precisely such reasons *L'Allegro* and *Il Penseroso* had attracted "so many admirers": [15] their language and imagery united to stir common associations in man leading to such pleasing and ennobling sensations that they could be said to contain the "very essence of poetry."

John E. Hall pressed much the same claim for *Comus*. Opening his critique by asserting that this masque possessed an enchanting "Ionic simplicity" and "Doric sweetness," he moved quickly into his main argument, finding tropes taken from painting more appropriate to his discourse than figures affected from architecture. If *Paradise Lost* partook of "the wild sublimity of Angelo," Hall declared, and *Paradise Regained* of "the mild and tender Raphael," then *Comus* blended "the romantic scenery of a Claude with the exquisite polish and splendor of a Titian." Now the accuracy of such comparisons is not here in question, though criticism of one art by reference to another is often unsound or misleading. What is important is Hall's tactic of citing painters to explain the pictorial effects of a poem. *Comus* had presented a series of bold images, and Hall could do no better than say that this masque exhibited the same "varied and beautiful excursions of fancy" that had decorated *L'Allegro*, where Milton had peopled the "colours of the rainbow," as later in *Paradise Lost* he was to people "the ideal waste and gloomy kingdoms of Chaos." Hall admitted that *Comus* could never be admired for its dramatic technique, but it possessed "such an elegance of expression" and "such compression of sentiment," its "col-

[15] *The New Haven Gazette and the Connecticut Magazine,* III, no. 10 (March 13, 1788); no. 11 (March 20, 1788); and no. 12 (March 27, 1788), [36–37]. The critical essay appeared in no. 12; *L'Allegro* and *Il Penseroso* in nos. 10 and 11 respectively.

ouring" was so "vivid" and its "scenery so picturesque," that it astonished, delighted, and enchanted mankind. For its language and imagery it deserved highest praise.[16]

In *The Bureau* a critic calling himself "Proclus" praised *Paradise Regained* on much the same grounds. Proclus began by saying that Milton had received less applause than he actually deserved—a sorry state of affairs, he believed, and accountable in great measure to the "solemnity" of his subjects and to the "religious gravity of his mind." But another and more important reason lay in his language. The *"unlearned reader,"* Proclus declared with Samuel Johnson, found himself upon perusing Milton *"surprised by a new language:* a language not easily intelligible to his understanding, nor immediately agreeable to his ear." No wonder so many Americans spoke of Milton by name only! Yet only those ignorant of his beauties or acquainted with his chief poems "no otherwise than by name" could "refrain from the repeated indulgence of the refined enjoyments" his poetry afforded. Such enjoyments sprang from the amplitude of his conceptions, from the observation of a mind rapid and full and "ever teeming," perpetually "pregnant with new combinations and original images." Milton's distinction lay in his power to mold through his unusual language and imagery "the most inflexible materials," Proclus explained: in his ability to decorate "with the fertility of his imagination the most denuded subjects."

*Paradise Lost* illustrated most fully such powers, the grandeur of its nature combining with the sublimest subject to make it at once "stupendous and imposing." But *Paradise Regained* possessed the same powers, Proclus went on, particularly as felt in "the pictorial description of the coming on of the third morning," which could not be "exceeded by the

[16] *The Port Folio*, I, no. 2, Third Series (February 1813), 174–176, under "The Adversaria; Or, Evening Recreations," signed by "J.E.H."

highest effort of the fancy," and in the great passages in Book IV, which caught some of the brilliance of execution and the solidity of precept moving through the whole poem. If *Paradise Lost* "constellated" the "highest of every degree of excellence," *Paradise Regained* ran a close second, ranking inferior only because of its brevity and less extensive design.

After a succinct appraisal of the "extraordinary elegance, sublimity, and harmony" of *Paradise Regained* Proclus closed down his argument. Time, he said, would crumble into oblivious dust all the edifices of dullness, but that same time would "add strength to the palaces of Milton." For men endued "with sensibility to feel, to taste or discriminate" would "in all ages applaud his works and reverence his genius"; and to "the pious, the learned and the good" he would "afford an unfailing source of exalted instruction and of pure pleasure." [17] The distinction of his language, the grandeur of his imagery, and the soundness of his precepts would always ensure Milton an audience, fit though few.

Critics of the early Republic occasionally included Milton's prose and the sonnets within their compass of praise. John Blair Linn thought Milton's prose a mine of intellectual gold, as already noticed; [18] and *The Analectic Magazine* and *The Literary Magazine and American Register* favored a sonnet or two.[19] Yet *Paradise Lost* clearly interested them most, followed by *L'Allegro* and *Il Penseroso*, *Comus*, and *Paradise Regained*. To say that praisers of Milton offered original insights or plumbed in depth the language and style of these

---

[17] *The Bureau Or Repository of Literature, Politics, and Intelligence*, I, no. 24 (September 5, 1812), 185–186, the lead article, "Essays After My Own Manner"; and *ibid.*, no. 25 (September 12, 1812), pp. 193–194.

[18] For further praise of Milton's prose, see *The Literary Magazine and American Register*, I, no. 3 (December 1803), 165–166.

[19] *The Analectic Magazine*, IV (November 1814), 418–419; and *The Literary Magazine and American Register*, VI, no. 35 (August 1806), 96. The latter magazine thought that Milton's sonnets, except for two or three, lacked grace and exactness.

poems would be far from the truth. Deriving their judgments from English critics and Scotch rhetoricians, they merit the general comment Ralph Waldo Emerson was later to make on American cultural dependence in *The American Scholar*. Nearly every judgment expressed in American journals could be traced to Samuel Johnson, or Hugh Blair, or Lord Kames. What is remarkable about American critics is not that they opened fresh vistas but that they adopted whatever hypothesis would argue their cause. Associationalism, pictorialism, neo-classic theories of language and style—all could be invoked to proclaim Milton's greatness. More than any writer they knew Milton fulfilled their highest, if often different, poetic ideals. In so arguing they sustained the popular clichés about Milton's supremacy, affirming his authority and his right to be heard.

## III

Yet at the very time critics praised Milton most, opposition to his poetry gathered strength. A student at Yale College in an essay "On Rhyme" spoke of the "loose manner" of *Lycidas*,[20] and *The Port Folio* called Milton's account of his blindness a "blemish." [21] Random comments reveal an increasing impatience with Milton idolatry and a growing uneasiness about his manner and matter.[22] If praisers of Milton deplored Samuel Johnson's critical strictures, his detractors welcomed their perceptive precision, often employing them as texts to guide further analysis. No consistent body of principles in-

[20] *Literary Cabinet*, I, no. 7 (Yale College, February 21, 1807), 52.
[21] *The Port Folio*, I, no. 12, New Series (March 29, 1806), 182, in the continuation of a discussion of *The Progress of Poesy*, by "The American Lounger."
[22] See, for example, *The Literary Magazine and American Register*, V, no. 32 (May 1806), 343–344; and *The Port Folio*, V, no. 1, Third Series (January 1815), 7. The idolatry of Shakespeare was also deplored. For special comment on Milton's prose, see *The Port Folio*, V, no. 15 (April 20, 1805), 117.

formed such critical sallies, but praisers and detractors of Milton faced each other across pretty well-defined lines: Was Milton's imagery natural, exact, and therefore effective, or was it extravagant, imprecise, and hence vain? Was his idiom strong and majestic, built to carry the weight of sublimity, or was it contrived and inflated, capable only of supporting grandiloquence? Was his poetic vision transcendentally viable, or was it moribund if not actually dead? Whether Milton was a pattern of perfection or a greatly flawed genius was a question of moment.

Detractors of Milton insisted that the minor poems abounded in faults. Like a number of critics today, they seemed less interested in the architectural whole of a poem than in its individual images and lines, which they appraised separately as good or bad, strong or weak, genuine or merely rhetorical. Thus in *The Monthly Anthology* "Silva" approached the *Nativity Ode* not so much to hear the music of Milton's hymn or to understand the argument of its two central movements as to evaluate separate parts. A few months later he was to extol in the same journal Milton's picture of the world as seen through Satan's eyes as a conception so sublime as not to be equalled in the whole body of poetry, but now he was much less impressed. Indeed, he said, Johnson had been too extravagant in implying that the seeds of *Paradise Lost* lay in the *Nativity Ode*, for were this poem not known to be Milton's it would have passed into oblivion long ago.

With this observation, Silva set the tone for his detailed analysis. He explained that in poetry as in painting an original must act as a standard—a face, for example, governs the stroke of a brush as well as the worth of that stroke in the design of the whole portrait. Norms in tradition and nature, or standards of common sense, allowed him to assert that the *Nativity Ode* abounded in the same "absurd conceits, forced analogies, vulgarisms and quibbles" that had deformed the pages of Shakespeare, Waller, and others of that age, and from which even *Paradise Lost* was "not entirely exempt." Consider, for instance, Milton's conceit "heaven's high council table," which appeared in the introductory lines to the *Ode*. This image recalled the "table of Jove" and hence burlesqued the awful subject of Christian Deity, Silva contended. Or consider a line from the hymn itself, "To wanton with the sun, her lusty paramour." This, Silva declared, was a forced analogy, a conceit so extended in the following stanza of the *Ode* as to become not simply absurd but "intolerable." In this manner Silva examined the *Nativity Ode*, sometimes finding an original and striking passage, such as the stanza beginning "So when the sun in bed," but more often pointing out artificialities and absurdities, which he implied structured the whole poem.[23]

Yet hard as Silva was on the *Nativity Ode* he reserved his harshest remarks for *The Passion*. No one would wish to quarrel with his appraisal of this unfinished imitation of Spenser, perhaps least of all Milton; the subject was beyond Milton's years and religious experience, and Milton confessed it. The significance of Silva's remarks lies not so much in his scorn for such lines as, "Had got a race of mourners on some pregnant cloud," as in the enunciation of his critical principles. A conceit, he said, should arise out of the order of nature, and should please by its novelty and appropriateness. The pleasures such a conceit should arouse in the reader could be likened to "a discovery in the ordinary properties of matter," a revelation so in keeping with the nature of things that one is surprised at not having known it before. The true poet therefore ever seeks to surprise in this manner. He "starts some fortunate conceit"; and "surrounding nature applies all her known principles in aid and illustration of it, as familiarly and as

---

[23] *The Monthly Anthology and Boston Review*, VIII (May 1810), 311–314.

fitly as if they were constructed for that identical purpose."
And as the reader surrendered to the "delightful deception"
the image presented, he contemplated "the symmetry, grace,
proportion and elegance" of the work to which it contributed,
"charmed with the ingenuity and skill of the architect."

Such was the nature of good imagery and such was its effect
on the reader. But imagery formulated *out of the order of
nature*, Silva went on, was a monstrous novelty only, requiring
no talent and having no boundaries; and since *The Passion*
abounded in unnatural images it therefore was a poor poem.
Neither decorum nor common sense would allow Silva to find
any pleasure in Milton's attempt to delineate Christ's passion;
but he concluded his remarks with praise for *Paradise Lost*.
Milton, he said, could be compared to an eagle, sluggish and
inert close to the ground but secure and strong as he rose to
his element near the dazzling beams of the sun. Even the
greatest men often produced work unworthy their genius.[24]

Two months after John Blair Linn had praised *Paradise
Lost* he turned a critical eye on *Il Penseroso*. By now he had
concluded that true poetry was archetypal and revelatory,
characterized by universalized imagery and generalized diction; and in view of such predispositions he found *Il Penseroso* filled with errors and poetic flaws. The principle of
associationalism, to be sure, allowed him to say that the outline
of the poem agreed "pretty accurately with the scheme of
every mind, habituated to the exercise of its faculties"; but
what of the "minuter particulars" of language and imagery?
Herein *Il Penseroso* failed the test of good poetry. Consider
the genealogy of Melancholy in the first part of the poem.
Why Saturn and Vesta on a "certain mountain in a certain isle
of the Mediterranean, should be fixed upon as the parents and
birthplace" of Melancholy, or what "legitimate gratification"
could or ought to derive from a tale of such a meeting be-

[24] *ibid.*, XIII (June 1810), 377–379, in an essay entitled "Milton."

tween father and daughter in the forests of Crete "while yet there was no fear of Jove," Linn found impossible to justify or explain. Passages so infused with classical learning rendered much of what Milton said unintelligible, he complained.

Linn complained further that *Il Penseroso* presented images foreign to American experience. Hearing the sweet song of a nightingale, for example, was a "privilege an American contemplatist must dispense with," since the groves of the New World sounded with "the music of nocturnal insects," which had "nothing in common with the notes of Philomena." Furthermore, the passage on the bee with honied thigh singing at *her* work contradicted scientific fact: Milton "was not physiologist enough to know that the working Bee is of no sex, that the honey is extracted by the tongue, and deposited for safe carriage, in the mouth of the insect."

Finally, Linn questioned the sentiment at the end of the poem. "The seriousness or melancholy here depicted," he argued, "has something in it unsocial, misanthropic and selfish, and though we may admire the portrait, *as* a portrait, yet, no man with a true taste for serious pleasures, will fully concur with the poet. . . ." Sometimes, to be sure, Linn found imagery of universal appeal or of unusual perception. Milton's image of the moon, he declared, "is congenial with every fancy, and is to be seen in every climate"; and his post-shower description, "With minute drops from off the eaves," he rightly admired as select and original. But such adulation he kept at a minimum. The burden of his analysis was that esoteric allusion, unrepresentative imagery, and inaccurate statement so flawed *Il Penseroso* that it could not be considered a good poem. What others had praised so highly and imitated so often, Linn roundly condemned.[25]

[25] *The Literary Magazine and American Register*, I, no. 3 (December 1803), 173–180, under "Critical Notices, No. III." According to Lewis Leary, this unsigned notice was by Linn.

Criticism of Milton's language and imagery in the minor poems carried over into *Paradise Lost*. Shortly after the turn of the century *The Literary Magazine* attacked Milton's famous pictures of Sin and Death, two portraits long admired by Americans and at least once declared among the finest descriptions in the annals of literature. The attack began with a partial quotation from the picture of Death:

> Black as night;
> Fierce as ten furies; terrible as hell.

Everyone knew that these lines referred to Milton's imaginary personage called Death, *The Literary Magazine* declared, but how many had stopped to "enquire into the propriety or reasonableness" of what they presented? Very few. Most had fallen back on general opinion that "this or that" was sublime and had taken "the work as a criterion of taste and excellence," seldom venturing "to judge for themselves, or to derive the reasons of their approbation from the unbiassed and original suggestions of their own minds." What others had not done, the critic for *The Literary Magazine* would do; and he would find more pleasure, he said, "in detecting faults, than in recognizing beauties."

Faults he found in abundance. He began by saying that "*Black as night* is an image the most trite, obvious, and unprecise imaginable." Everyone should know that *night* is not *black* absolutely, but only relatively, since nights on earth may be star-lit or moon-lit, and even Tartarian night, he said, calling on ancient tradition, is constantly irradiated by upper, nether, and surrounding fires. Had Milton chosen to say "black as ebony" he might have elicited smiles, but such a gain in precision would be a loss in sublimity. And what could be said of the remaining line? "The ferocity of ten furies," *The Literary Magazine* continued, might seem "more formidable or destructive than that of one, as *ten hells* are more *terrible* than *one hell;* but *degrees* of ferocity are entirely distinct from the *multitude* of the fierce." Thus to say as "swift as ten race-horses" would be to speak nonsense. "As poetical as ten Homers, infallible as ten popes, brave as ten Diomeds, wise as ten Newtons, tall as ten giants, are all similes, the grotesqueness and absurdity of which are evident at first sight." Yet "Milton's *ten* furies are exactly parallel to these."

Even Milton's "terrible as hell" seemed nonsensical to the critic of *The Literary Magazine.* "That Death should be as terrible as hell" was "not an unnatural thought"; but this was "just as if one should say, that a hangman is as hateful as the gallows, a dun as the bailiff, or a bailiff as the prison." In short, *The Literary Magazine* believed that reason and good sense should proclaim Milton's portrait of Death neither admirable nor sublime but trite, imprecise, and ineffective.[26]

Before long such a critical approach encompassed the whole of *Paradise Lost.* Somewhat earlier *The American Monthly Review* had echoed Samuel Johnson in saying that the pedantry of Milton's style was a fault not a merit, a view other journals not only supported but began to embellish after the turn of the century. Taking its cue directly from Johnson's dictum on Milton, *The Literary Magazine* now spoke of Milton's inversions and stiff diction, artifices which robbed his poetry of animation and ease, such as had run through the verses of Homer and Virgil. Milton's lighter verse displayed a fulness of such grace and spirit, *The Literary Magazine* declared; but in *Paradise Lost,* sensing the inferiority of English over the classical languages, Milton had created an idiom of inverted periods, which, had he succeeded, would have improved poetry and eloquence, but which, because of

---

[26] *ibid.,* II, no. 9 (June 1804), 176–179. Internal evidence argues, as Lewis Leary said, that this critical notice No. VIII was not by Linn. See also *The Monthly Magazine and American Review,* III, no. 6 (December 1800), 413–416 for the same critical view of Milton's portrait of Death.

the nature of English, could only fail, costing him "half the price of his labour."

The very characteristic which John Quincy Adams praised in his *Rhetoric*, and which *The Bureau* asserted as the distinctive merit of his verse, *The Literary Magazine* now deplored as a fault. But Milton's idiom had not only marred his own poetry; it had left an unfortunate print on the effusions of others. By the "natural course of critical idolatry," the argument went on, critics had praised Milton's defects and poets in turn had imitated them, with the result that they threw such a "stiff and cumbrous pedantry" over their poetry that nothing was natural.[27] Recollection of imitations like *The Gospel Tragedy* or *The Propitiation* makes such a judgment seem but a litotes.

As critics probed deeper into the language and imagery of *Paradise Lost* the epic itself began to lose caste.[28] Perhaps most Americans still believed this genre to be the grandest the mind of man had ever conceived; some specifically said so.[29] But the rationality of the age militated against supernatural machinery and archetypal personages and events. *The Port Folio* made this quite clear in some "Desultory Observations on Poetry," an essay directed to an appraisal of the epic in general and of *Paradise Lost* in particular. Here it was argued that an epic poem seldom succeeds, unless in a barbarous or semi-barbarous age, that such a genre could exist only before

[27] *The Literary Magazine and American Register*, V, no. 32 (May 1806), 343–344, in an essay, "Milton, His Metre and His Imitators."

[28] See, for example, *The Monthly Magazine and American Review*, I, no. 3 (June 1799), 225–229, in a review of Southey's *Joan of Arc;* and *The Literary Magazine and American Register*, VII, no. 42 (March 1807), 223–228, in a reprint of the Reverend Walker's views "On the Machinery of the Ancient Epic Poem." The essay is continued in the April issue, pp. 269–271. See also Donald M. Foerster, "Homer, Milton, and the American Revolt Against Epic Poetry: 1812–1860," *Studies in Philology*, LIII (January 1956), 75–100.

[29] See, for example, *The Port Folio*, III, no. 5, Third Series (May 1810), 377–392, in a continuation of some lectures on Rhetoric.

a general diffusion of philosophical knowledge. What *The Port Folio* objected to most was supernatural machinery, particularly where Milton had "rashly exhibited the Divine Being himself as taking a part in the action, promising, threatening, and discussing *knotty* questions in divinity." Such an appearance of God could result only in "complete failure." For who could read this part of the poem "without being astonished at its absurdity, or shocked at its manifest impiety"?

The appearance of angels caused less concern, since their activities had been partly depicted in Scripture; but to have them "fight with the weapons of mortals, or contend after the manner of men" was ridiculous, *The Port Folio* maintained. Who in the modern age "would venture to lend assistance to his hero, by the sword of Michael, or snatch him from danger through the friendship of Gabriel"? No rational poet would. But the main defect of supernatural epic machinery was that it simply could no longer hold interest. "The guardian genii of states are very dull personages," the critic in *The Port Folio* asserted, focusing squarely on Hesper in Joel Barlow's *The Columbiad;* and whenever he heard Columbia or Britannia mentioned, he felt an overpowering "inclination to doze."[30] Perhaps *The Monthly Anthology* was right: after the first two books, except for parts of Book IX, *Paradise Lost* could weary the mind with metaphysics no longer viable in a rational world.[31] To some Americans Milton's epic was becoming, as Sir Walter Raleigh was to say nearly a century later, a monument to dead ideas.

Such attacks on the language, imagery, and thought of the minor poems and of *Paradise Lost* opened a schism among Milton critics that later became irreconcilable. Even today admirers and detractors of Milton face each other across the identical lines from which critics of the early Republic de-

[30] *The Port Folio*, VIII, no. 3, New Series (September 1812), 256–257, in an essay, "Desultory Observations on Poetry."

[31] *The Monthly Anthology and Boston Review*, V (March 1808), 148–149, in an essay on "Milton."

ployed, arguing the old issues in fresh contexts but saying little essentially new. Such positions will probably see little change in the future since they mark basic differences about the name and nature of poetry. But the schism evidenced in literary journals of the early Republic apparently had little discernible effect on Milton's popular image of greatness. He still lived in schools, shaped ideals of marriage and love, dramatized religious experience, enlivened political disputes, and dominated mood poetry and epic expression.

As yet, most Americans saw him as a combined scholar and genius, as a witness for Christianity and a spokesman for God, as a poet of titanic stature, without peer in the ancient or modern worlds. That sharp attacks on his idiom and thought only presaged a diminution in stature and a lessening of his authority testifies to the tenacity of popular idolatry, as well as to the power of his art. He was not to be easily toppled from his position of eminence.

## I V

Diminution of Milton's stature during the nineteenth century and hence a narrowing of his influence in American life proceeded so gradually that few seemed aware of the change the passage of years made.[32] Journals such as *The Yale Literary Magazine* and *The North American Review* continued to carry critical essays on his poetry and thought; [33] and he still spoke with a commanding authority to some of the most

[32] For commentary on the diminution of Milton's reputation, with relevant and informative glances at American authors, see James E. Thorpe, Jr., "The Decline of the Miltonic Tradition" (Unpublished dissertation, Harvard University, 1941). See also Thorpe's *Milton Criticism* (Rinehart, 1950), which grew out of his earlier work; James G. Nelson, *The Sublime Puritan* (Madison, 1963); and John A. Weigel, "The Milton Tradition in the First Half of the Nineteenth Century" (Unpublished dissertation, Western Reserve University, 1939).

[33] See Ruth W. Gregory, "American Criticism of Milton 1800–1938" (Unpublished thesis, University of Wisconsin, 1938); and Lester Fred Zimmerman, "Some Aspects of Milton's American Reputation to 1900" (Unpublished dissertation, University of Wisconsin, 1950).

distinguished literary men of the day. Edgar Allan Poe and Ralph Waldo Emerson, as well as Nathaniel Hawthorne, John Greenleaf Whittier, Herman Melville, and James Russell Lowell often professed his power and greatness, either openly in praise of the man and his works or silently in borrowed language and imagery.[34] Neoclassic imitation of his diction and forms soon disappeared; but Romantic commitments in the Renascence of American literature hardly meant that his person and style could not inspire a body of poetry and prose for decades to come. Yet the new age called for fresh modes of expression, asked for a less formal and a more individual style—a shift in taste that placed Milton more on the shelf with classical authors than in the hands of everyday readers. His grand, rhetorical sweep no longer carried the wide appeal it once had possessed.

Such changes in taste, foreshadowed in earlier critical conflicts and destined to lessen his fame, now joined with an event that began to raise doubts about the orthodoxy of his Christian belief: the discovery and publication of his controversial *De Doctrina Christiana*. Even the most liberal American found his approval of polygamy here and his seemingly Arian positions somewhat alarming, despite William Ellery Channing's defense of the document; and the more pious

---

[34] William Cullen Bryant, Margaret Fuller, Jones Very, and others also succumbed to the spell of Milton's poetry. See Jacob H. Adler, "A Milton-Bryant Parallel," *The New England Quarterly*, XXIV (1951), 377–380; Harry Glickman, "Lowell on Milton's *Areopagitica*," *Modern Language Notes*, XXXV (March 1920), 185–186; Thomas P. Haviland, "How Well Did Poe Know Milton?," PMLA, LXIX (1954), 841–860; Richard C. Pettigrew, "Emerson and Milton," *American Literature*, III (1931–1932), 45–59; *idem*, "Lowell's Criticism of Milton," *American Literature*, III (1931–1932), 457–464; *idem*, "Milton in the Works of Emerson, Lowell, and Holmes" (Unpublished dissertation, Duke University, 1930); Henry F. Pommer, *Milton and Melville* (Pittsburgh, 1950); and Joe D. Pollitt, "Ralph Waldo Emerson's Debt to John Milton," *Marshall Review*, III (1939), 13–21. For an analysis of the commentary of Poe, Emerson, Lowell, and Whitman on Milton, see Norman Foerster, *American Criticism* (Boston, 1928), pp. 32, 51, 78, 92, 96, 121, 164.

recoiled from what they thought was immorality and rank heresy. By mid-century the image of greatness Americans had cherished so long had become definitely flawed; Milton could no longer serve as a pattern of poetic perfection, nor stand as an incorrupt witness for God.

Manifest destiny conspired to confine his name even more. As the frontier spread to the Mississippi River and to reaches beyond, to be stopped only by the shores of the Pacific, Americans marched to the rhythm of a fresh epic dream. Their current journey into the wilderness purposed less to establish a new spiritual Canäan [35] than to subdue and exploit a vast, virgin land. To such an ambitious enterprise Milton's story of man's disobedience and Fall apparently had little to say. The great scenes in *Paradise Lost* which had permitted Cotton Mather to invest the wars of New England with a transcendent significance, or Timothy Dwight to envision the glories of the "Western Millennium," the spiritual vision which had allowed men of the Revolution and of the early Republic to formulate ideals or assess events of their day, no longer presented living analogies with worldly existence.

Milton's pictures remained etched on men's minds, but they now seemed more pertinent to private than to public experience; they still dramatized a persistent old piety, but no longer served as archetypes of action and thought to inform a vital, existential activity. The old analogies between heaven and earth, between Old Testament prophecy and new national hope, had ceased to be generally viable.[36] If scholars and critics admired and published Milton's works in this later

[35] For a discussion of the religious purpose in founding New England, see Samuel Eliot Morison, *The Intellectual Life of Colonial New England*, pp. 6–7. See also Perry Miller, *Errand into the Wilderness*.

[36] Jean H. Hagstrum, in *The Sister Arts* (Chicago, 1958), p. 128, speaks of Milton's "sacramental pictorialism," that is, "the pictorial was a gate that opened not primarily upon visible nature but upon transcendent and invisible reality."

time, the public largely ignored them; references to Milton in almanacs, popular journals, and fugitive tracts gradually lessened until he lived mainly within the confines of literary circles and schools. America had simply become too vast a land, had become too diverse in its aims and too transformed in its tastes, beliefs, and modes of feeling and thought for Milton to traverse the wide front he had earlier ranged.[37]

A glance backward reveals that he reached the peak of his influence and fame in the first few decades of the Republic. Perhaps his prose never greatly affected American thought, even at the height of Revolutionary activity, when statesmen and ministers found his positions on civil and ecclesiastical freedom especially congenial. His arguments impressed men more for their idealism and their rhetorical skill than for their originality or their practical relevance. But by the early years of the Republic his poetry had become and was to remain for some while an inextricable part of American culture: his imagery had turned by that time into a mode of popular thinking, had become in truth archetypal, assaying wide varieties of American experience. The rationalism of the Enlightenment could not exorcise wholly ancient habits of analogical and anagogical thought. Milton's portrayal of the Infernal Council and of the great throne of God, of warfare in Heaven and of tortures in Hell, of the Garden of Eden and of Adam and Eve's idyllic estate, so dramatized the old transcendent view of man and the world that Americans, for a brief span at least, habitually read life in its manifold colors and shapes against his vision of spiritual truth. Early Americans quite rightly maintained that his power to move and instruct lay in his sublime, prophetic scenes. Perhaps such images still inform American habits of mind, particularly among Christians, who

[37] For an analysis of why the epic lost ground in America, see Donald M. Foerster, *The Fortunes of Epic Poetry* (Washington, D. C., 1962), Chapter 4, "The Epic in an Epic Land: American Theory, 1812–1860."

304

occasionally animate Biblical story and myth with Miltonic figures, many of which have long since been enlivened by illustrators of *Paradise Lost* from William Blake to Paul Gustave Doré.[38]

Such speculation, however, is idle. What is clear is that Americans discovered in Milton a manner and matter which fulfilled the needs of their national youth. If his rhetoric overwhelmed much serious verse of that time, divesting it of originality and life, that same art quickened ideals and values, dramatized faiths and beliefs, and even shaped dreams of an American Millennium. John Locke remained on the scene as an esteemed, oft-cited philosopher; Sir Isaac Newton stood as an unchallenged titan in science. But among great names of the past acclaimed in that early day Milton ranged more variously over the moral, spiritual, and intellectual life of the country than any one man. Schoolmaster and poet, statesman and prophet and priest, he spoke with singular effectiveness on countless occasions to Americans of widely differing talents, interests, and tastes. Few authors in any age have moved so pervasively over the sensibilities of a nation, and odds argue that Milton himself will never do so again with the same sweep and power. Milton idolatry, national ambition, and paradoxes born of the Enlightenment converged to make his imprint in early America unique.

[38] For an illuminating article on the imagery of *Paradise Lost* and painting, see Kester Svendsen, "John Martin and the Expulsion Scene in Paradise Lost," *Studies in English Literature 1500–1900*, I (1961), 63–73. See the bibliography of this article for reference to items discussing the relation of Milton's imagery to the graphic arts. See also Merritt Y. Hughes, "Some Illustrators of Milton: The Expulsion From Paradise," JEGP, LX (1961), 670–679.

# INDEX

Abercrombie, James, 195n.
Adair, Douglass, 124n.
Adams, Abijah, 249, 250 and note
Adams, Charles Francis, 7n., 128n.
Adams, Daniel, 187, 192; *The Thorough Scholar*, 187; *The Understanding Reader*, 192
Adams, Hannah, 24; *The Truth and Excellence of the Christian Religion Exhibited*, 24n.
Adams, John (the poet), 9, 85, 86, 87, 88, 218; *Poems on Several Occasions, Original and Translated*, 86 and note; *To A Gentleman at the Sight of Some of His Poems*, 85; *The Revelation of St. John the Divine*, 86
Adams, John (2nd President of the United States), 3, 12, 127–135, 240, 248; *A Defence of the Constitutions of Government of the United States of America*, 12n., 131, 133n., 135n.; *Thoughts on Government*, 129, 131n.
Adams, John Quincy, 29, 30, 187, 192–194, 299; *Lectures on Rhetoric and Oratory*, 29, 30n., 192–194, 299
Adams, M. Ray, 182n.
Adams, Samuel, 128
Addison, Joseph, 5n., 20, 37, 87, 96, 111, 285; *The Spectator*, 96
*Address to Melancholy*, 273
Adler, Jacob H., 302n.
Aikin, John, 195n.; *The Calendar of Nature*, 195n.
Alden, Abner, 194n.; *The Reader*, 194n.
Allen, Jonathan, 23; *A Poem, On the Existence of God*, 23n.

Allen, Paul, 265; *Original Poems, Serious and Entertaining*, 265n.
Alline, Henry, 234; *Two Mites, Cast into the Offering to God*, 234n.
*Almanack for the Year of Christian Account, An*, 67n.
*Almanack For the Year of Our Lord Christ, 1761, An*, 67n., 72n.
*Almanack of Poor Richard the Second, The*, 223n.
Alsop, Richard, 246, 247 and note, 249; *Aristocracy: An Epic Poem*, 246, 247n.; *The Political Greenhouse, For the Year 1798*, 249
Alspach, Russell K., 110n.
*American Almanac, The*, 67n.
*American Lady's Preceptor, The*, 197, 198, 205n.
*American Magazine, The*, 15n., 175n., 179n.
*American Magazine [and Historical Chronicle]*, 9, 42, 43n., 92n.
*American Magazine and Monthly Chronicle, The*, 92n., 93, 94n., 95n.
*American Monthly Review, The*, 298
*American Museum Or Repository of Ancient and Modern Fugitive Pieces, Prose and Poetical*, 117n., 123n., 147n., 167n., 212n.
*American Museum Or Universal Magazine, The*, 184n., 185n., 196, 201, 206n., 208n., 224, 225n., 230n.
*American Review and Literary Journal*, 231n.
Ames, Fisher, 253n.

307